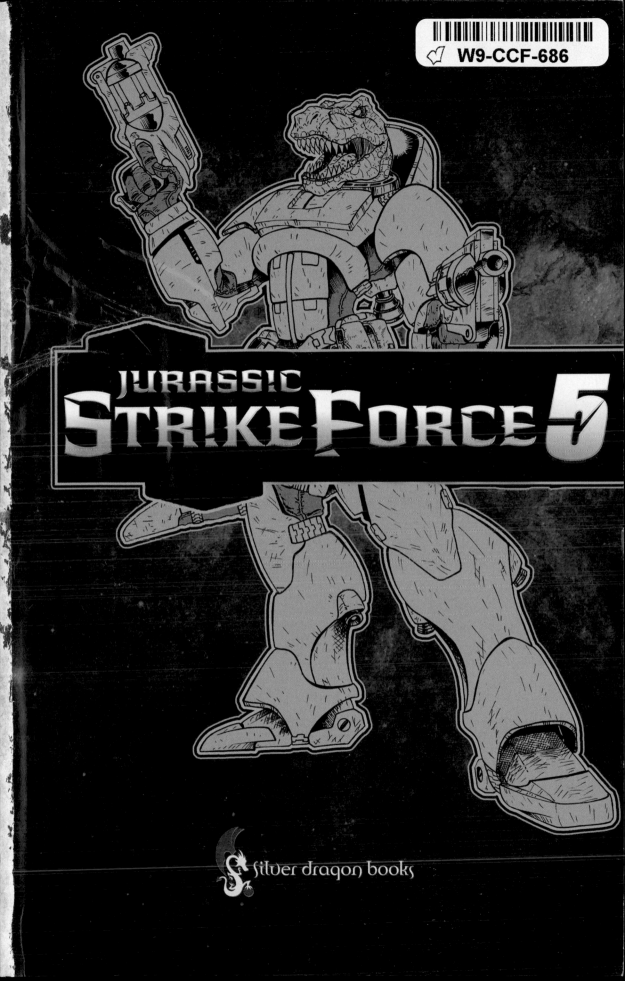

JURASSIC
STRIKE FORCE 5

silver dragon books

JURASSIC STRIKE FORCE 5
Volume One

STORY
JOE BRUSHA

WRITERS
JOE BRUSHA (CHAPTER 1)
NEO EDMUND (CHAPTERS 2-6)

ARTWORK
JULIAN AGUILERA (CHAPTER 1)
JL GILES-RIVERA (CHAPTERS 2-5)
RYAN HOWE (CHAPTER 6)
ARMANDO RILLO (CHAPTER 6)

COLORS
THOMAS MASON (CHAPTER 1)
JEFF BALKE (CHAPTERS 2-6)

LETTERS
ARTMONKEYS (CHAPTER 1)
JIM CAMPBELL (CHAPTERS 2-6)

ART DIRECTION
ANTHONY SPAY

TRADE DESIGN
CHRISTOPHER COTE

EDITOR
RALPH TEDESCO

ASSISTANT EDITOR
MATT ROGERS

THIS VOLUME REPRINTS THE
COMIC SERIES JURASSIC STRIKE FORCE
5 ISSUES #0-5 PUBLISHED BY SILVER
DRAGON BOOKS.

WWW.SILVERDRAGONBOOKS.COM

FIRST EDITION, JUNE 2013
ISBN: 978-1-937068-43-1

silver dragon books

WWW.SILVERDRAGONBOOKS.COM
FACEBOOK.COM/SILVERDRAGONBOOKS

SILVER DRAGON BOOKS, INC.
Joe Brusha • President & Publisher
Jennifer Bermel • VP Business Affairs
Ralph Tedesco • Executive Editor
Anthony Spay • Art Director
Christopher Cote • Production Manager

JURASSIC STRIKE FORCE 5

Volume One

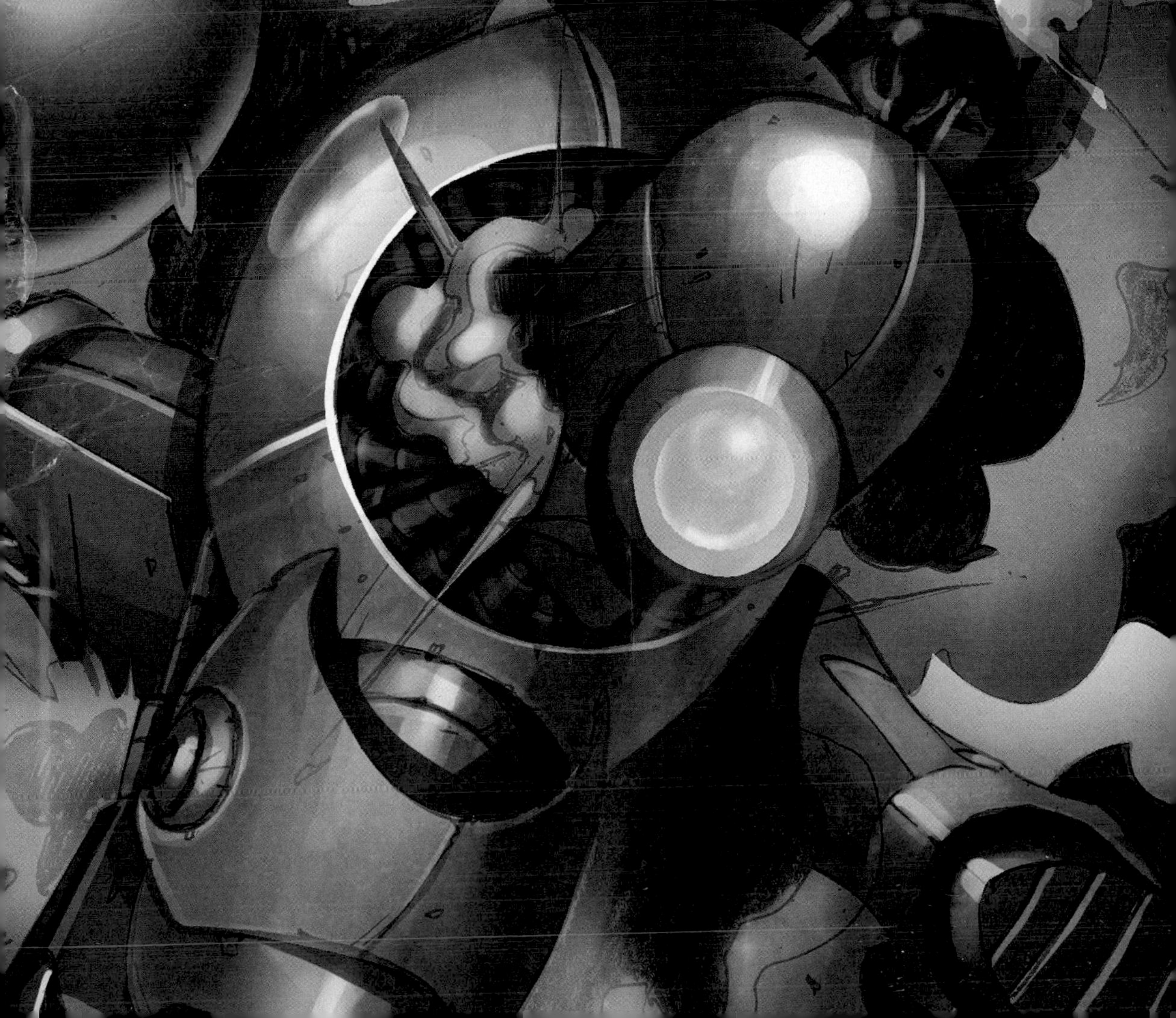

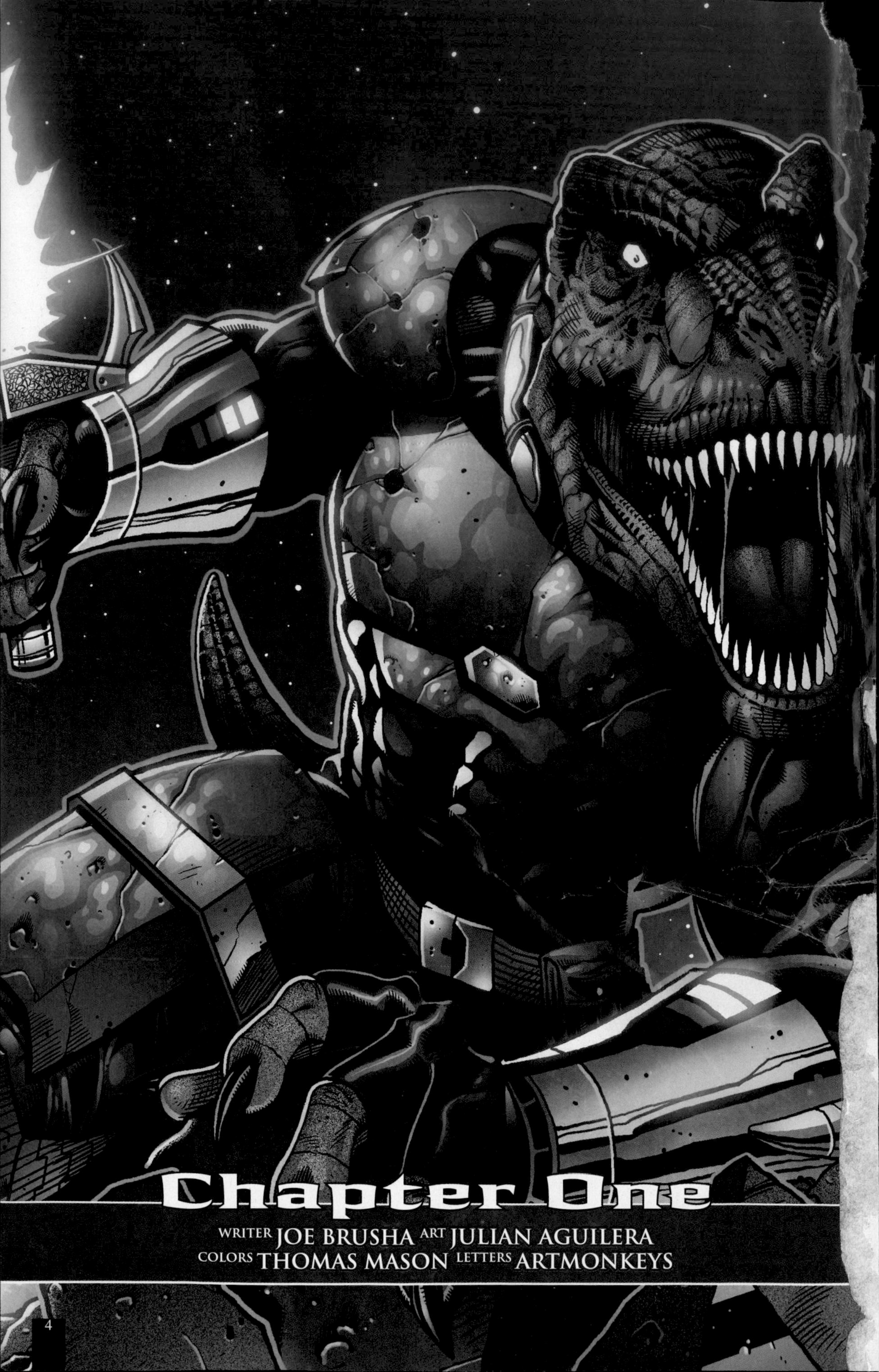

Chapter One

WRITER JOE BRUSHA ART JULIAN AGUILERA
COLORS THOMAS MASON LETTERS ARTMONKEYS

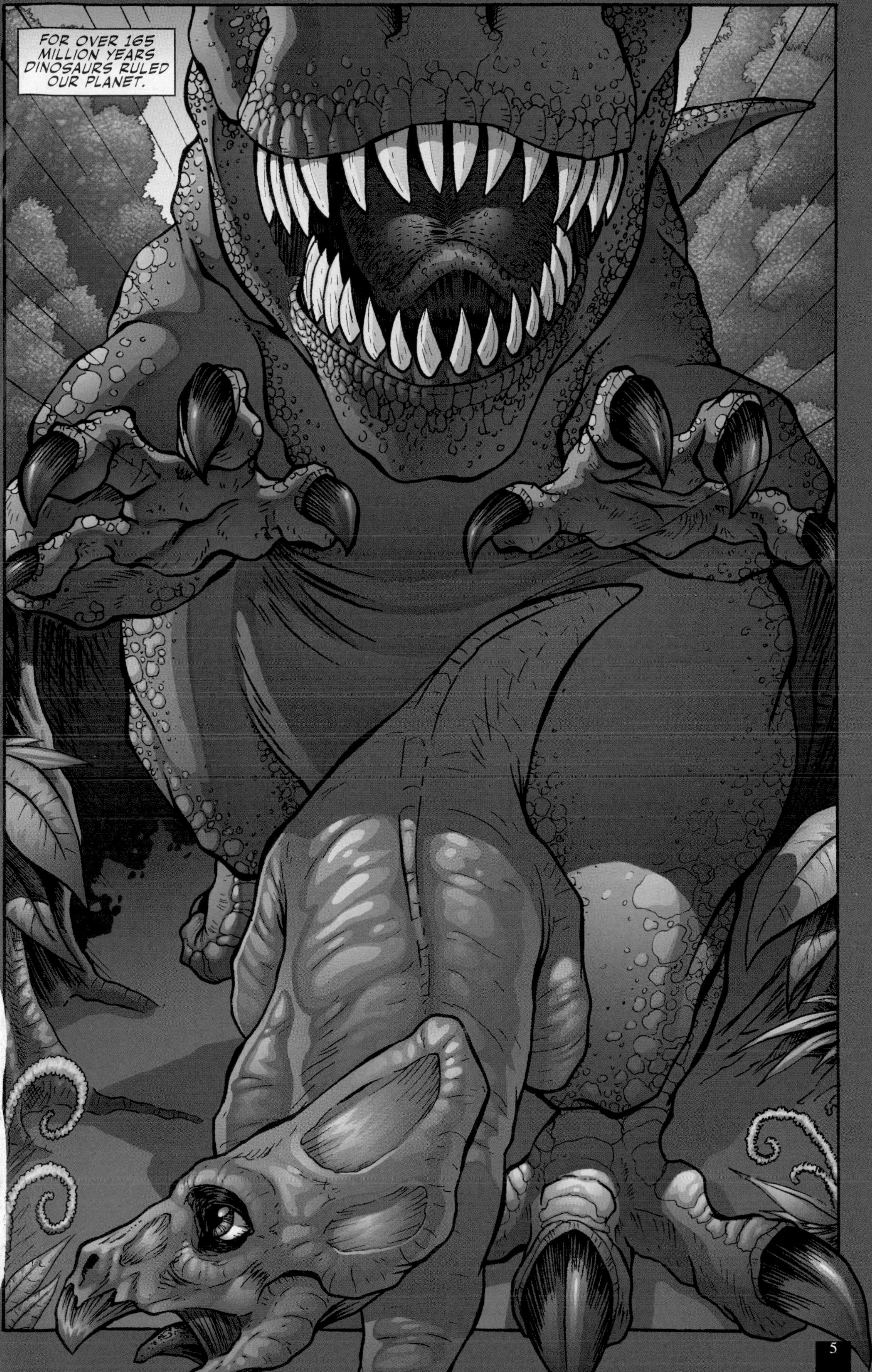
FOR OVER 165 MILLION YEARS DINOSAURS RULED OUR PLANET.

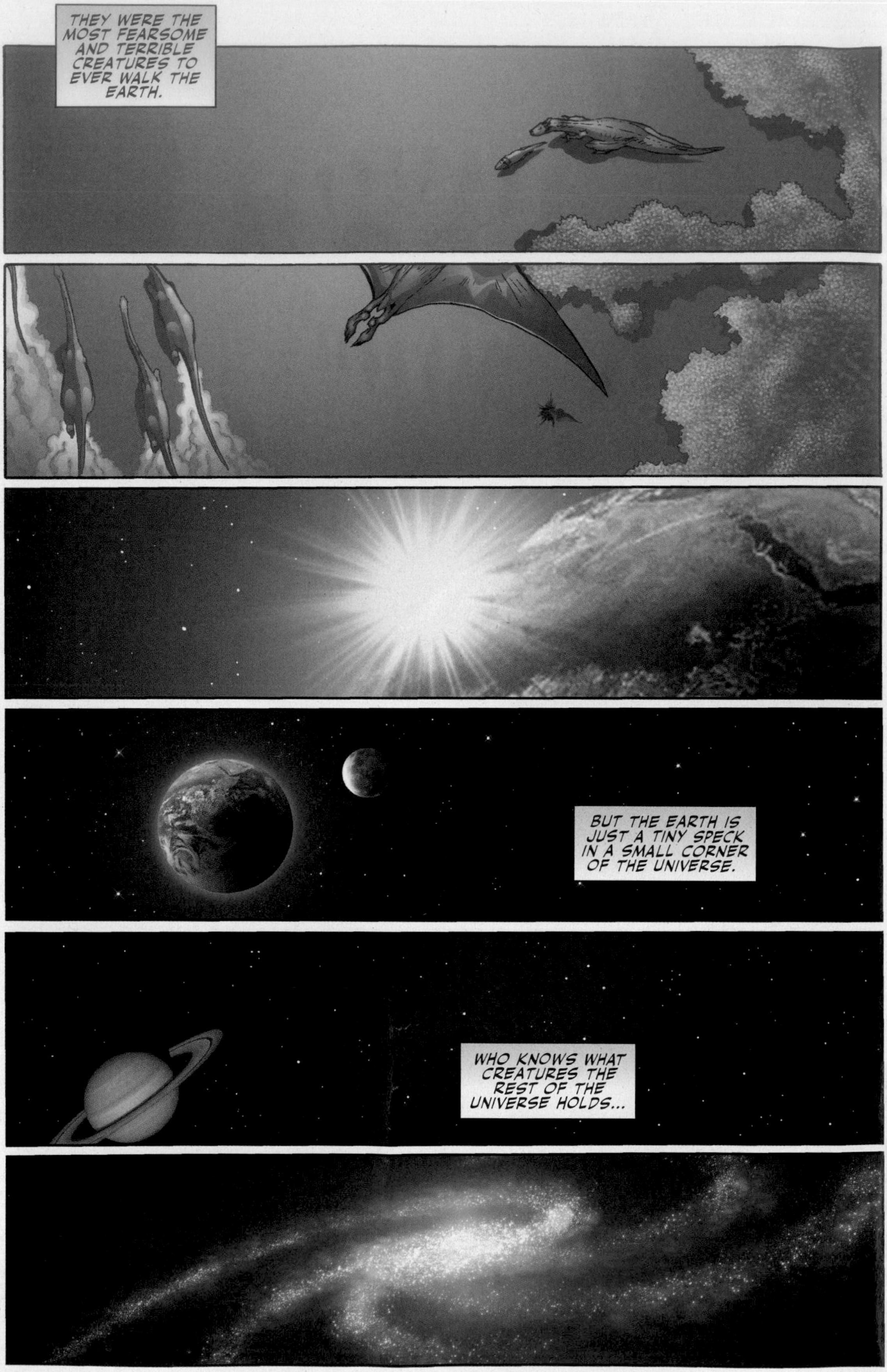
THEY WERE THE MOST FEARSOME AND TERRIBLE CREATURES TO EVER WALK THE EARTH.
BUT THE EARTH IS JUST A TINY SPECK IN A SMALL CORNER OF THE UNIVERSE.
WHO KNOWS WHAT CREATURES THE REST OF THE UNIVERSE HOLDS...

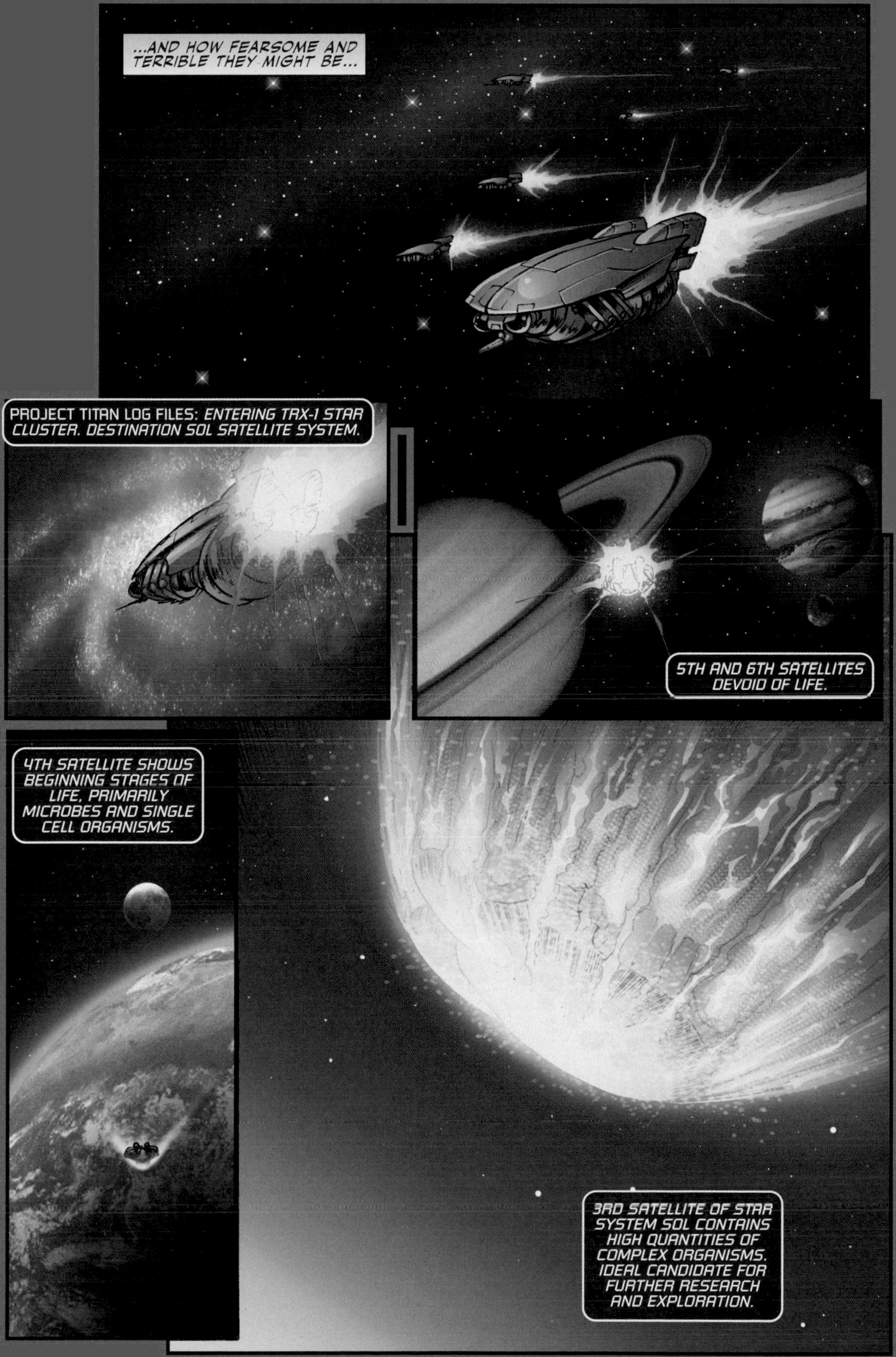
...AND HOW FEARSOME AND TERRIBLE THEY MIGHT BE...
PROJECT TITAN LOG FILES: ENTERING TRX-1 STAR CLUSTER. DESTINATION SOL SATELLITE SYSTEM.
5TH AND 6TH SATELLITES DEVOID OF LIFE.
4TH SATELLITE SHOWS BEGINNING STAGES OF LIFE, PRIMARILY MICROBES AND SINGLE CELL ORGANISMS.
3RD SATELLITE OF STAR SYSTEM SOL CONTAINS HIGH QUANTITIES OF COMPLEX ORGANISMS. IDEAL CANDIDATE FOR FURTHER RESEARCH AND EXPLORATION.

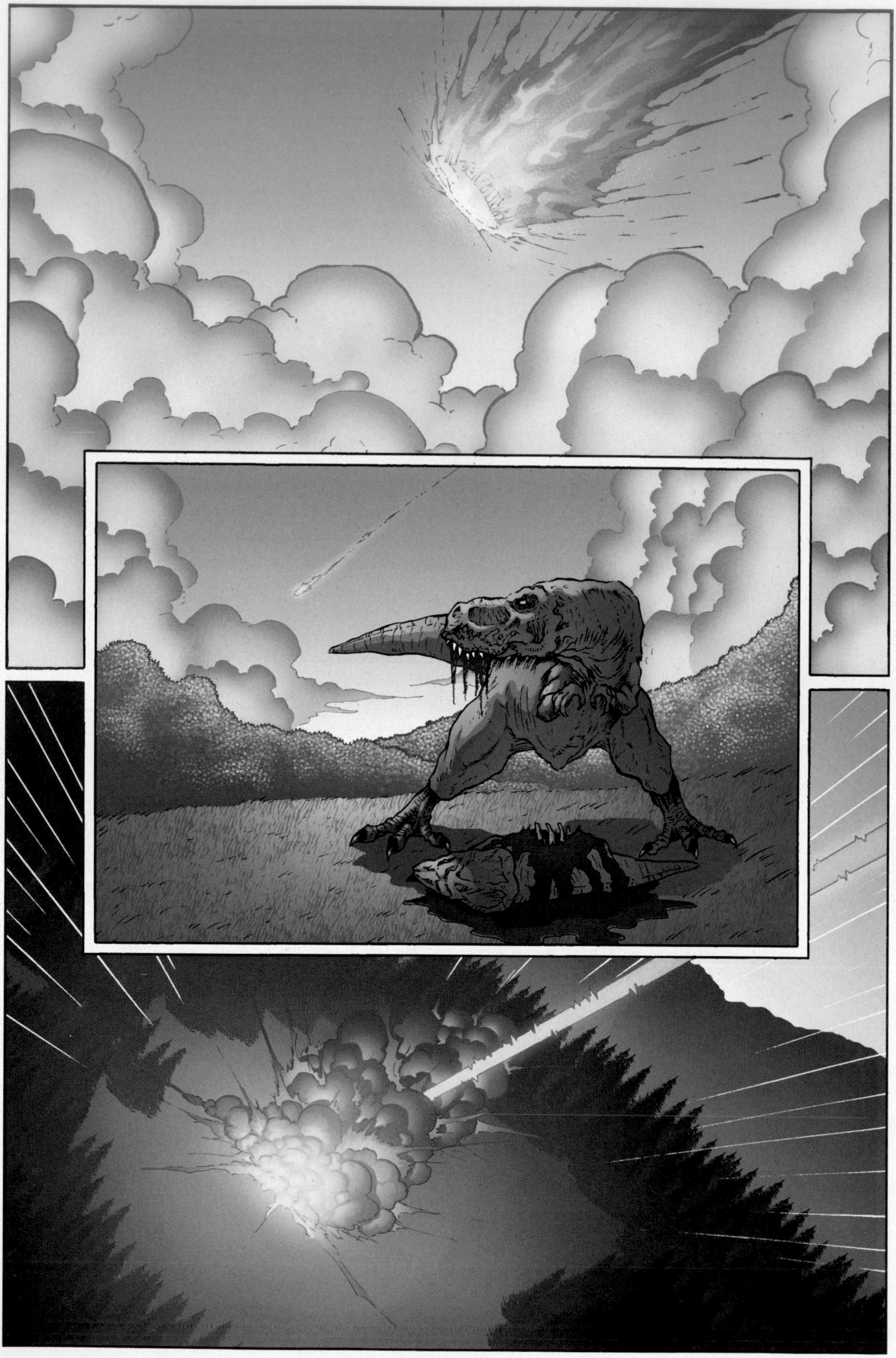

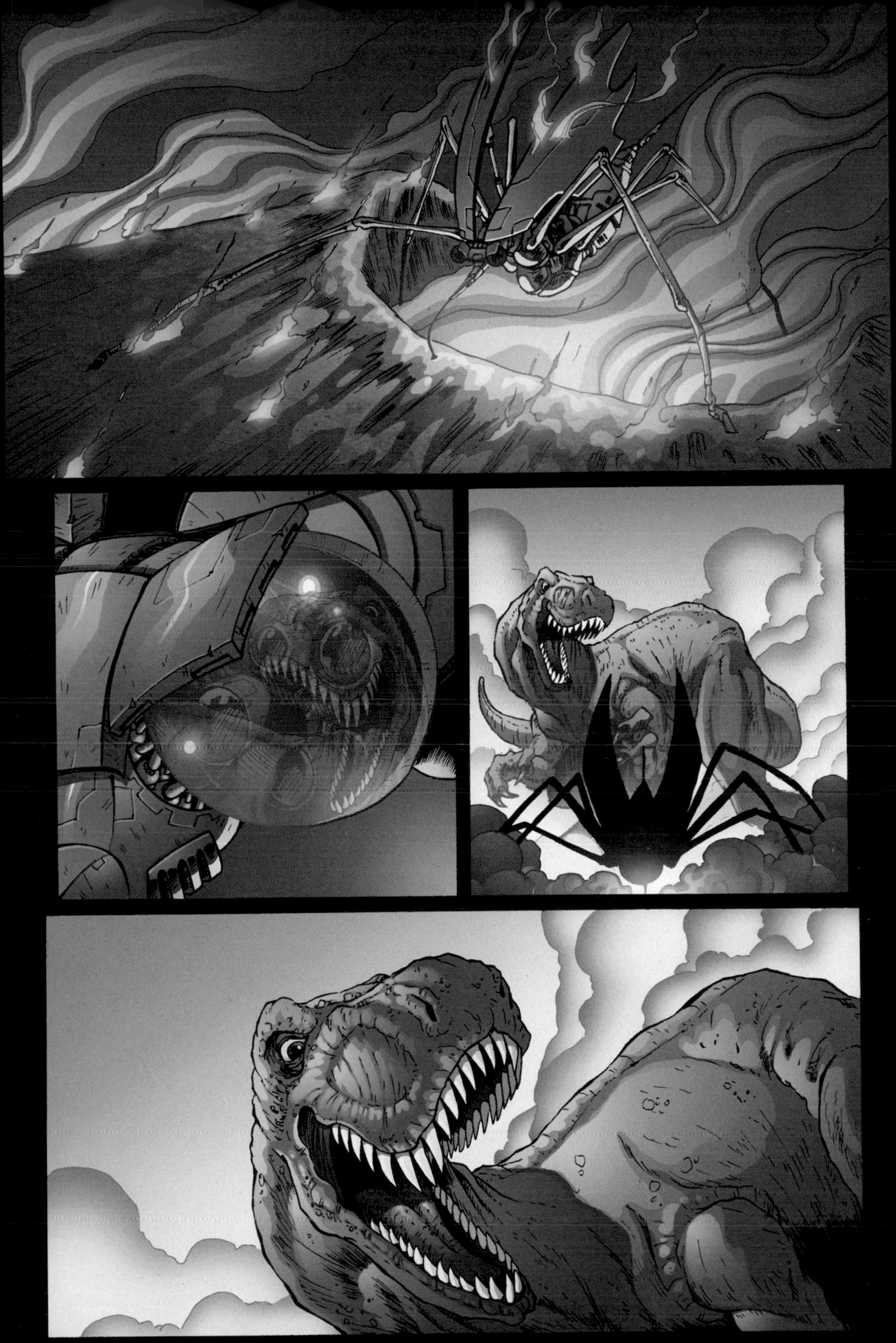

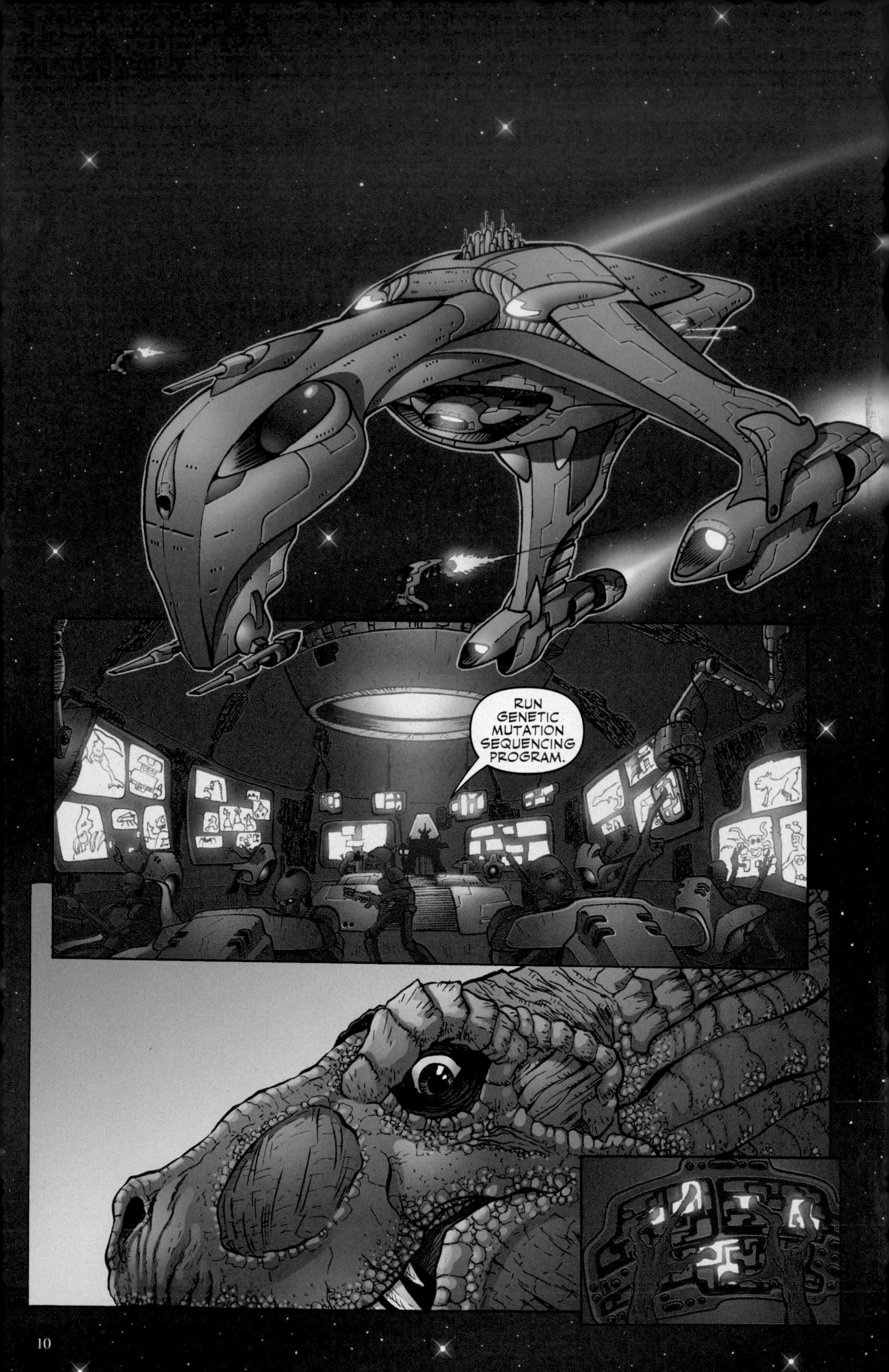
RUN GENETIC MUTATION SEQUENCING PROGRAM.

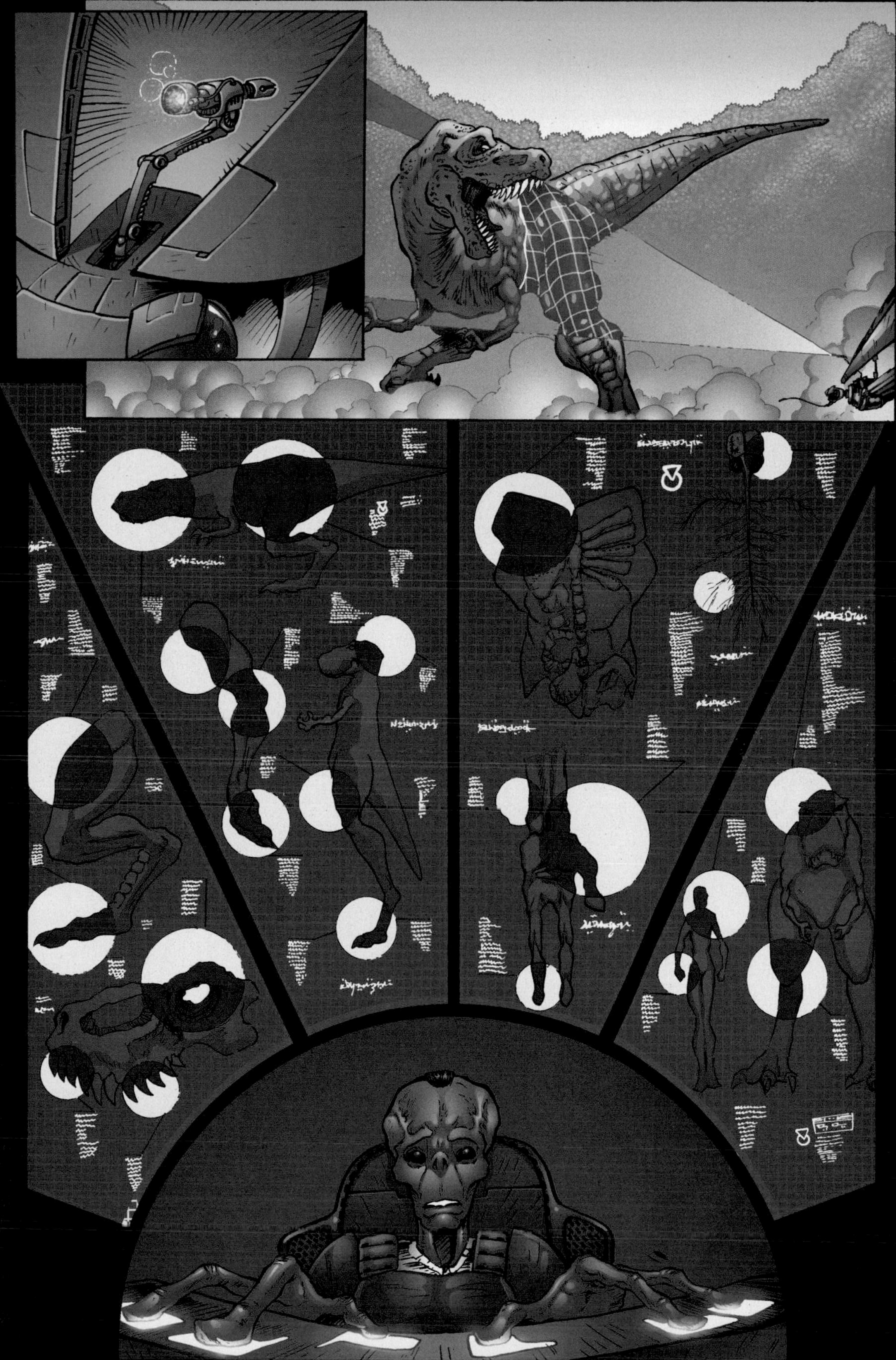

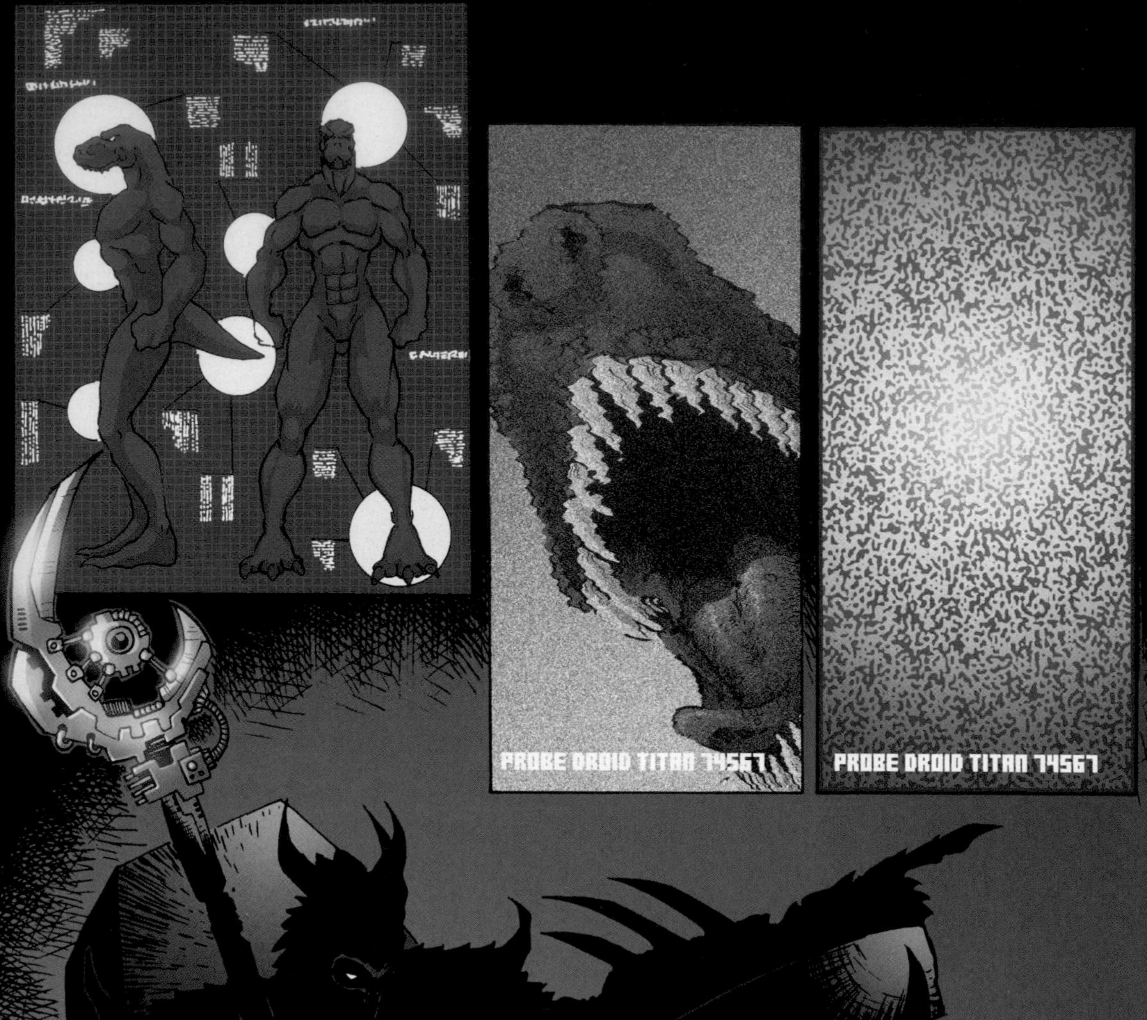
PROBE DROID TITAN 74567
PROBE DROID TITAN 74567

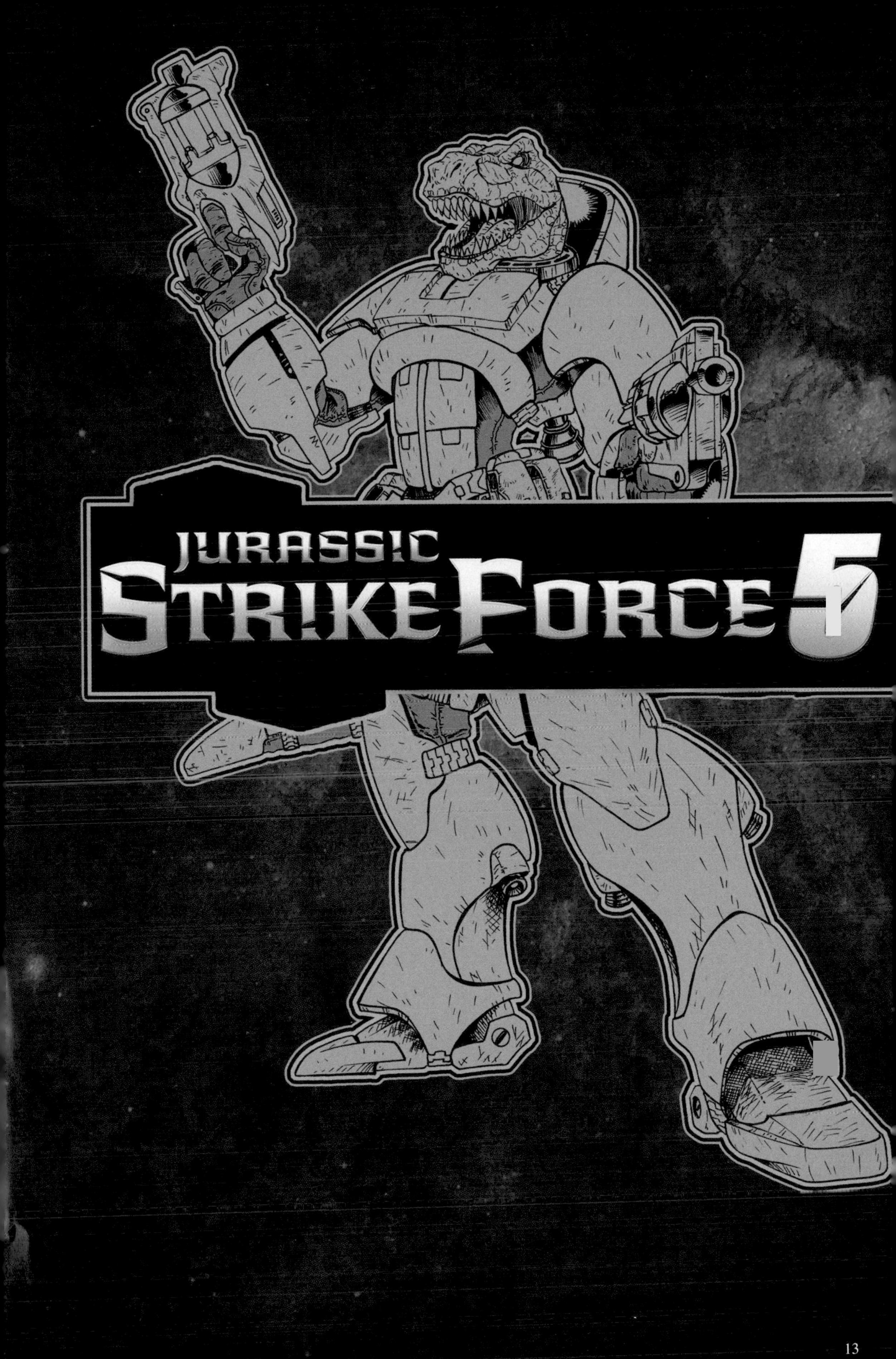
JURASSIC
STRIKE FORCE 5

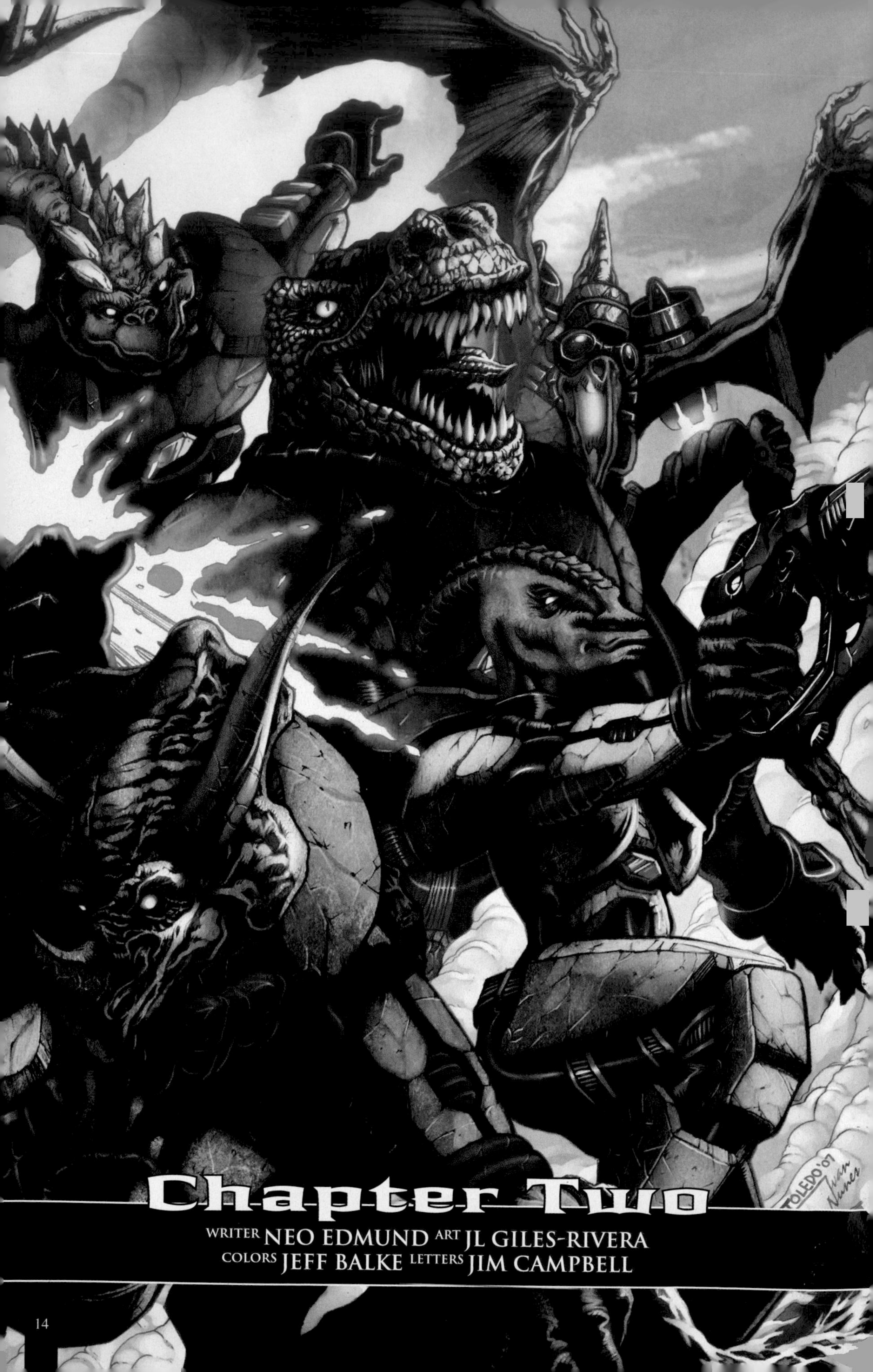

Chapter Two

WRITER NEO EDMUND ART JL GILES-RIVERA
COLORS JEFF BALKE LETTERS JIM CAMPBELL

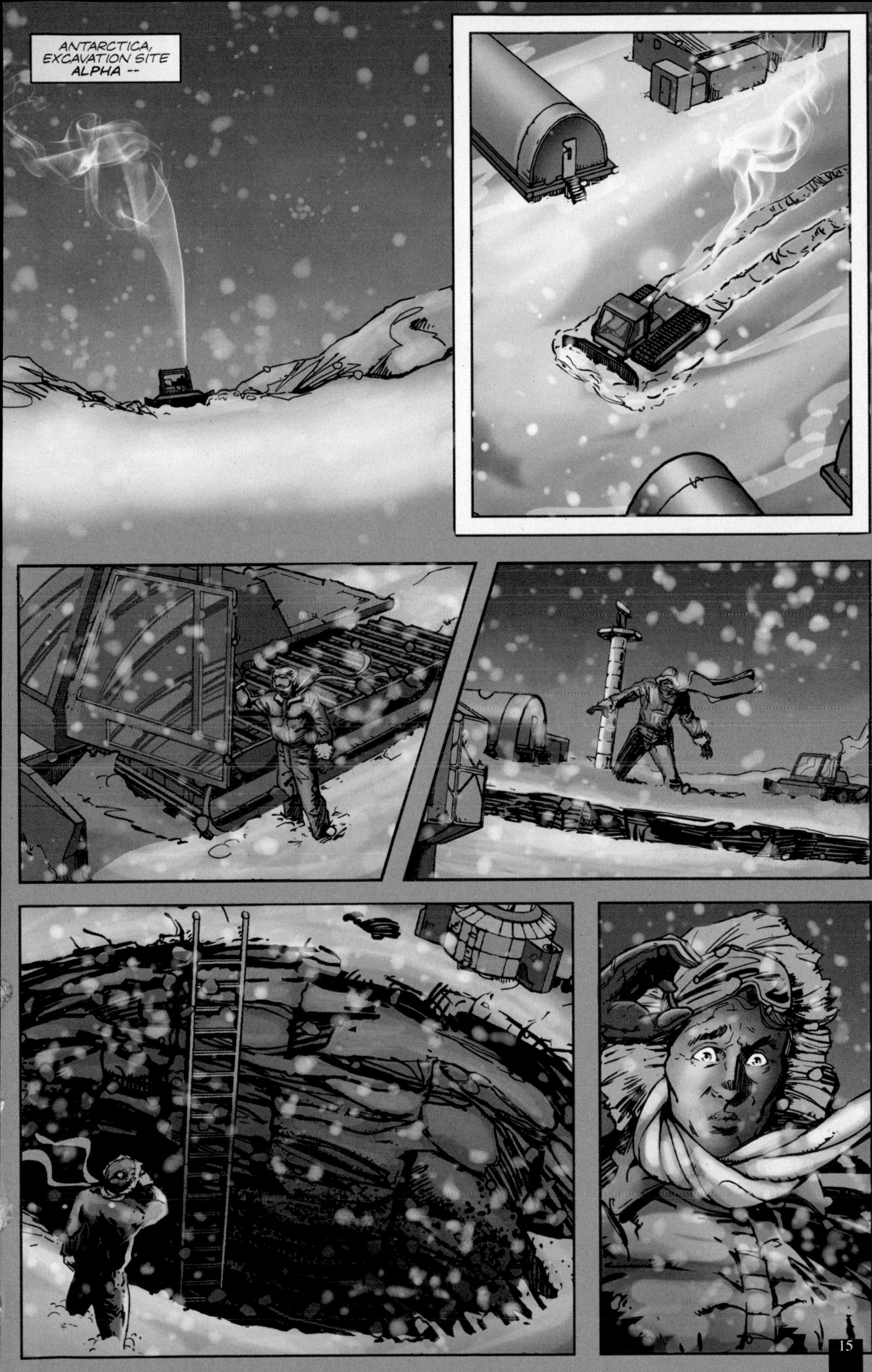
ANTARCTICA, EXCAVATION SITE ALPHA --

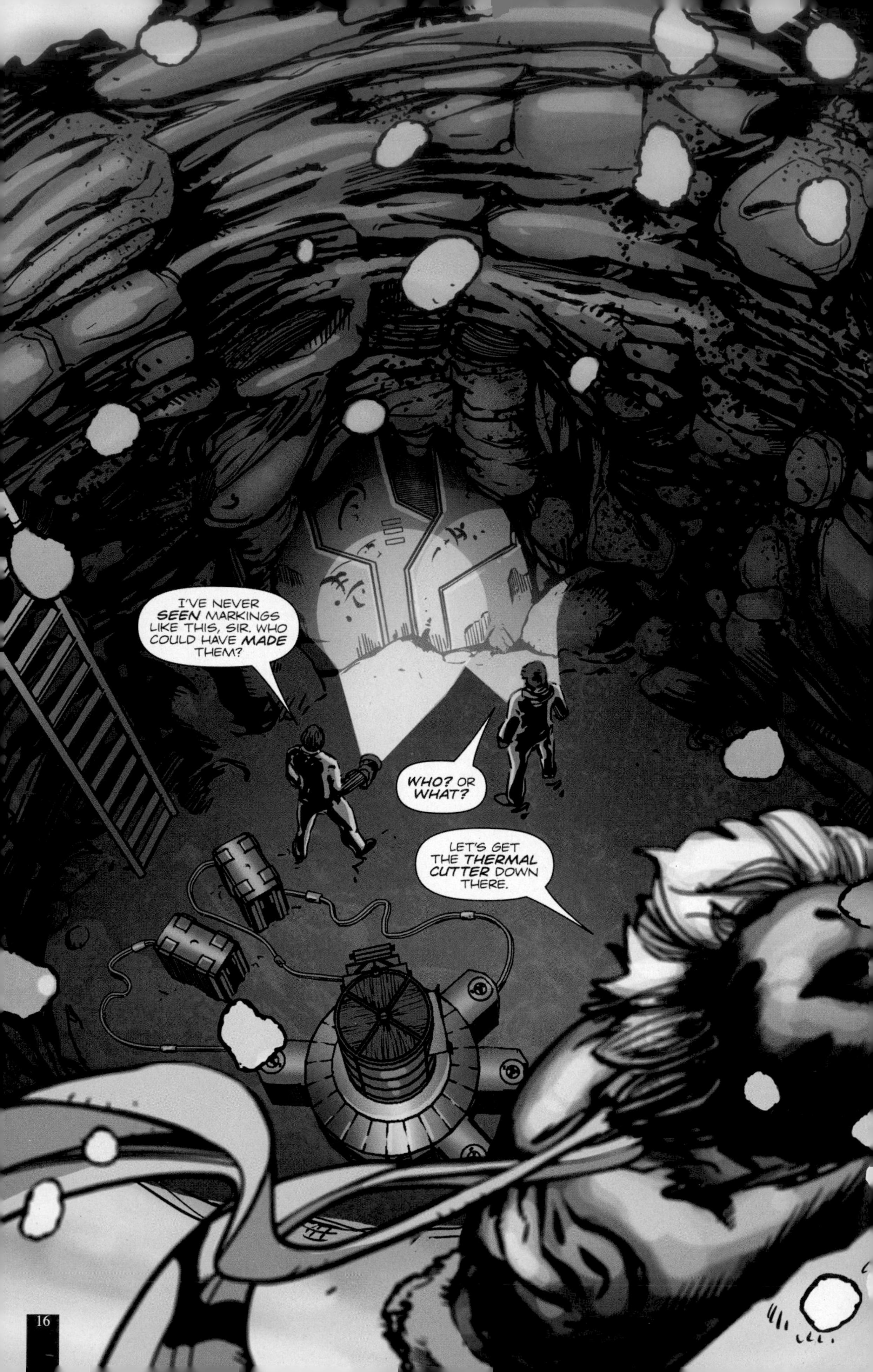
I'VE NEVER SEEN MARKINGS LIKE THIS, SIR. WHO COULD HAVE MADE THEM?
WHO? OR WHAT?
LET'S GET THE THERMAL CUTTER DOWN THERE.

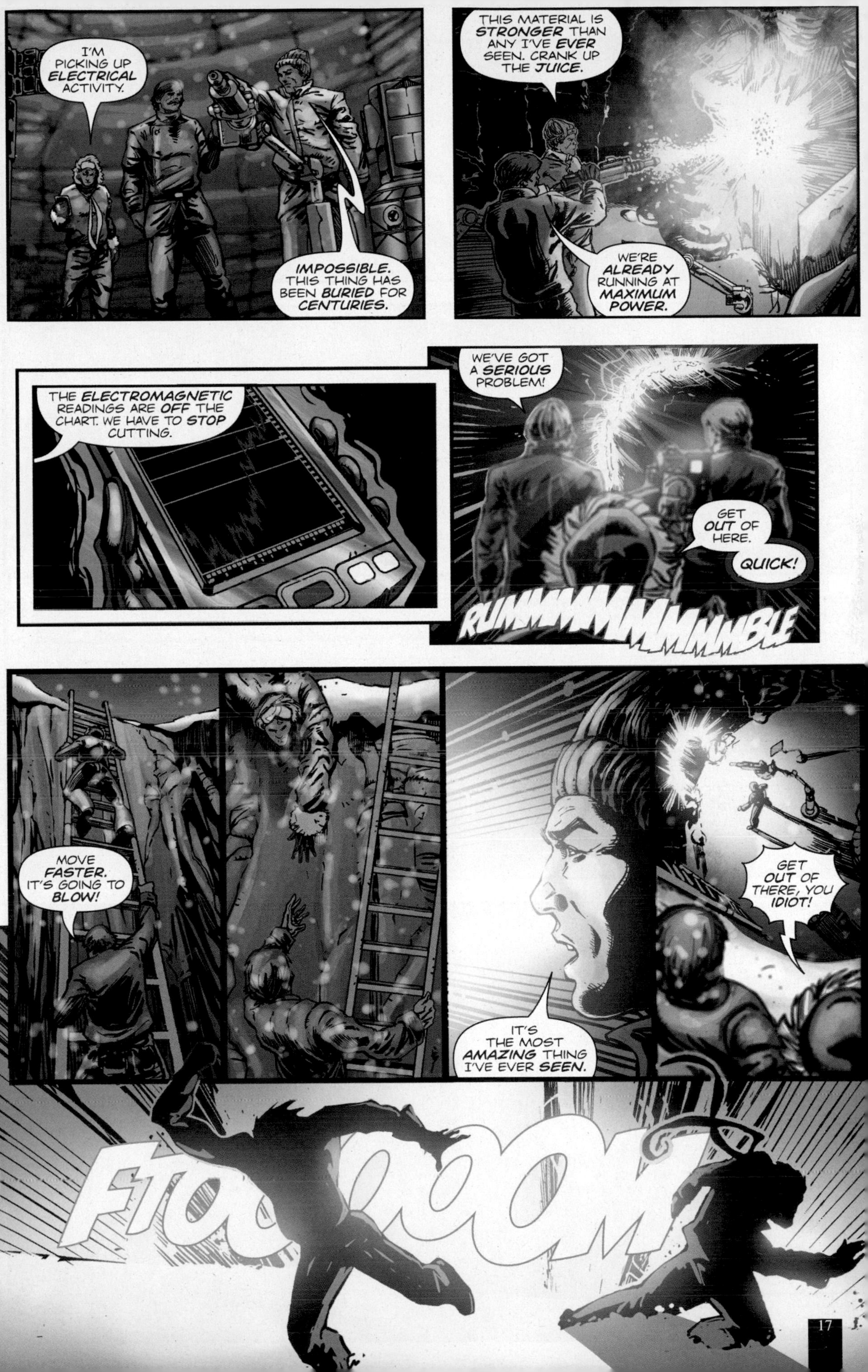

I'M PICKING UP ELECTRICAL ACTIVITY.
IMPOSSIBLE. THIS THING HAS BEEN BURIED FOR CENTURIES.
THIS MATERIAL IS STRONGER THAN ANY I'VE EVER SEEN. CRANK UP THE JUICE.
WE'RE ALREADY RUNNING AT MAXIMUM POWER.
THE ELECTROMAGNETIC READINGS ARE OFF THE CHART. WE HAVE TO STOP CUTTING.
WE'VE GOT A SERIOUS PROBLEM!
GET OUT OF HERE.
QUICK!
RUMMMMMMMMMMMBLE
MOVE FASTER. IT'S GOING TO BLOW!
IT'S THE MOST AMAZING THING I'VE EVER SEEN.
GET OUT OF THERE, YOU IDIOT!
FTOOOOOM

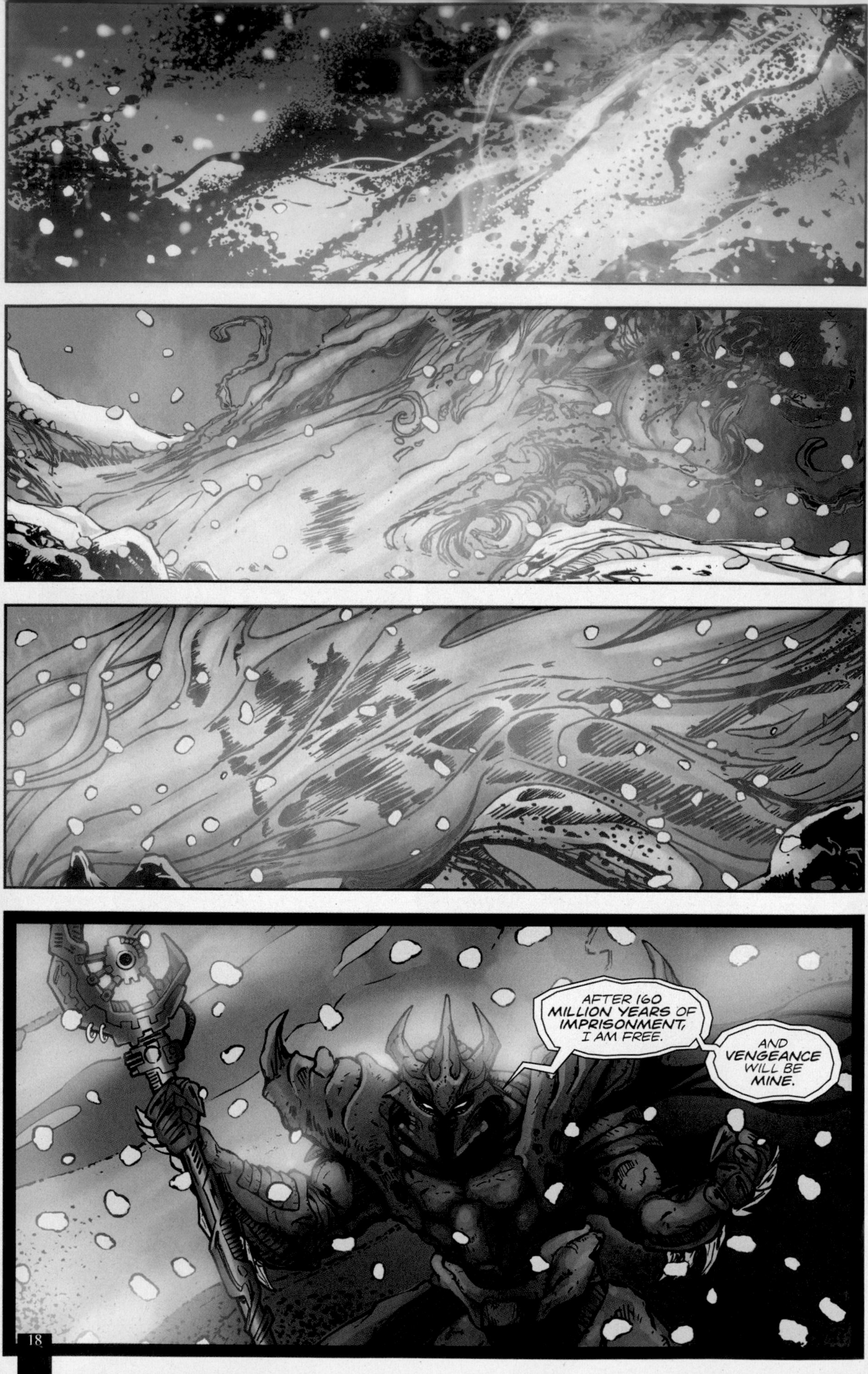
AFTER 160 MILLION YEARS OF IMPRISONMENT, I AM FREE.
AND VENGEANCE WILL BE MINE.

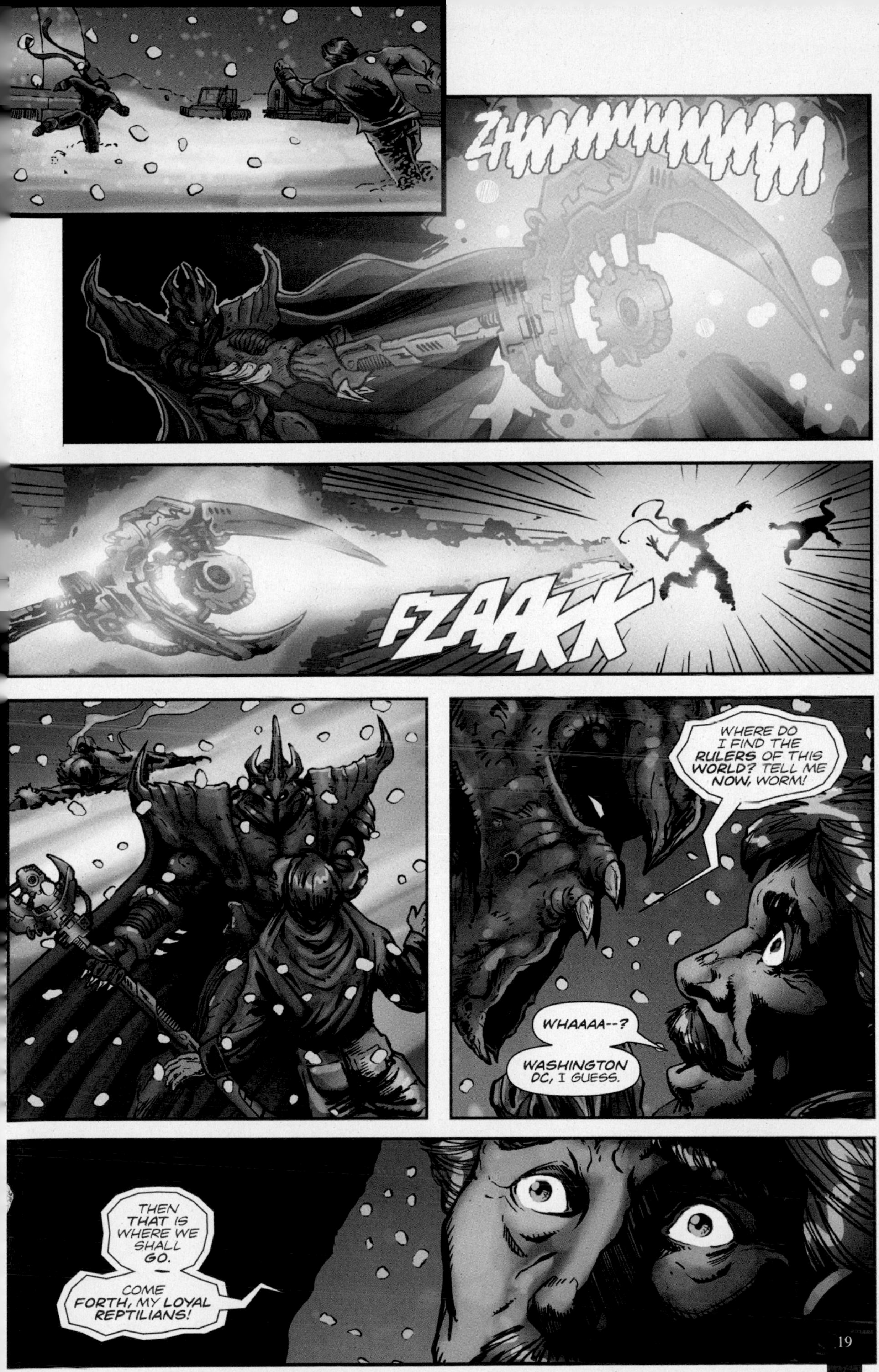
ZHMMMMMMM
FZAAKK
WHERE DO I FIND THE RULERS OF THIS WORLD? TELL ME NOW, WORM!
WHAAAA--?
WASHINGTON DC, I GUESS.
THEN THAT IS WHERE WE SHALL GO.
COME FORTH, MY LOYAL REPTILIANS!

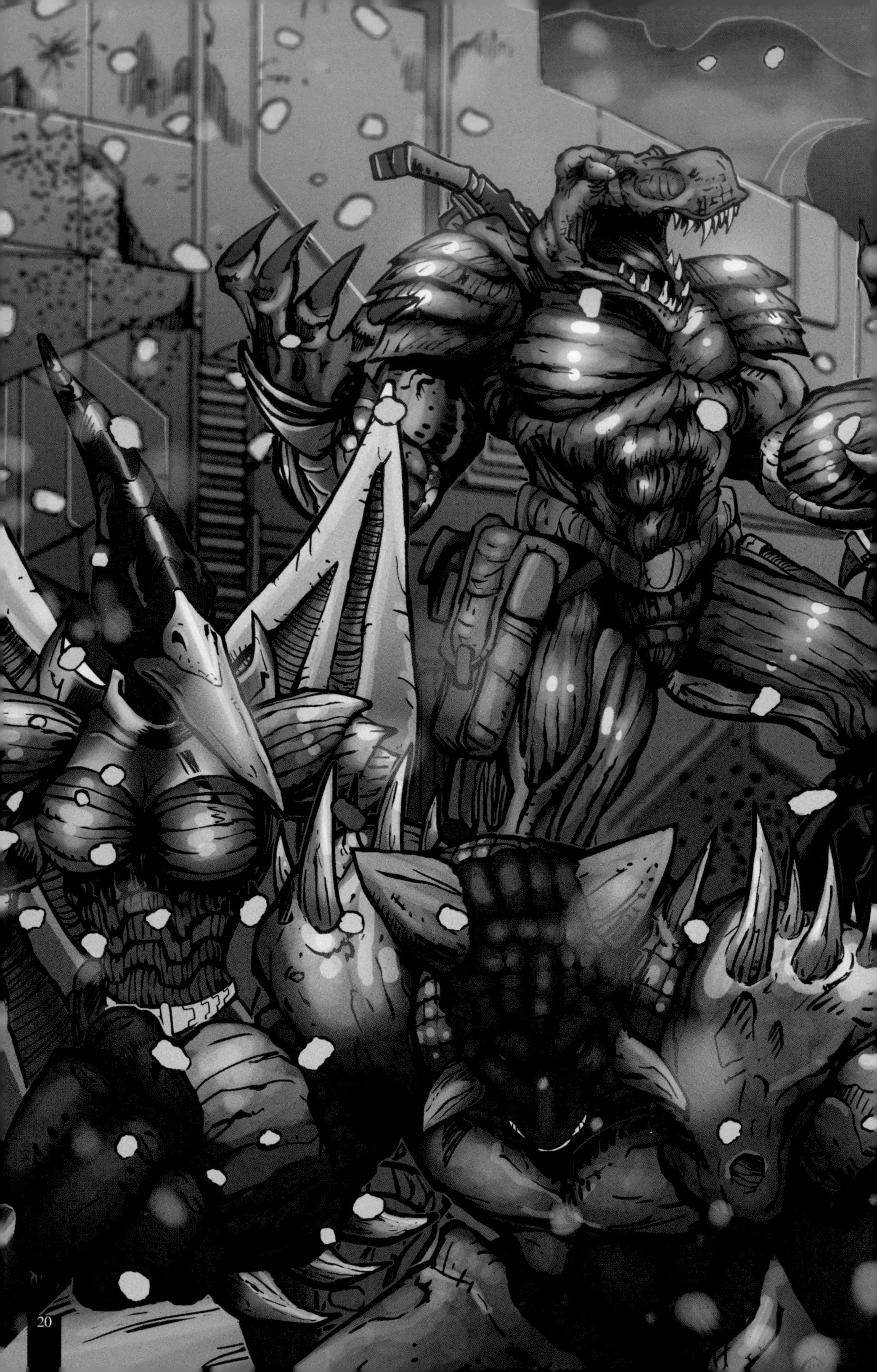

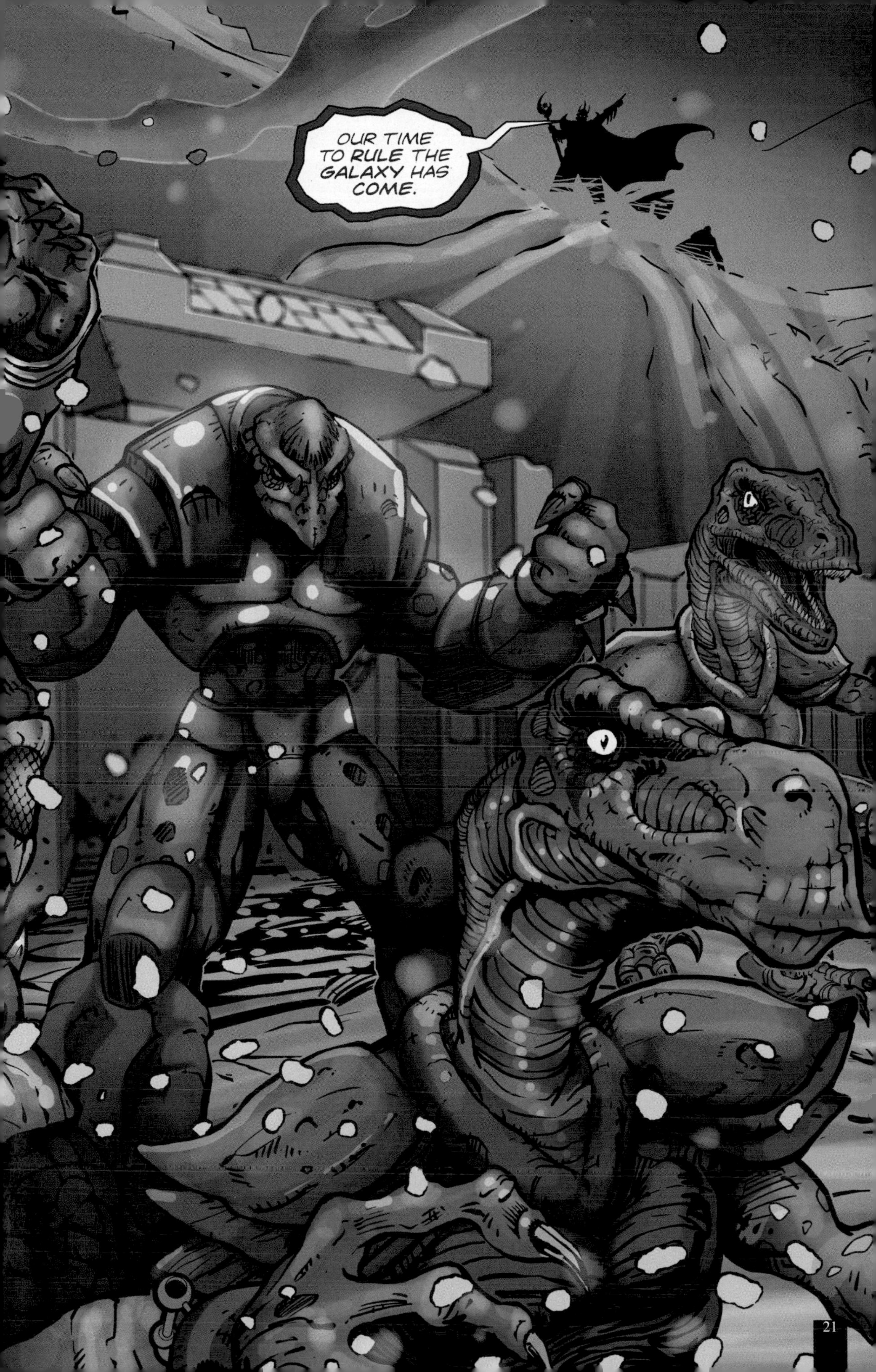
OUR TIME TO RULE THE GALAXY HAS COME.

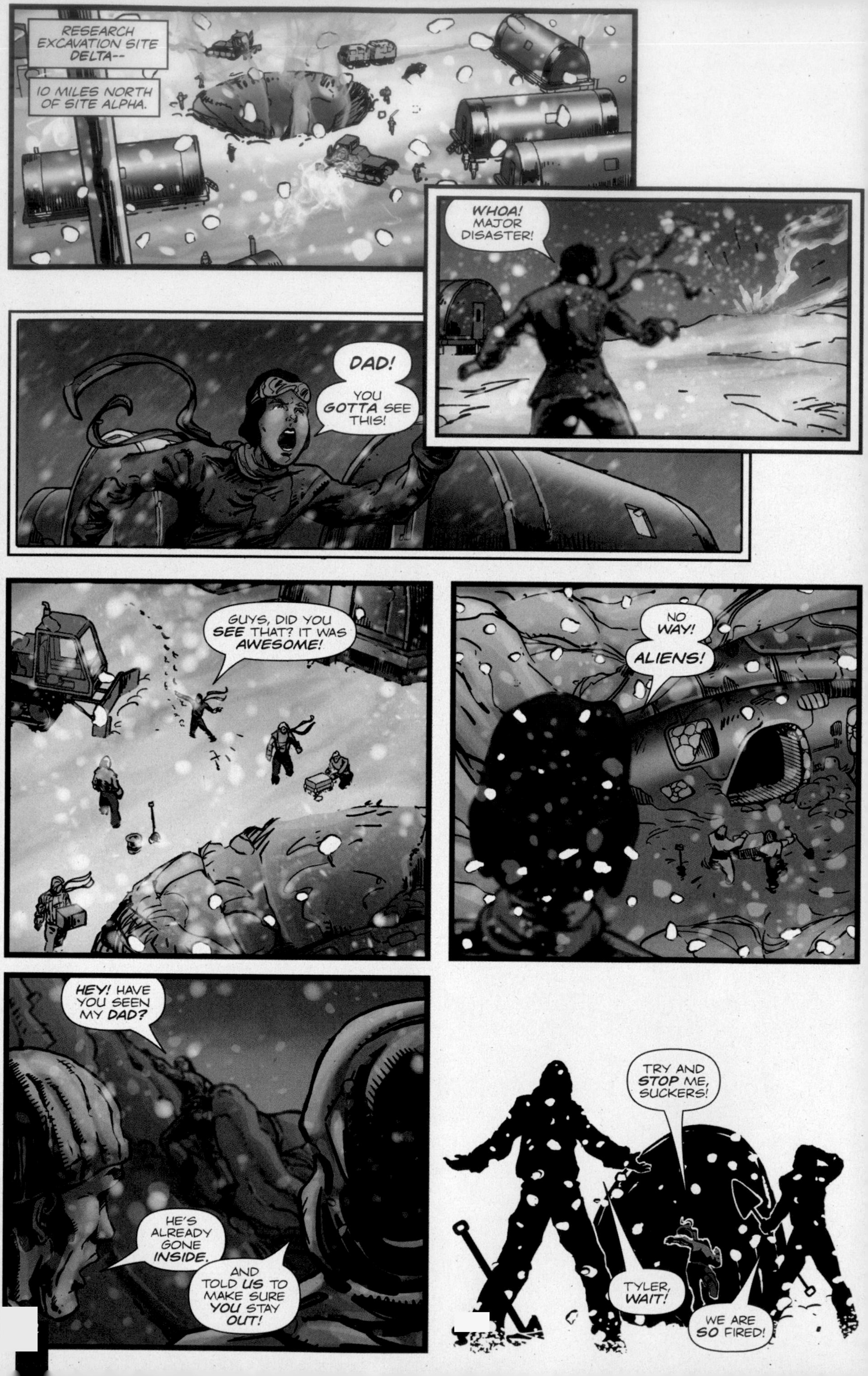
RESEARCH EXCAVATION SITE DELTA--
10 MILES NORTH OF SITE ALPHA.
WHOA! MAJOR DISASTER!
DAD!
YOU GOTTA SEE THIS!
GUYS, DID YOU SEE THAT? IT WAS AWESOME!
NO WAY!
ALIENS!
HEY! HAVE YOU SEEN MY DAD?
HE'S ALREADY GONE INSIDE.
AND TOLD US TO MAKE SURE YOU STAY OUT!
TRY AND STOP ME, SUCKERS!
TYLER, WAIT!
WE ARE SO FIRED!

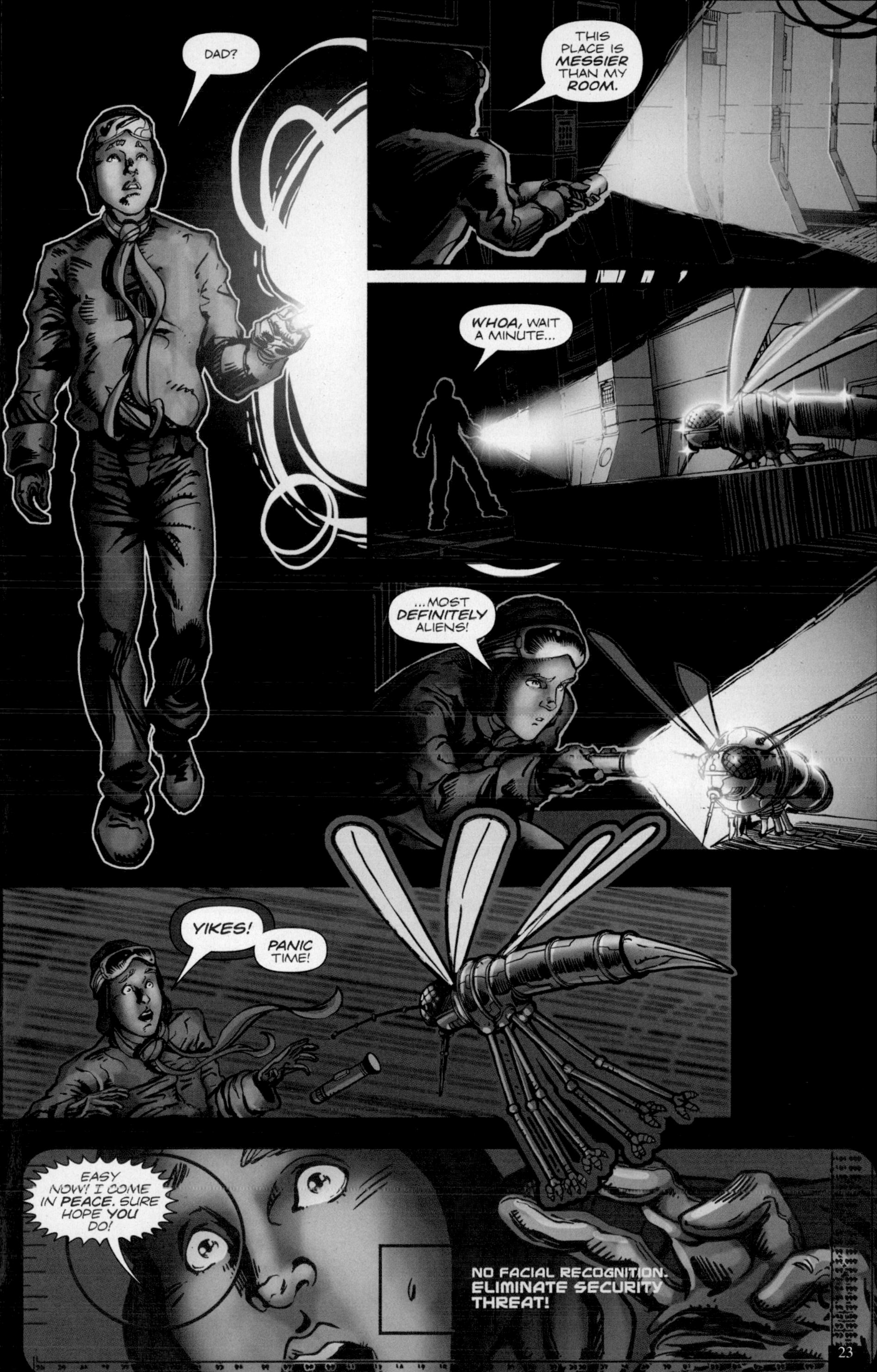
DAD?
THIS PLACE IS MESSIER THAN MY ROOM.
WHOA, WAIT A MINUTE...
...MOST DEFINITELY ALIENS!
YIKES!
PANIC TIME!
EASY NOW! I COME IN PEACE. SURE HOPE YOU DO!
NO FACIAL RECOGNITION. ELIMINATE SECURITY THREAT!

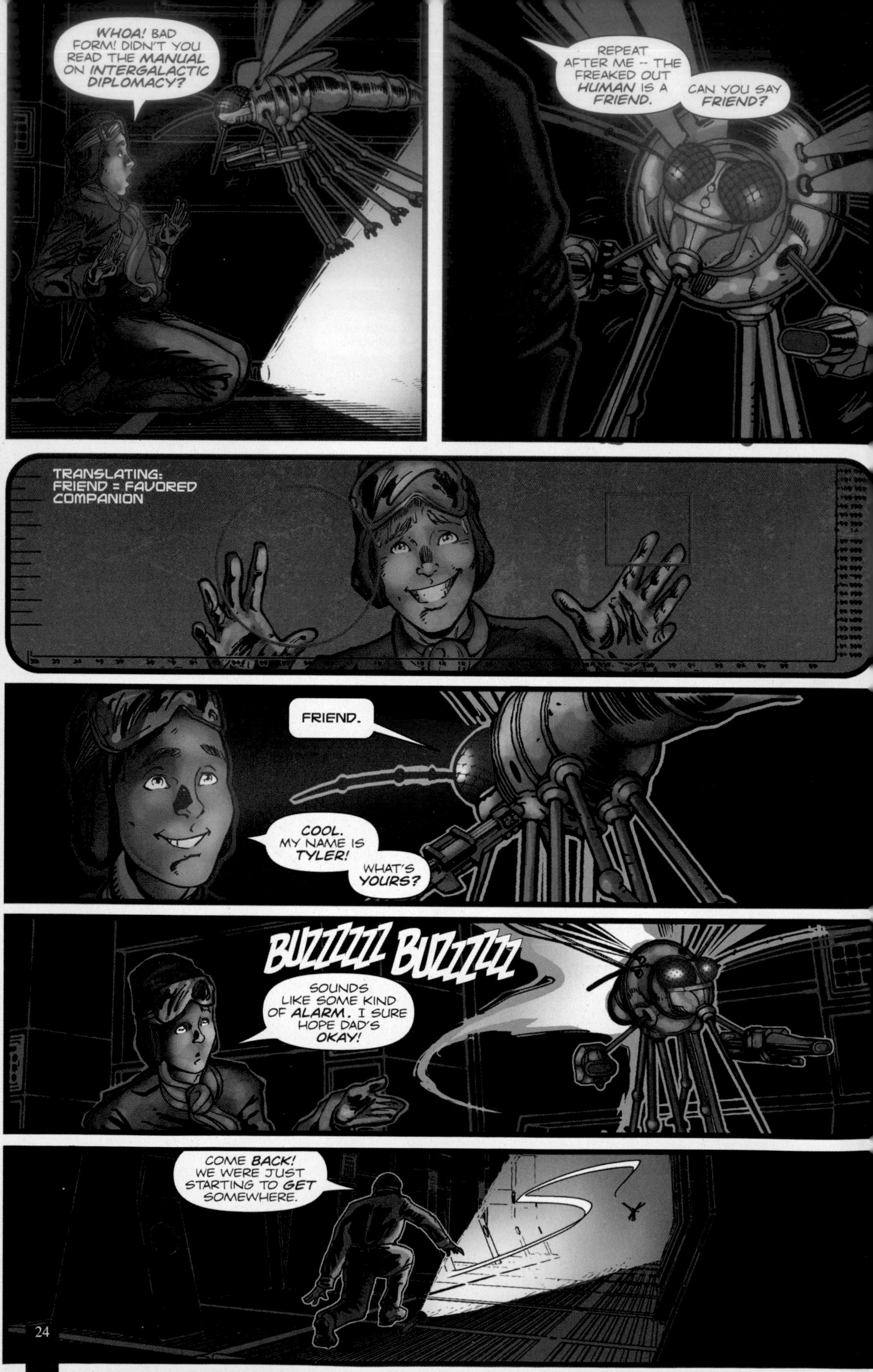
WHOA! BAD FORM! DIDN'T YOU READ THE MANUAL ON INTERGALACTIC DIPLOMACY?
REPEAT AFTER ME -- THE FREAKED OUT HUMAN IS A FRIEND.
CAN YOU SAY FRIEND?
TRANSLATING: FRIEND = FAVORED COMPANION
FRIEND.
COOL. MY NAME IS TYLER!
WHAT'S YOURS?
BUZZZZZ BUZZZZZ
SOUNDS LIKE SOME KIND OF ALARM. I SURE HOPE DAD'S OKAY!
COME BACK! WE WERE JUST STARTING TO GET SOMEWHERE.

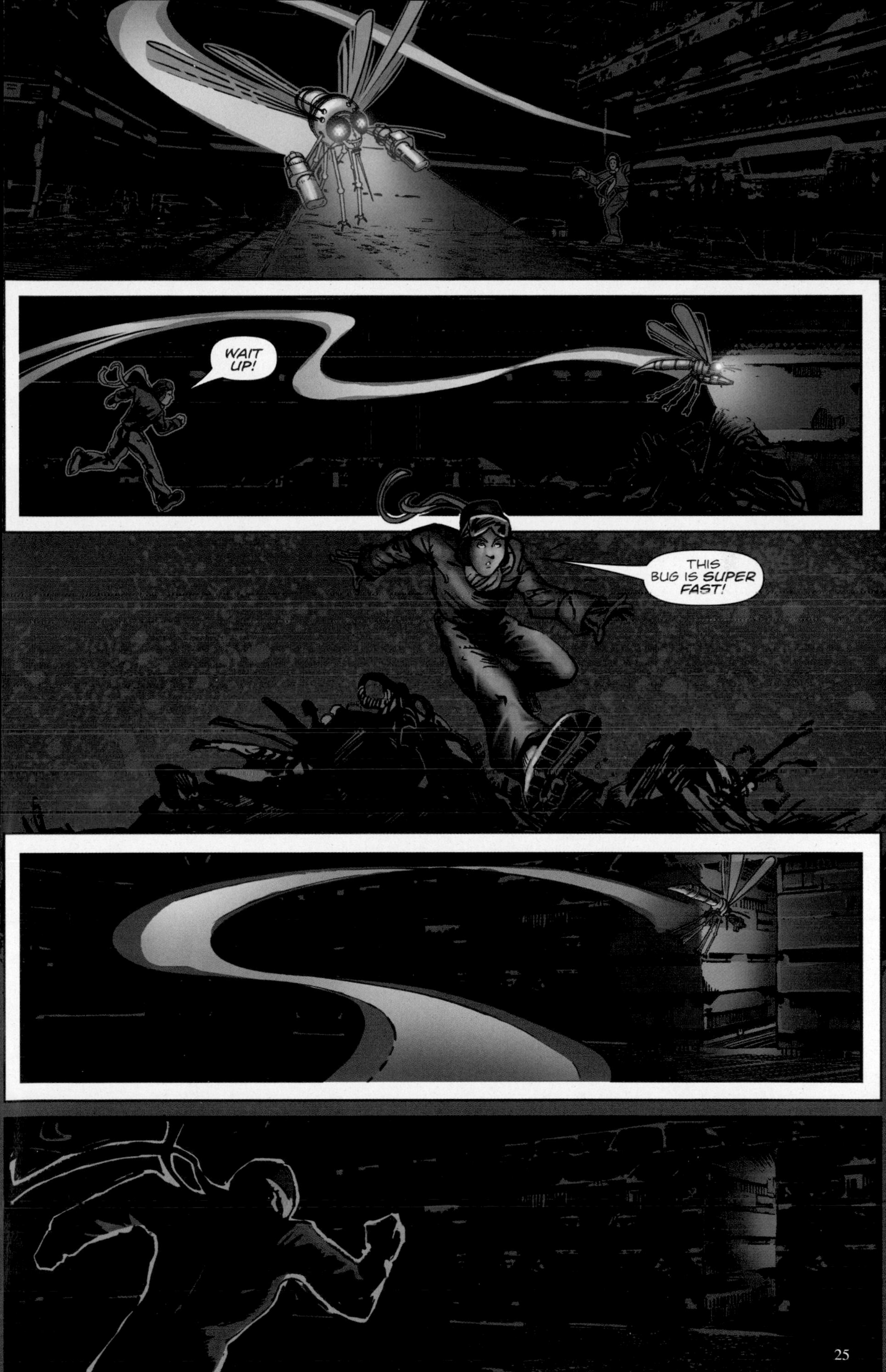
WAIT UP!
THIS BUG IS SUPER FAST!

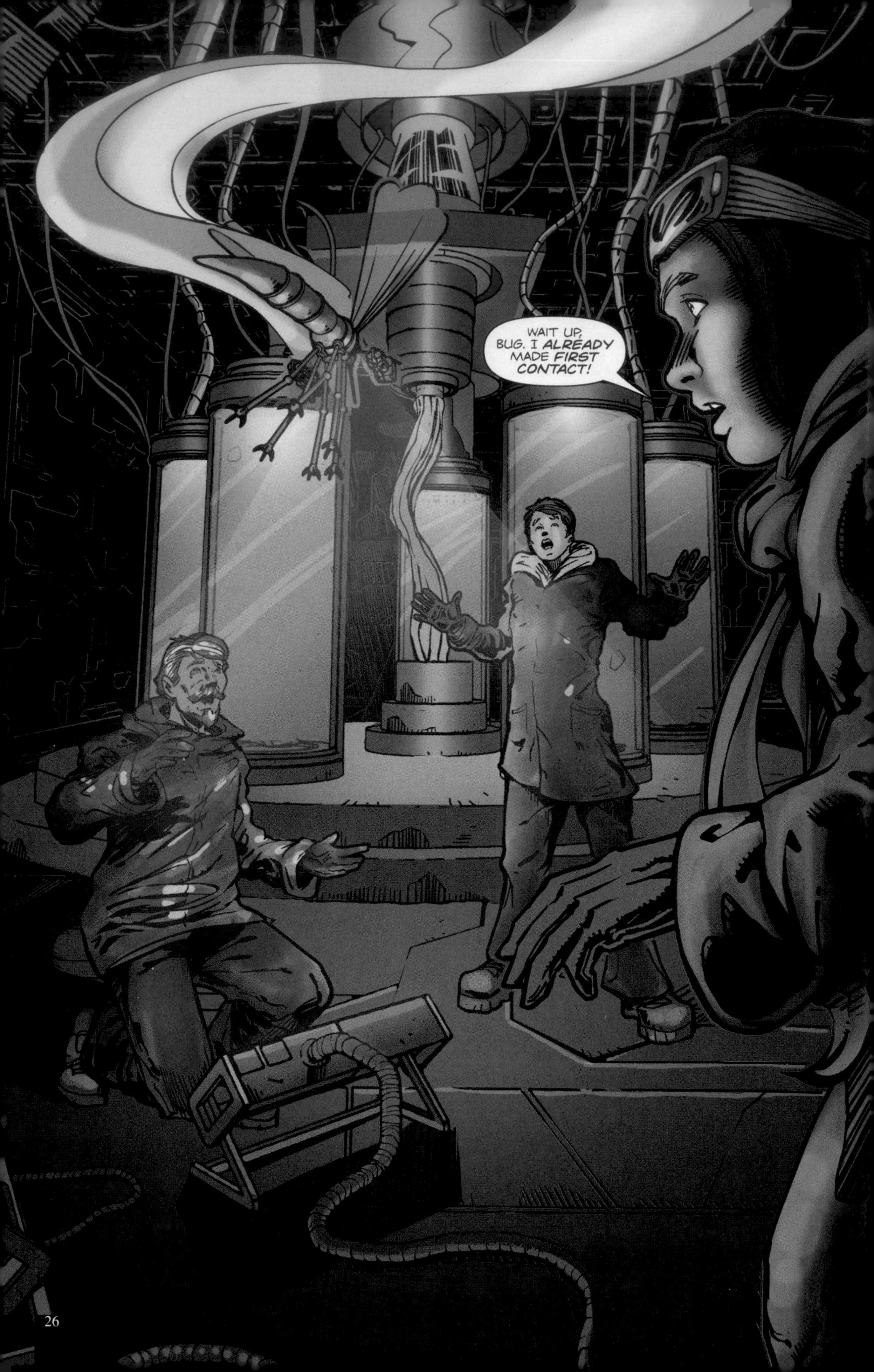
WAIT UP, BUG. I ALREADY MADE FIRST CONTACT!

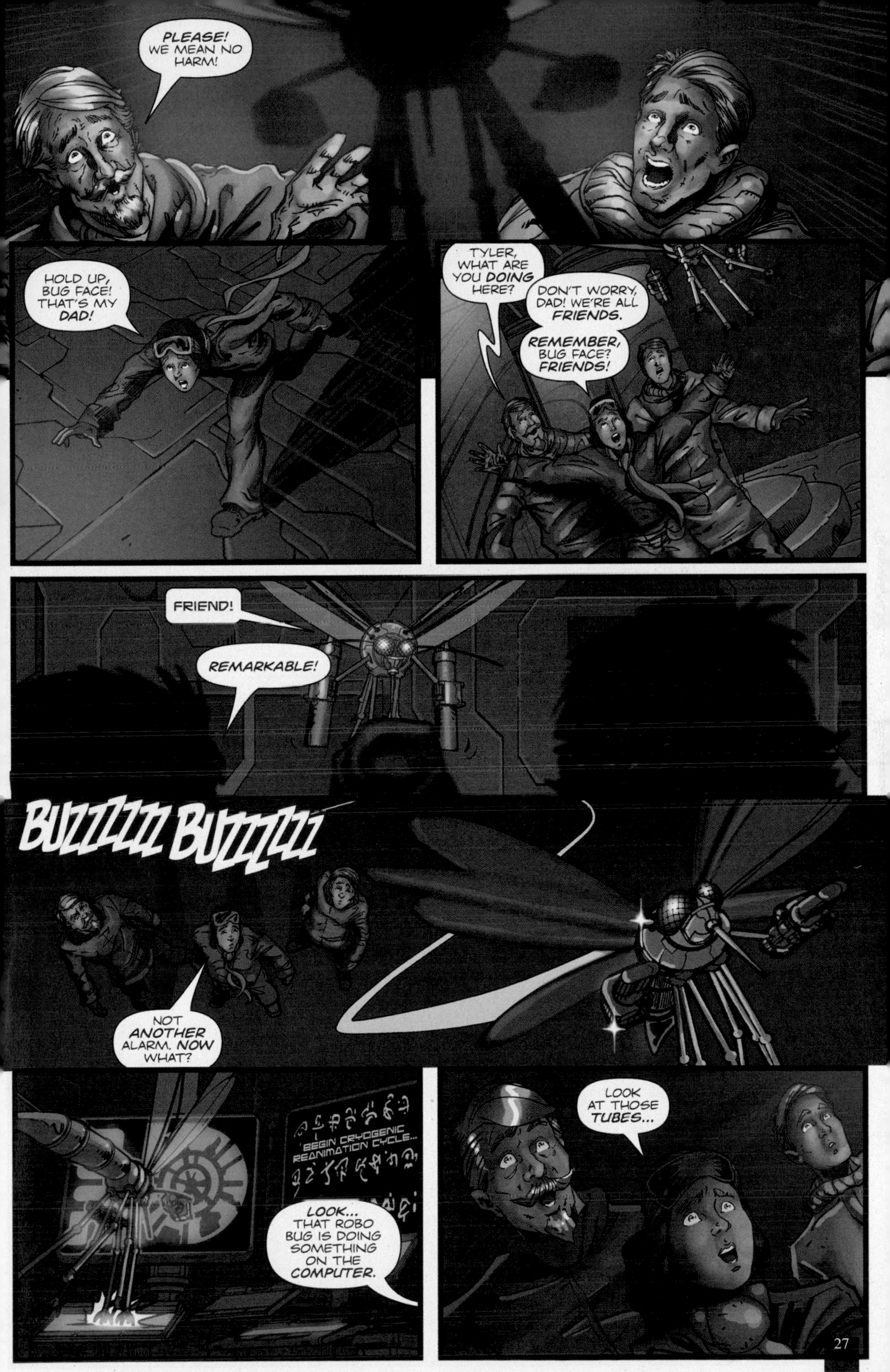
PLEASE! WE MEAN NO HARM!
HOLD UP, BUG FACE! THAT'S MY DAD!
TYLER, WHAT ARE YOU DOING HERE?
DON'T WORRY, DAD! WE'RE ALL FRIENDS.
REMEMBER, BUG FACE? FRIENDS!
FRIEND!
REMARKABLE!
BUZZZZZ BUZZZZZ
NOT ANOTHER ALARM. NOW WHAT?
BEGIN CRYOGENIC REANIMATION CYCLE...
LOOK... THAT ROBO BUG IS DOING SOMETHING ON THE COMPUTER.
LOOK AT THOSE TUBES...

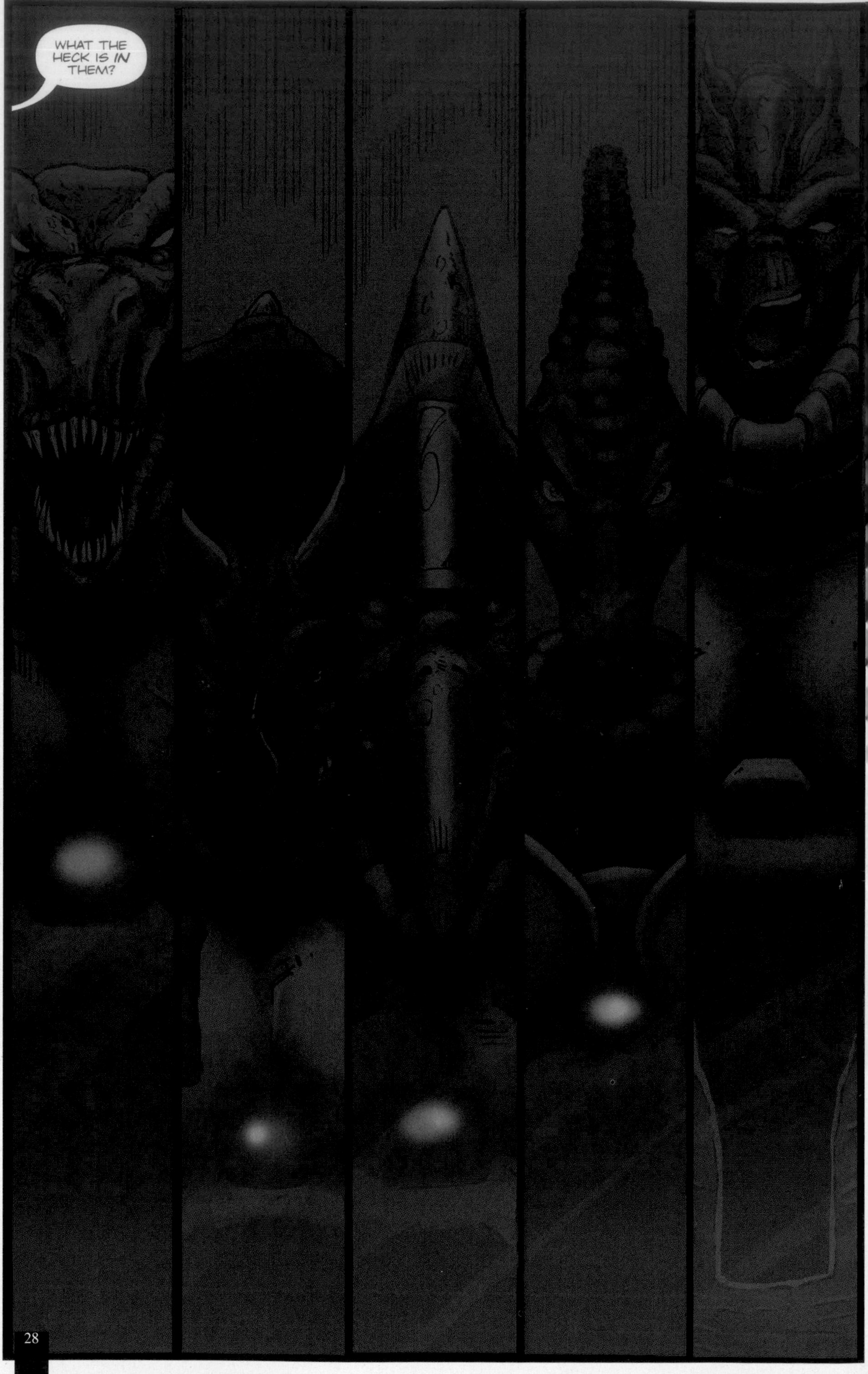
WHAT THE HECK IS IN THEM?

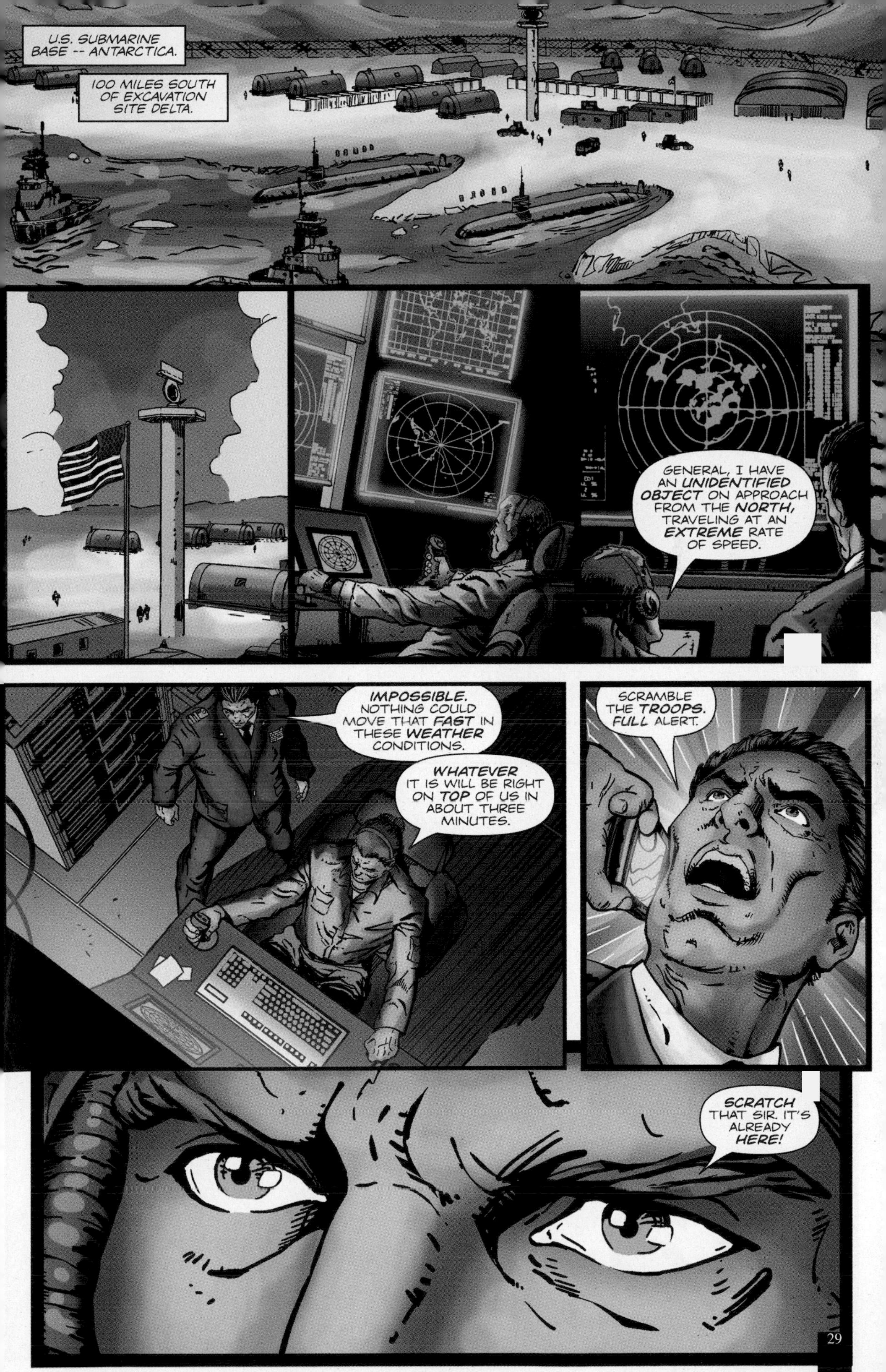
U.S. SUBMARINE BASE -- ANTARCTICA.
100 MILES SOUTH OF EXCAVATION SITE DELTA.
GENERAL, I HAVE AN UNIDENTIFIED OBJECT ON APPROACH FROM THE NORTH, TRAVELING AT AN EXTREME RATE OF SPEED.
IMPOSSIBLE. NOTHING COULD MOVE THAT FAST IN THESE WEATHER CONDITIONS.
WHATEVER IT IS WILL BE RIGHT ON TOP OF US IN ABOUT THREE MINUTES.
SCRAMBLE THE TROOPS. FULL ALERT.
SCRATCH THAT SIR. IT'S ALREADY HERE!

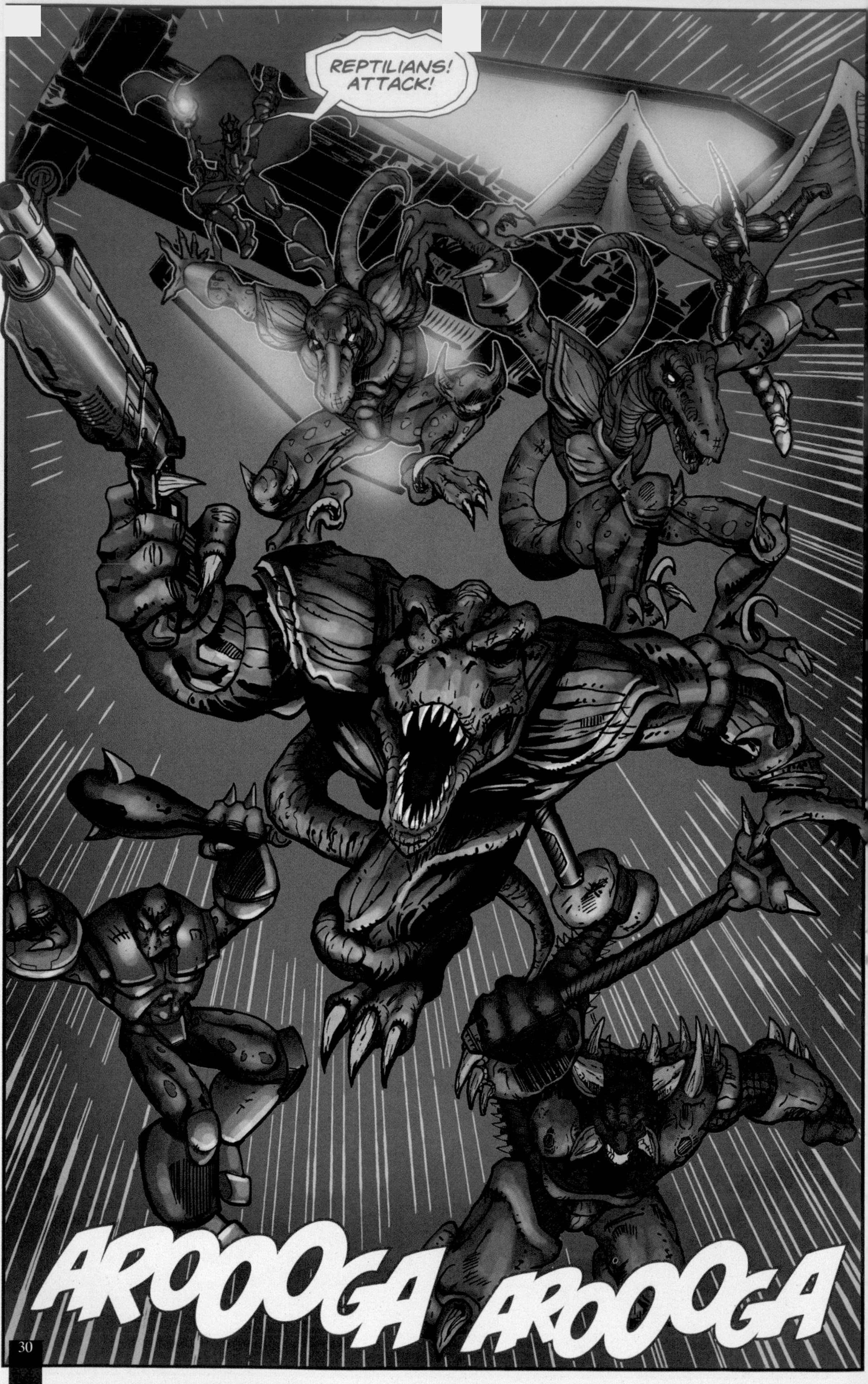

REPTILIANS! ATTACK!
AROOOGA AROOOGA

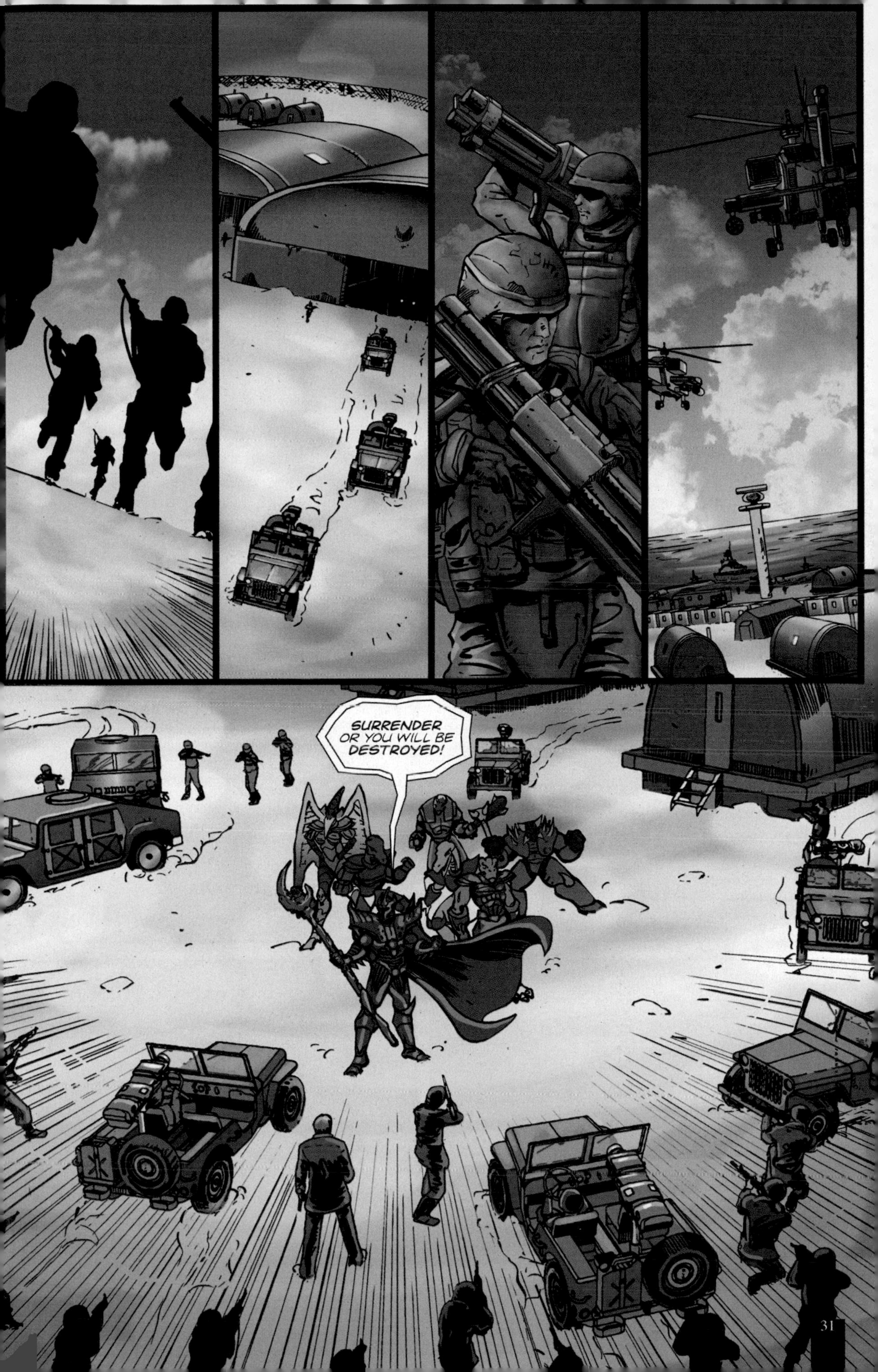
SURRENDER OR YOU WILL BE DESTROYED!

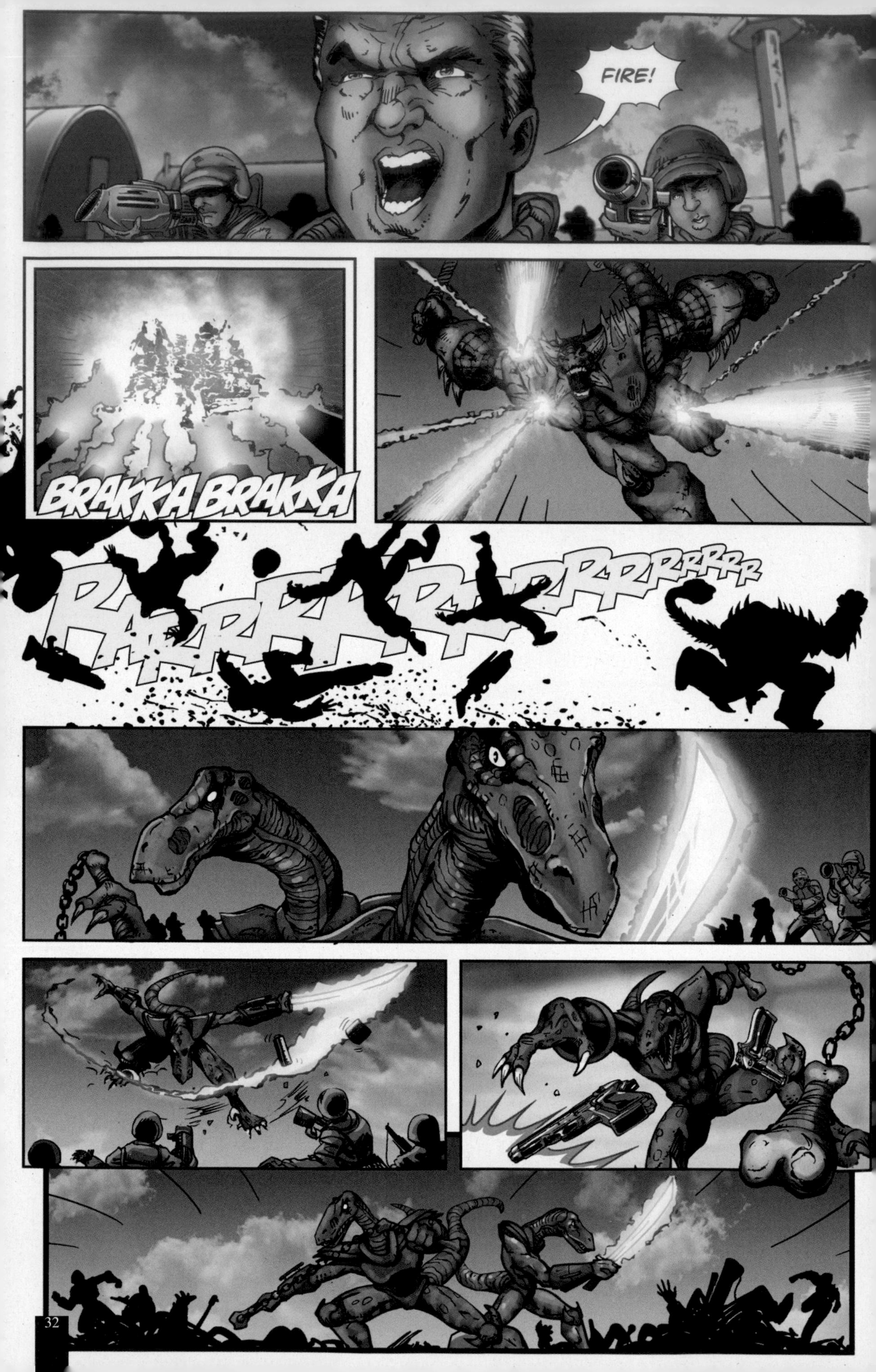
FIRE!
BRAKKA BRAKKA
RARRRRRRRRRRRRRR

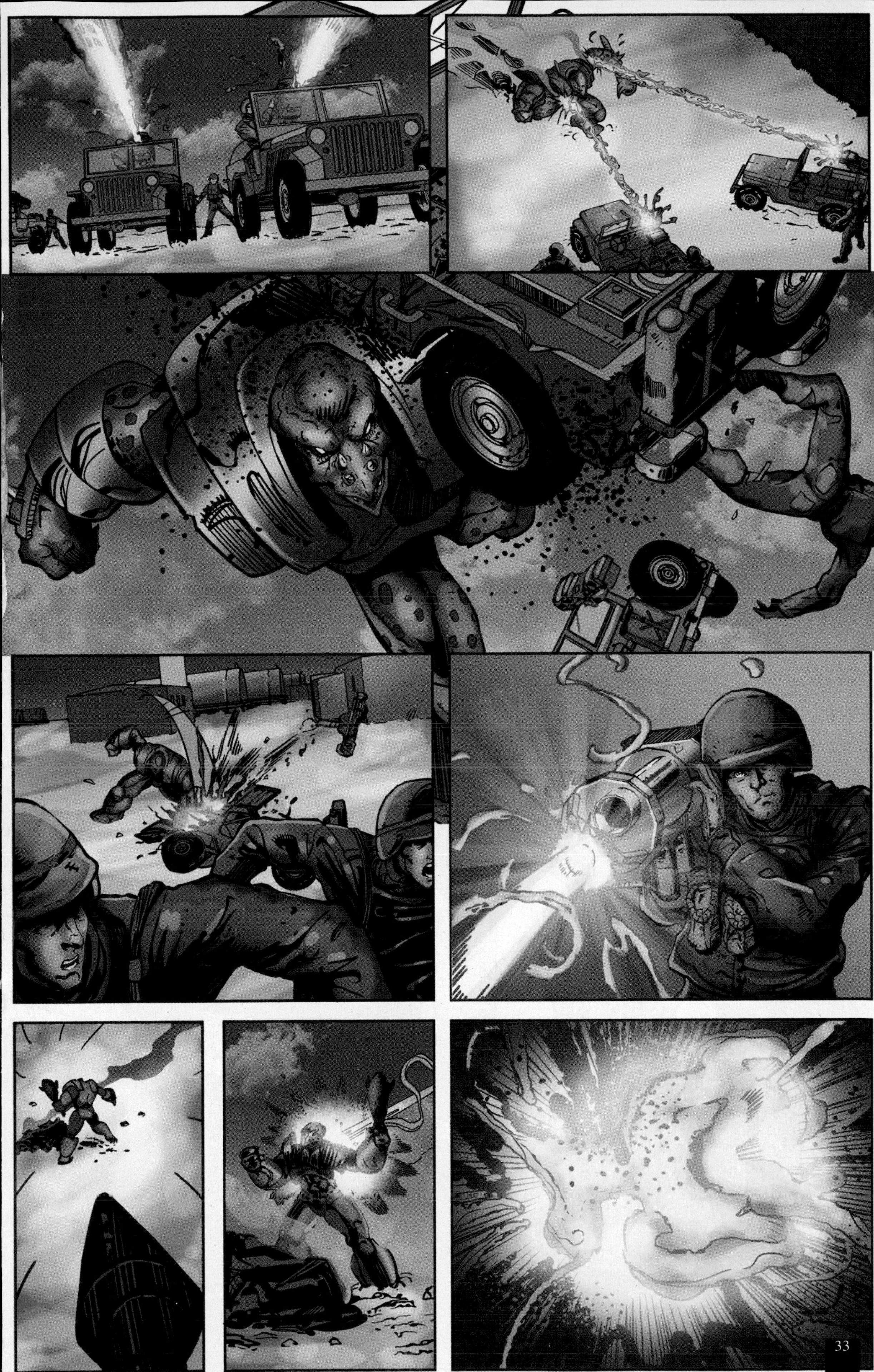

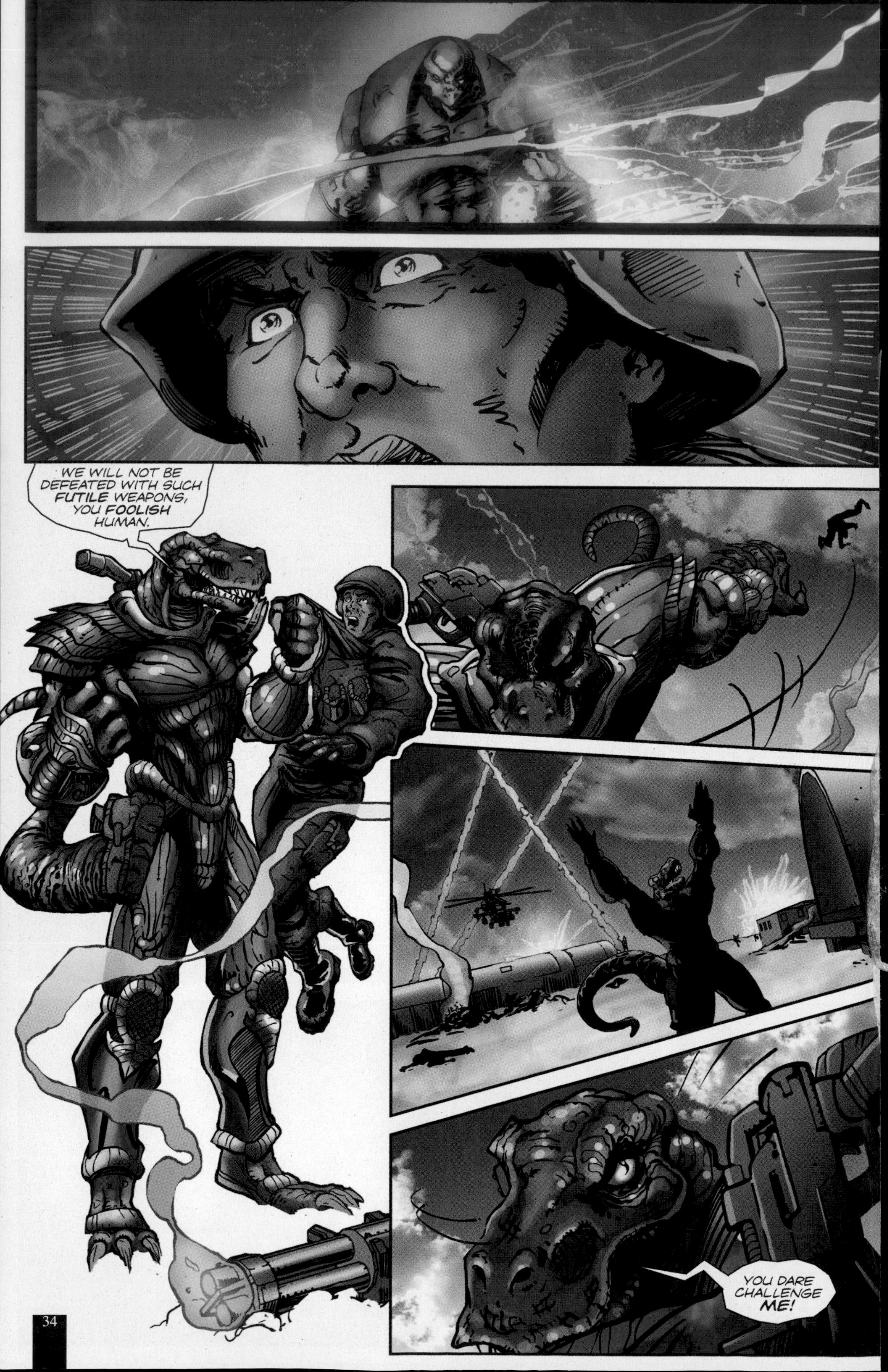
WE WILL NOT BE DEFEATED WITH SUCH FUTILE WEAPONS, YOU FOOLISH HUMAN.
YOU DARE CHALLENGE ME!

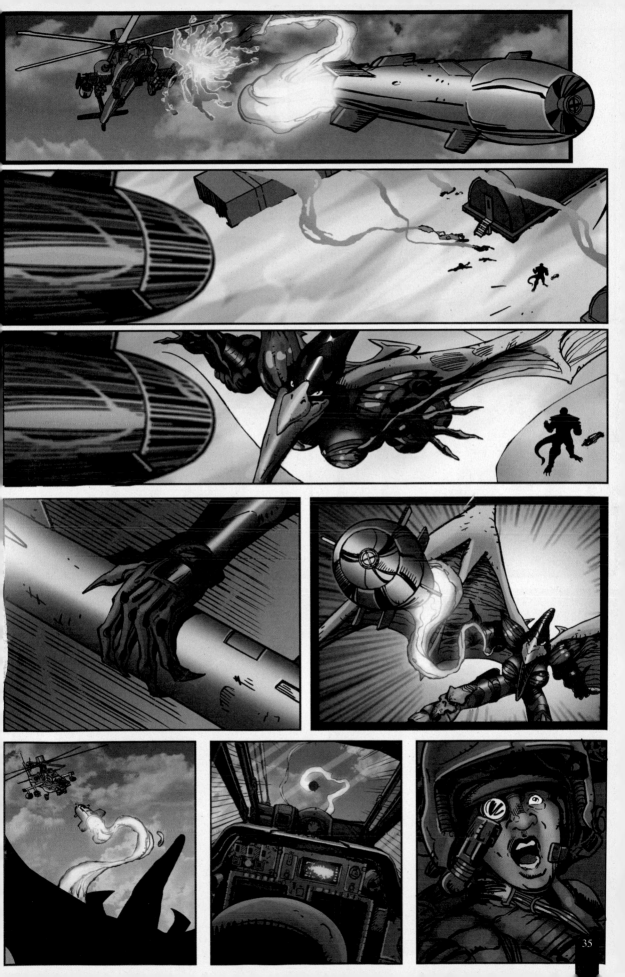

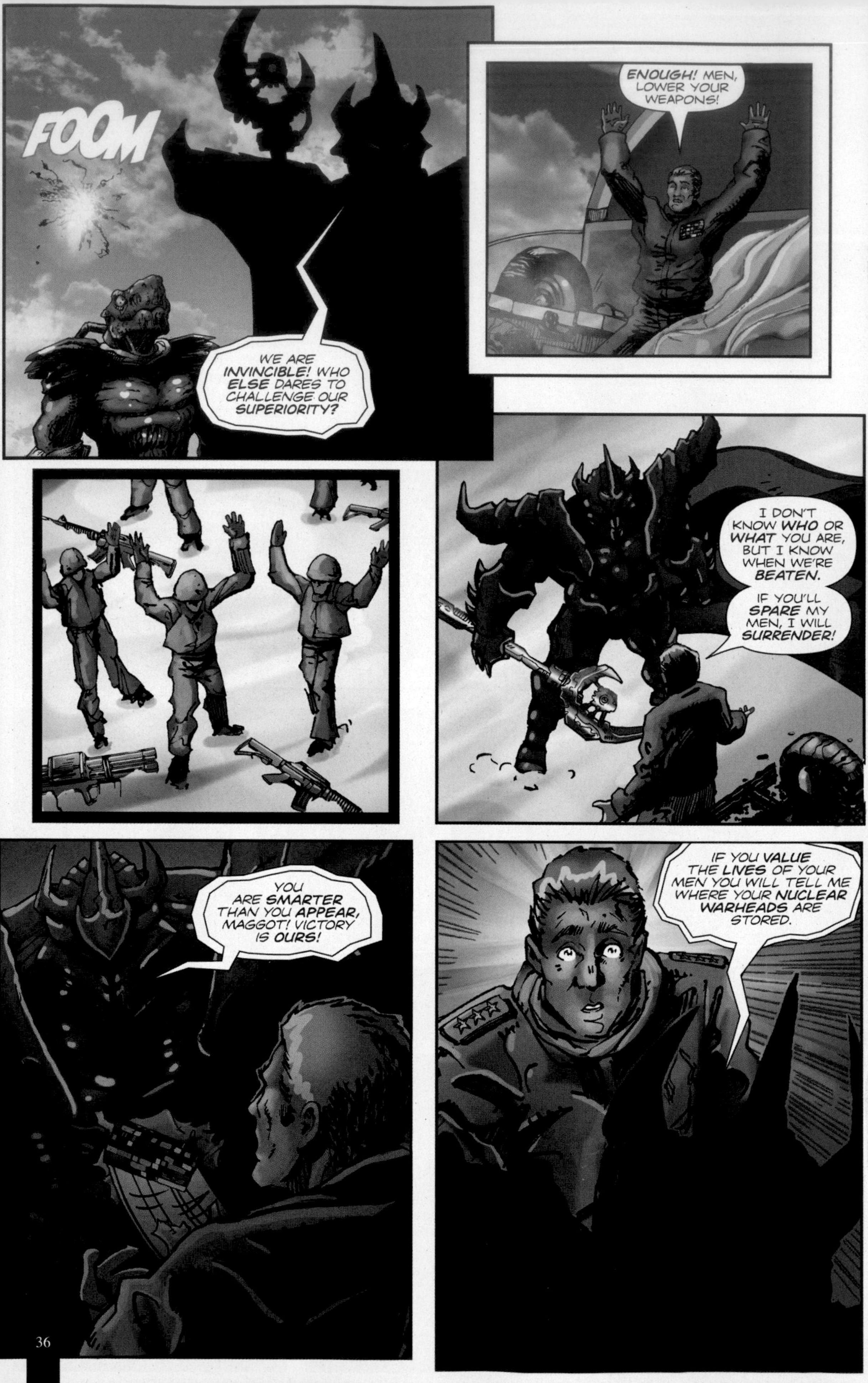
FOOM
WE ARE INVINCIBLE! WHO ELSE DARES TO CHALLENGE OUR SUPERIORITY?
ENOUGH! MEN, LOWER YOUR WEAPONS!
I DON'T KNOW WHO OR WHAT YOU ARE, BUT I KNOW WHEN WE'RE BEATEN.
IF YOU'LL SPARE MY MEN, I WILL SURRENDER!
YOU ARE SMARTER THAN YOU APPEAR, MAGGOT! VICTORY IS OURS!
IF YOU VALUE THE LIVES OF YOUR MEN YOU WILL TELL ME WHERE YOUR NUCLEAR WARHEADS ARE STORED.

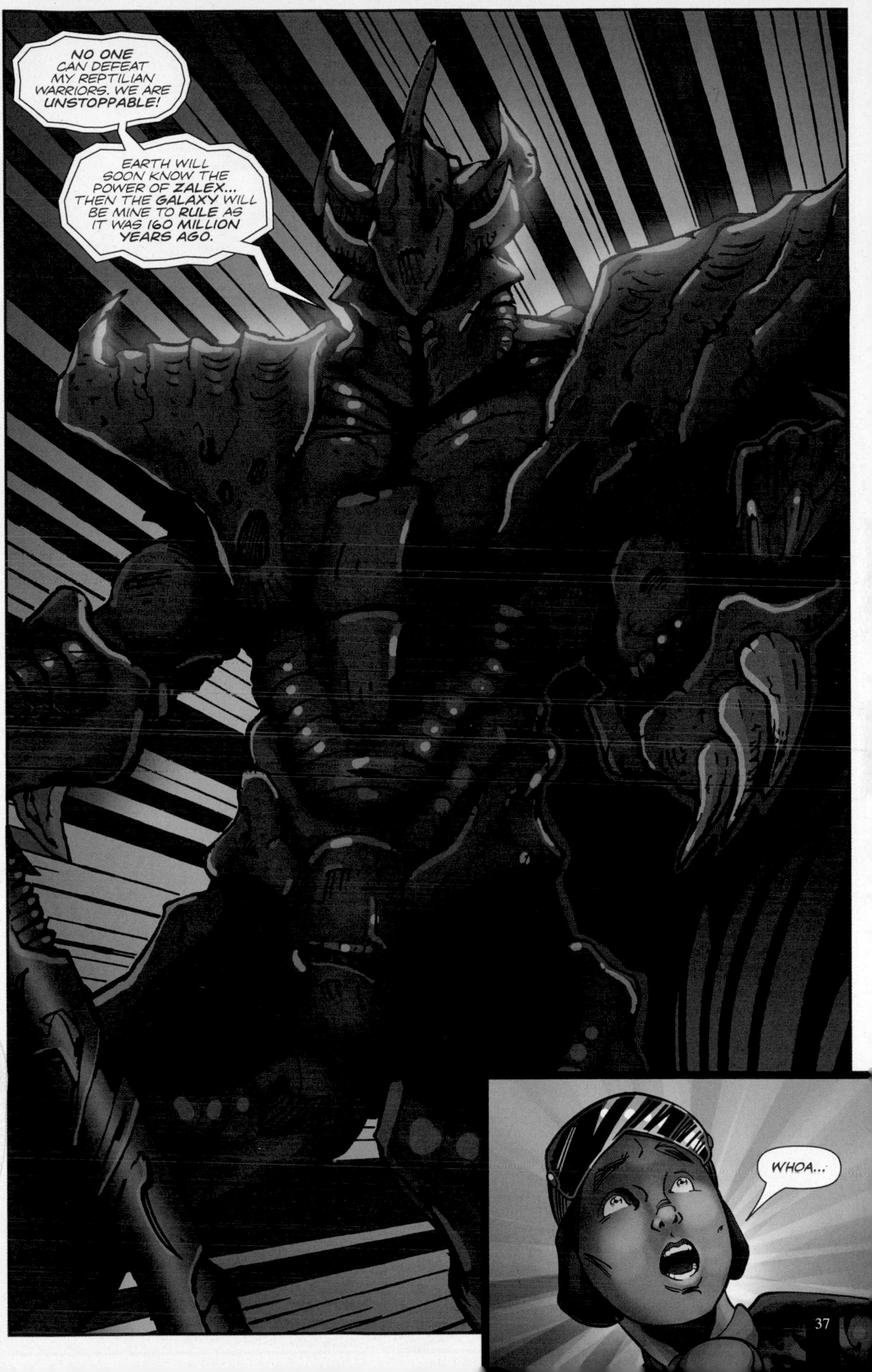
NO ONE CAN DEFEAT MY REPTILIAN WARRIORS. WE ARE UNSTOPPABLE!
EARTH WILL SOON KNOW THE POWER OF ZALEX... THEN THE GALAXY WILL BE MINE TO RULE AS IT WAS 160 MILLION YEARS AGO.
WHOA...

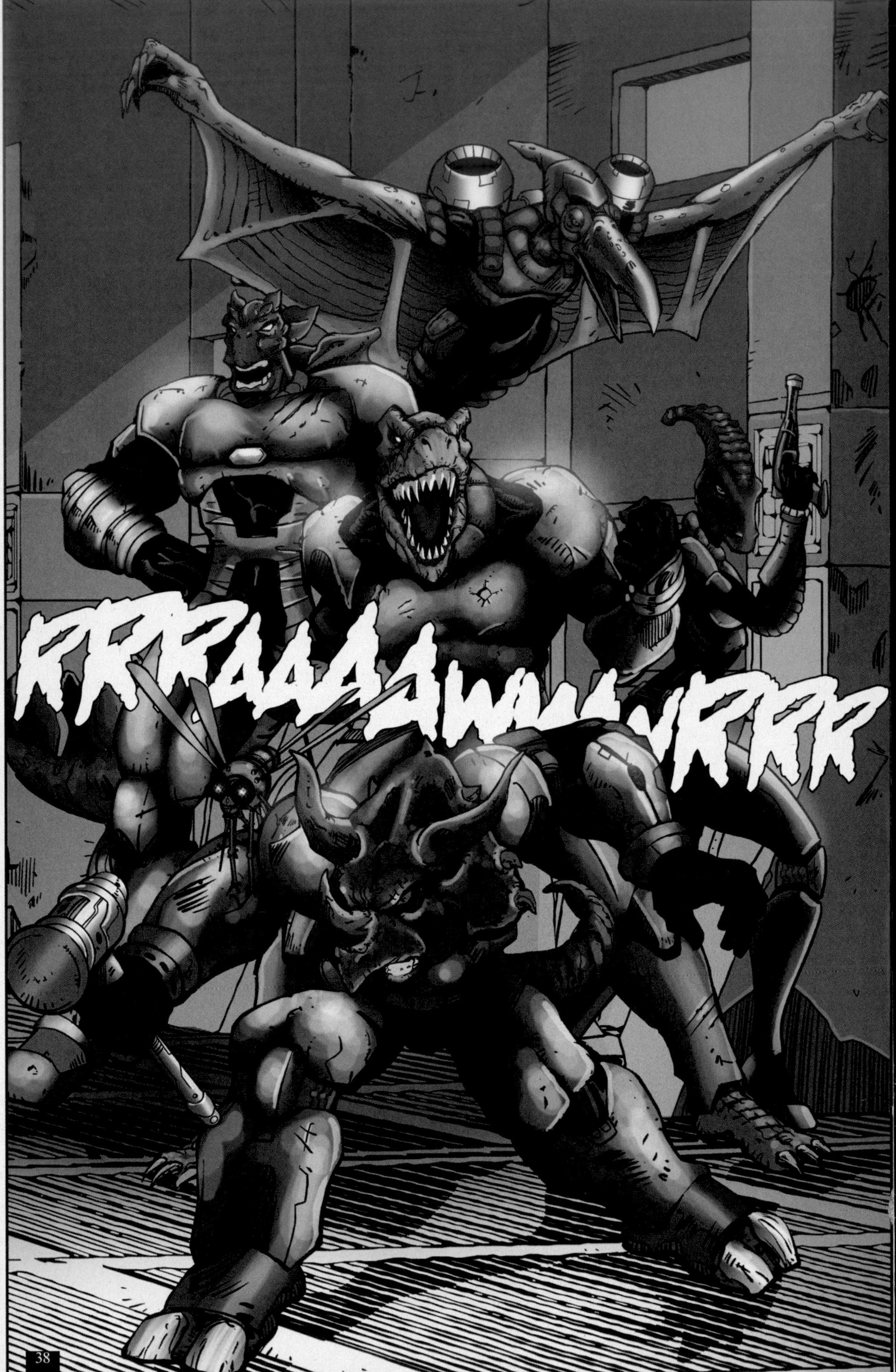
RRRAAAAWWWWRRRR

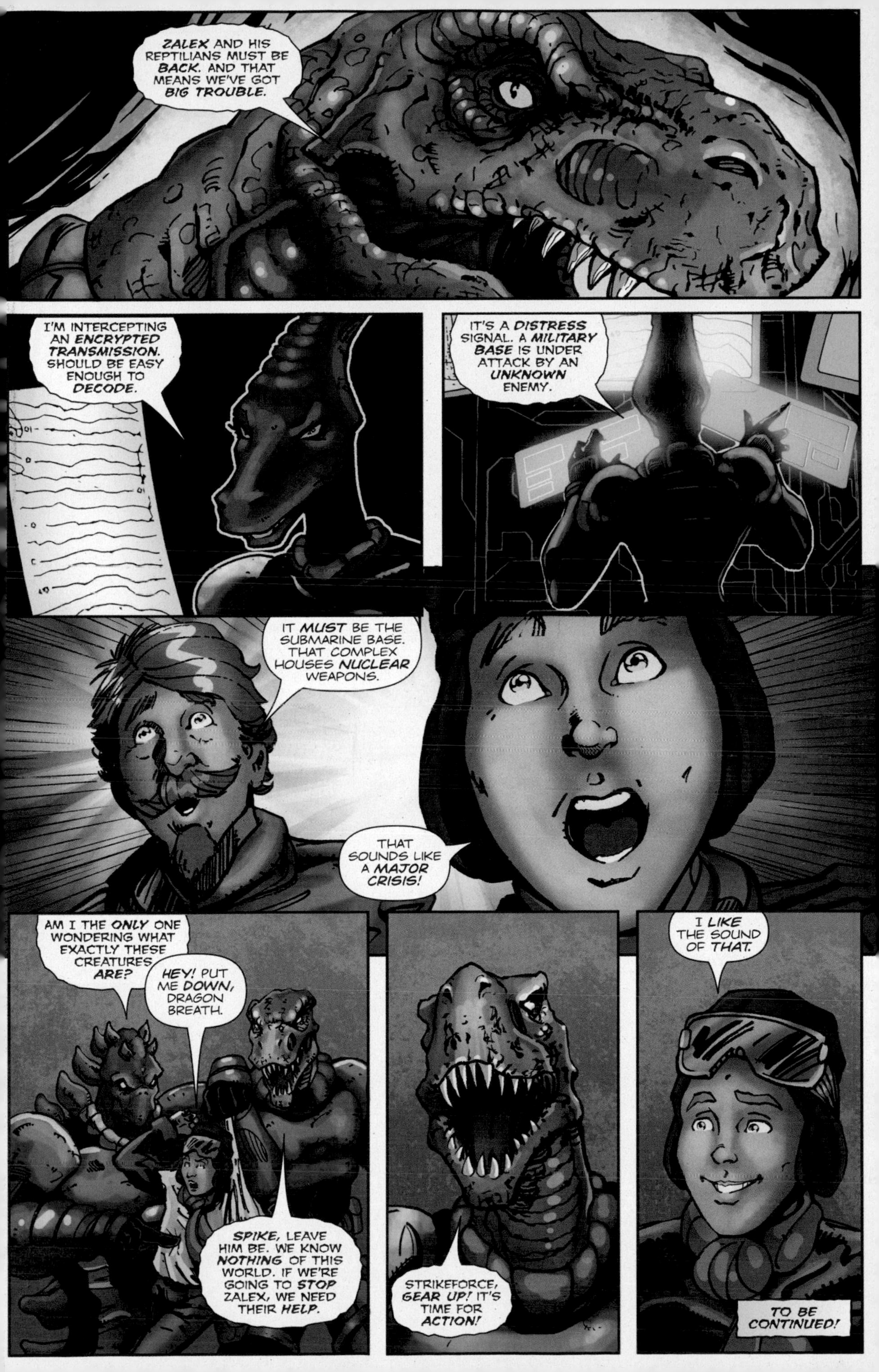
ZALEX AND HIS REPTILIANS MUST BE BACK. AND THAT MEANS WE'VE GOT BIG TROUBLE.
I'M INTERCEPTING AN ENCRYPTED TRANSMISSION. SHOULD BE EASY ENOUGH TO DECODE.
IT'S A DISTRESS SIGNAL. A MILITARY BASE IS UNDER ATTACK BY AN UNKNOWN ENEMY.
IT MUST BE THE SUBMARINE BASE. THAT COMPLEX HOUSES NUCLEAR WEAPONS.
THAT SOUNDS LIKE A MAJOR CRISIS!
AM I THE ONLY ONE WONDERING WHAT EXACTLY THESE CREATURES ARE?
HEY! PUT ME DOWN, DRAGON BREATH.
SPIKE, LEAVE HIM BE. WE KNOW NOTHING OF THIS WORLD. IF WE'RE GOING TO STOP ZALEX, WE NEED THEIR HELP.
STRIKEFORCE, GEAR UP! IT'S TIME FOR ACTION!
I LIKE THE SOUND OF THAT.
TO BE CONTINUED!

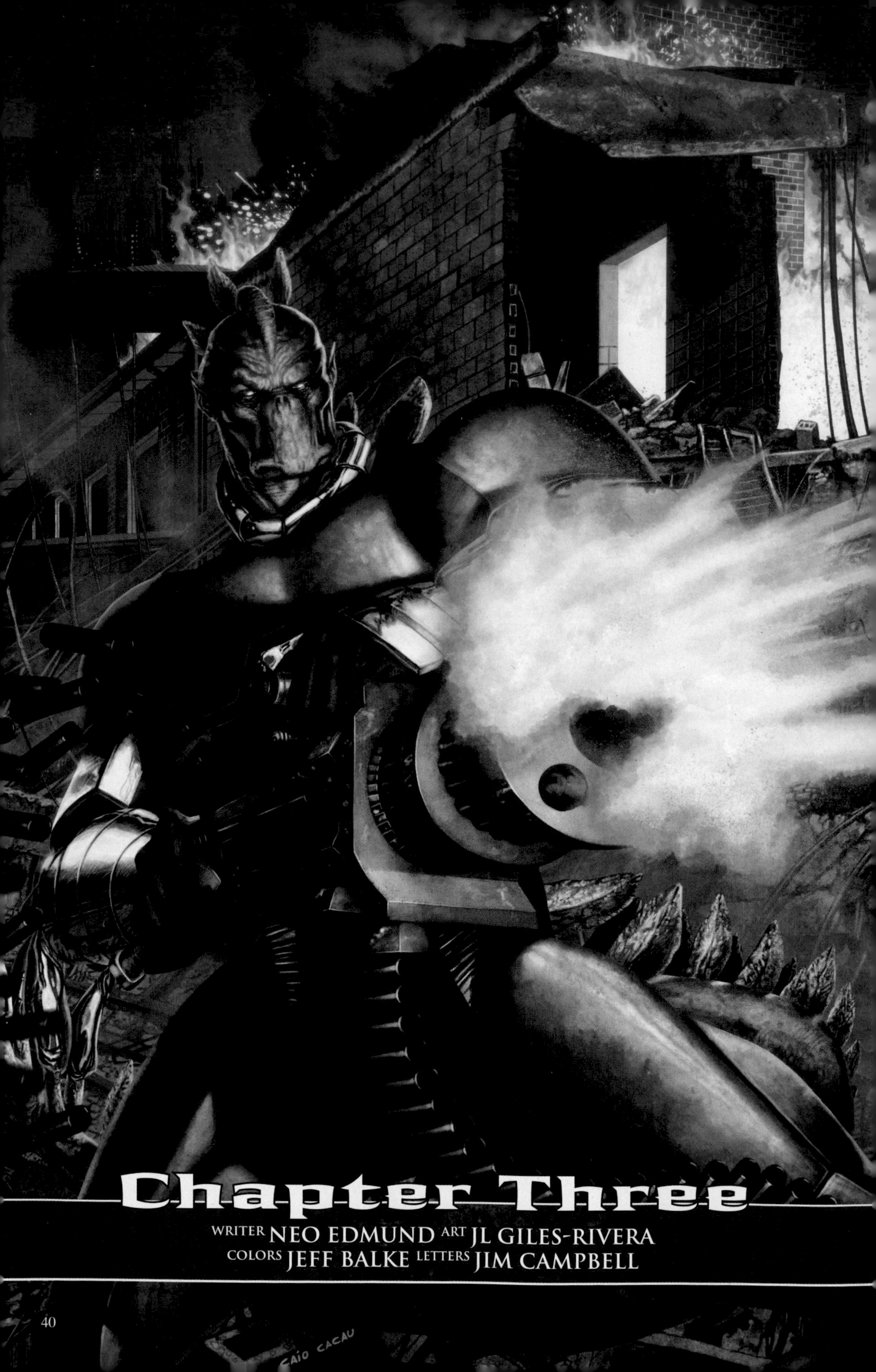
CAIO CACAU

Chapter Three

WRITER NEO EDMUND ART JL GILES-RIVERA
COLORS JEFF BALKE LETTERS JIM CAMPBELL

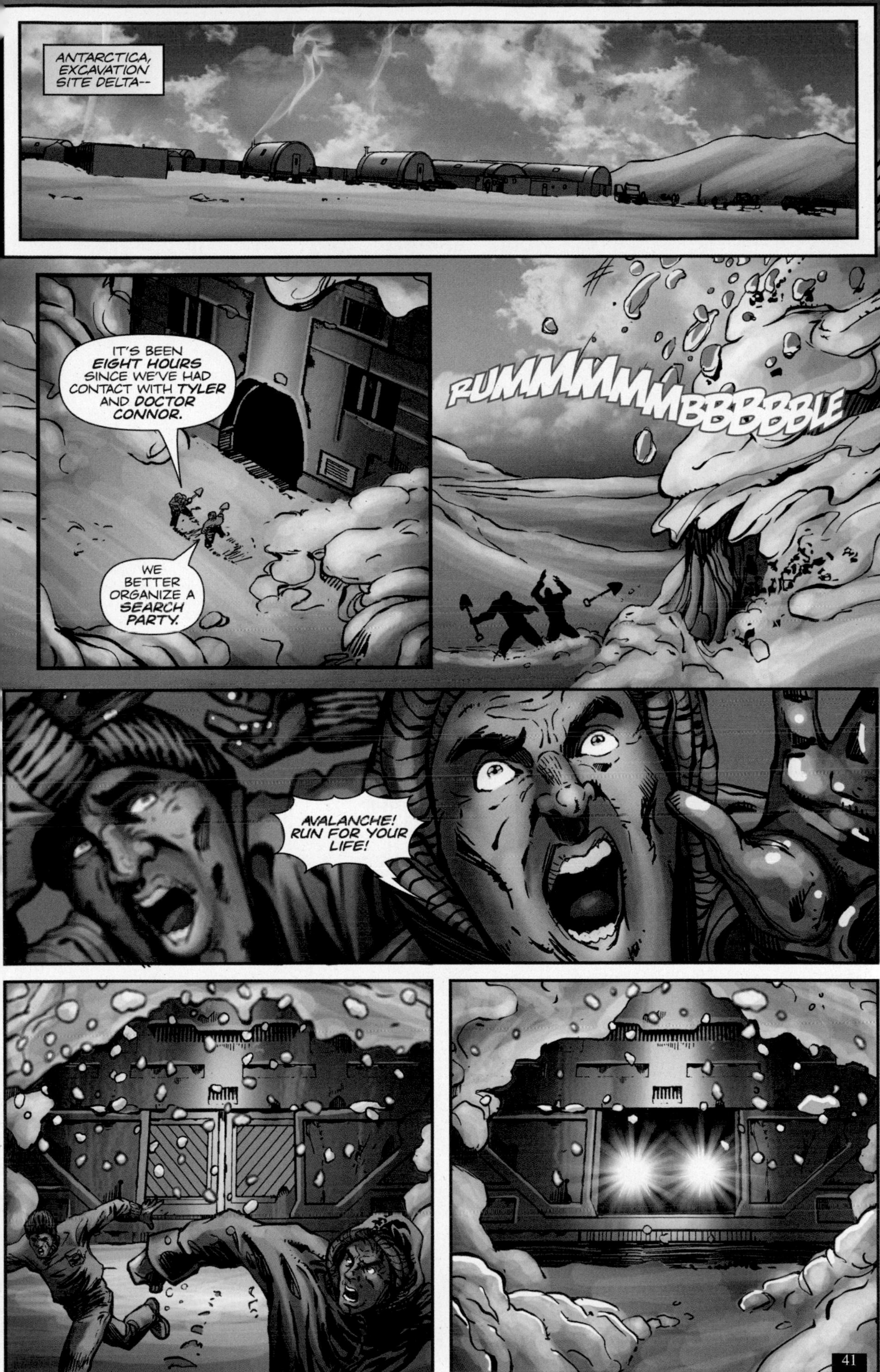
ANTARCTICA, EXCAVATION SITE DELTA--
IT'S BEEN EIGHT HOURS SINCE WE'VE HAD CONTACT WITH TYLER AND DOCTOR CONNOR.
WE BETTER ORGANIZE A SEARCH PARTY.
RUMMMMMMBBBBBLE
AVALANCHE! RUN FOR YOUR LIFE!

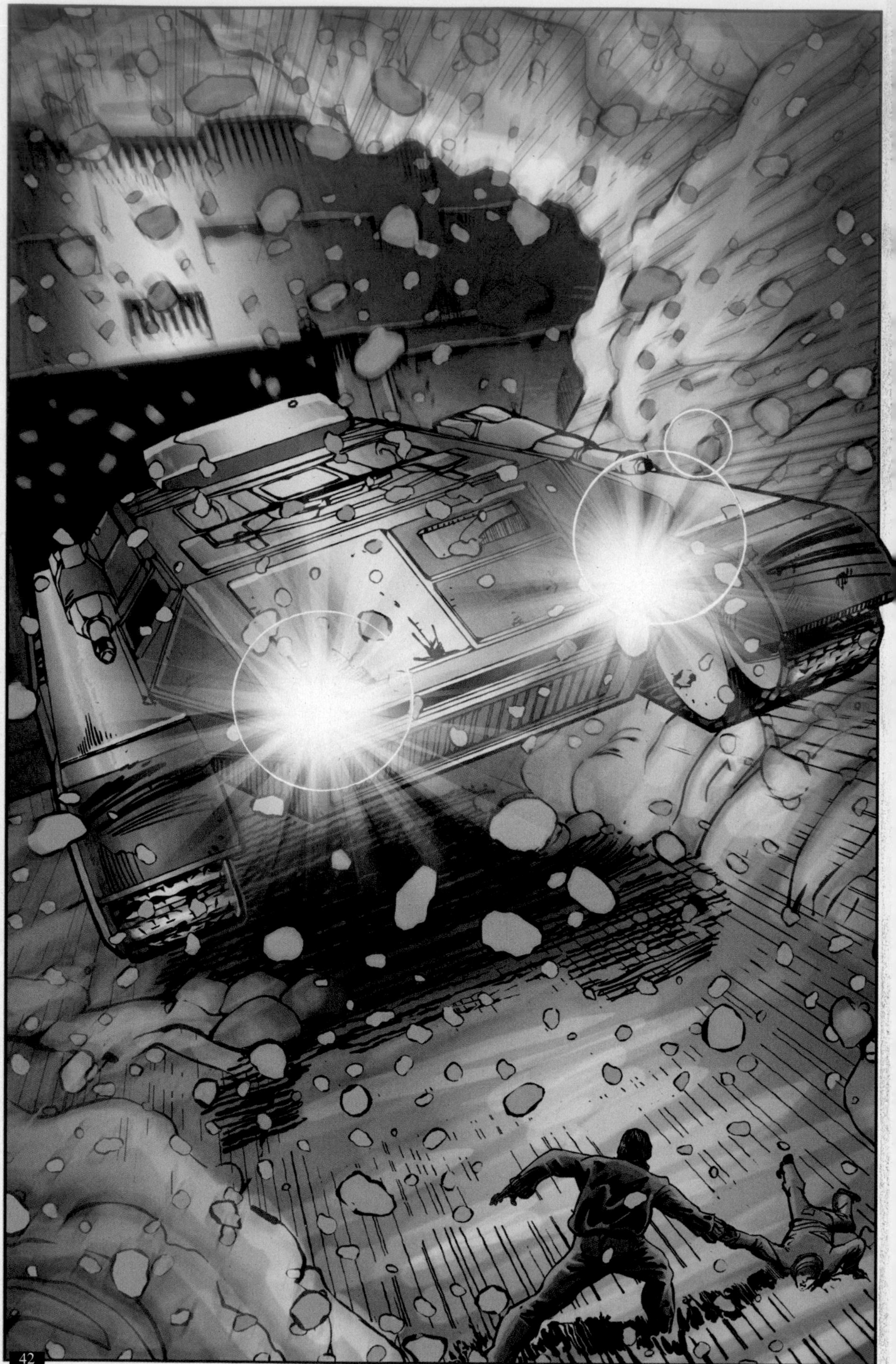

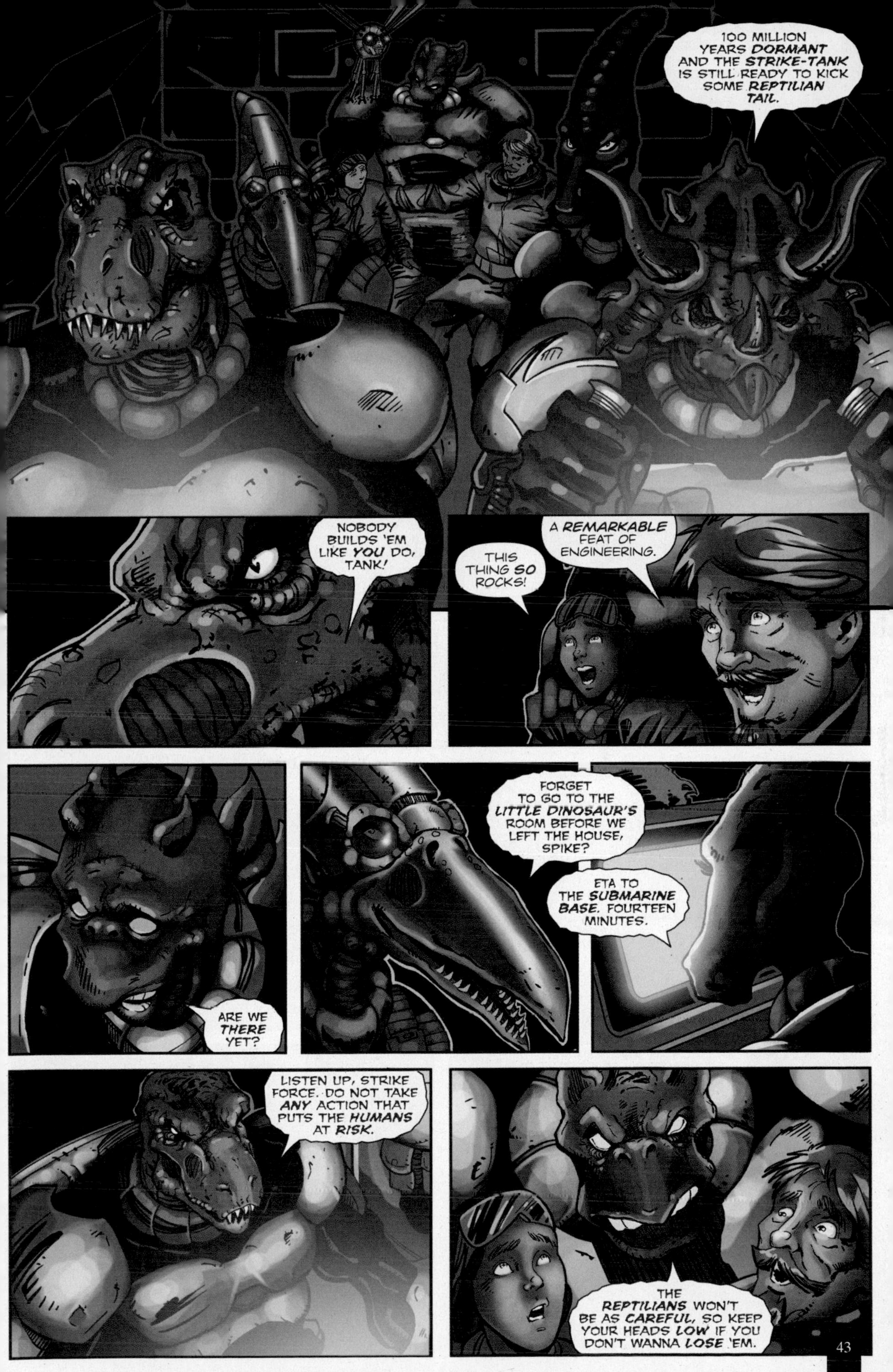
100 MILLION YEARS DORMANT AND THE STRIKE-TANK IS STILL READY TO KICK SOME REPTILIAN TAIL.
NOBODY BUILDS 'EM LIKE YOU DO, TANK!
A REMARKABLE FEAT OF ENGINEERING.
THIS THING SO ROCKS!
ARE WE THERE YET?
FORGET TO GO TO THE LITTLE DINOSAUR'S ROOM BEFORE WE LEFT THE HOUSE, SPIKE?
ETA TO THE SUBMARINE BASE. FOURTEEN MINUTES.
LISTEN UP, STRIKE FORCE. DO NOT TAKE ANY ACTION THAT PUTS THE HUMANS AT RISK.
THE REPTILIANS WON'T BE AS CAREFUL, SO KEEP YOUR HEADS LOW IF YOU DON'T WANNA LOSE 'EM.

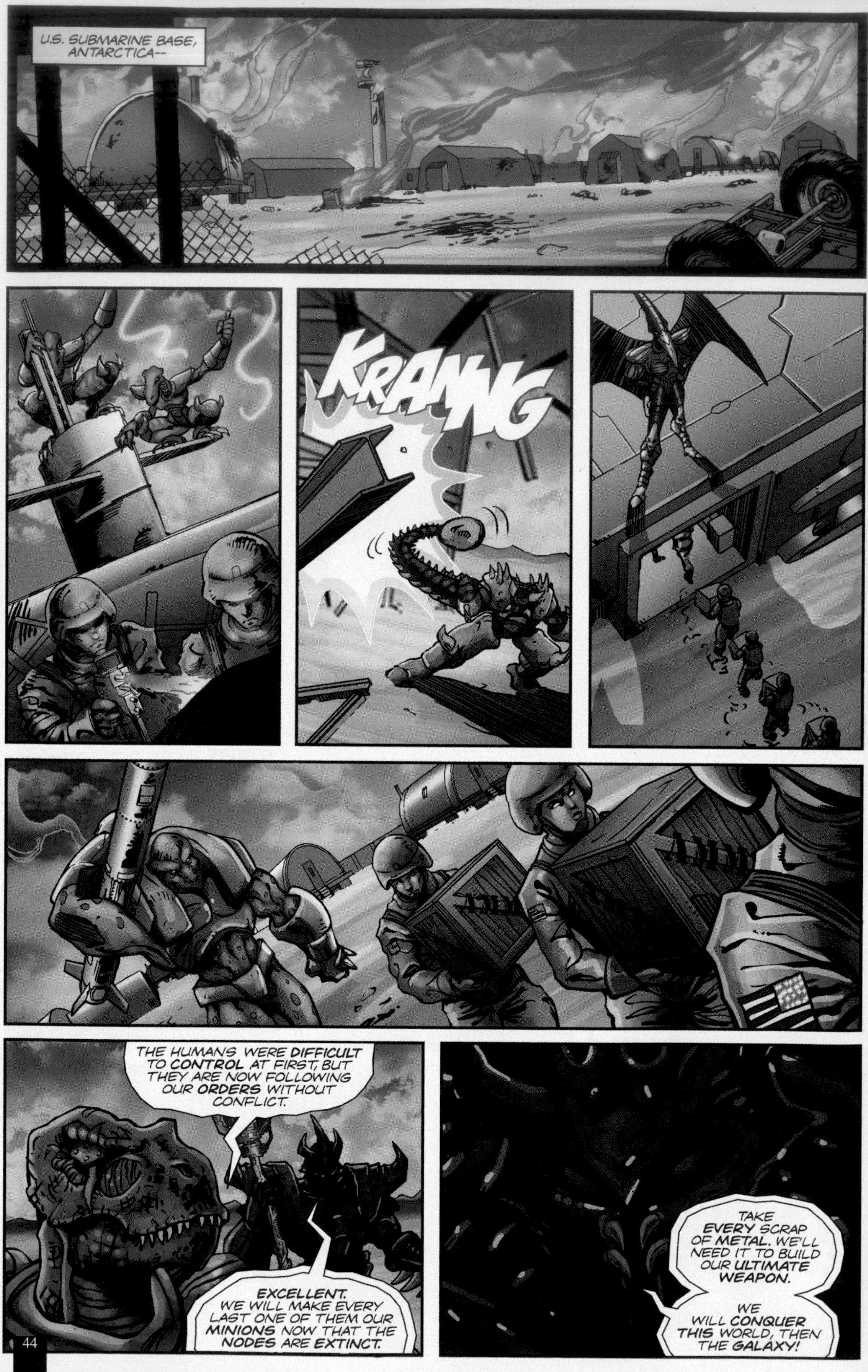

U.S. SUBMARINE BASE, ANTARCTICA--
KRANNG
THE HUMANS WERE DIFFICULT TO CONTROL AT FIRST, BUT THEY ARE NOW FOLLOWING OUR ORDERS WITHOUT CONFLICT.
EXCELLENT. WE WILL MAKE EVERY LAST ONE OF THEM OUR MINIONS NOW THAT THE NODES ARE EXTINCT.
TAKE EVERY SCRAP OF METAL. WE'LL NEED IT TO BUILD OUR ULTIMATE WEAPON.
WE WILL CONQUER THIS WORLD, THEN THE GALAXY!

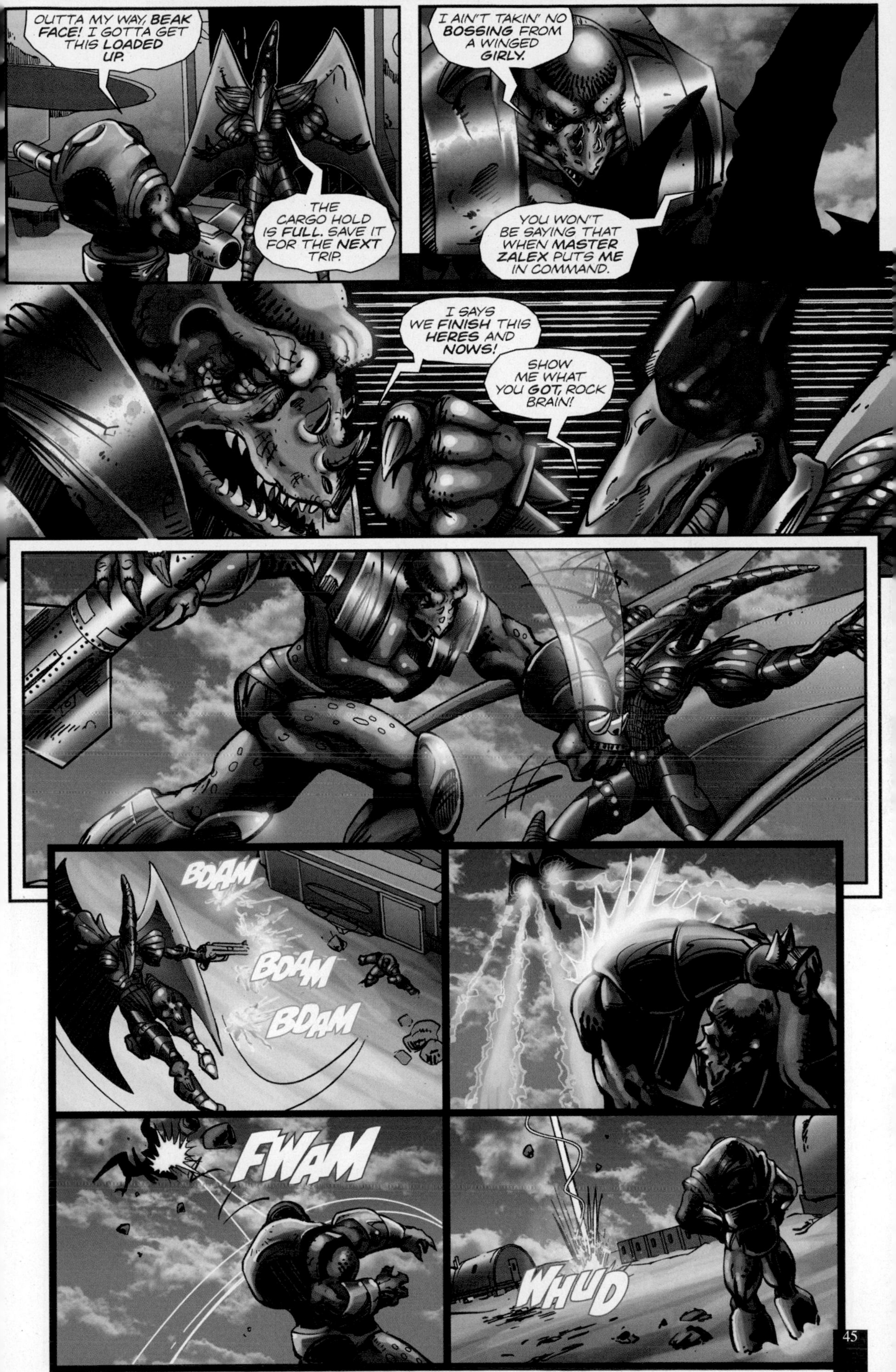

OUTTA MY WAY, BEAK FACE! I GOTTA GET THIS LOADED UP.
THE CARGO HOLD IS FULL. SAVE IT FOR THE NEXT TRIP.
I AIN'T TAKIN' NO BOSSING FROM A WINGED GIRLY.
YOU WON'T BE SAYING THAT WHEN MASTER ZALEX PUTS ME IN COMMAND.
I SAYS WE FINISH THIS HERES AND NOWS!
SHOW ME WHAT YOU GOT, ROCK BRAIN!
BDAM
BDAM
BDAM
FWAM
WHUD

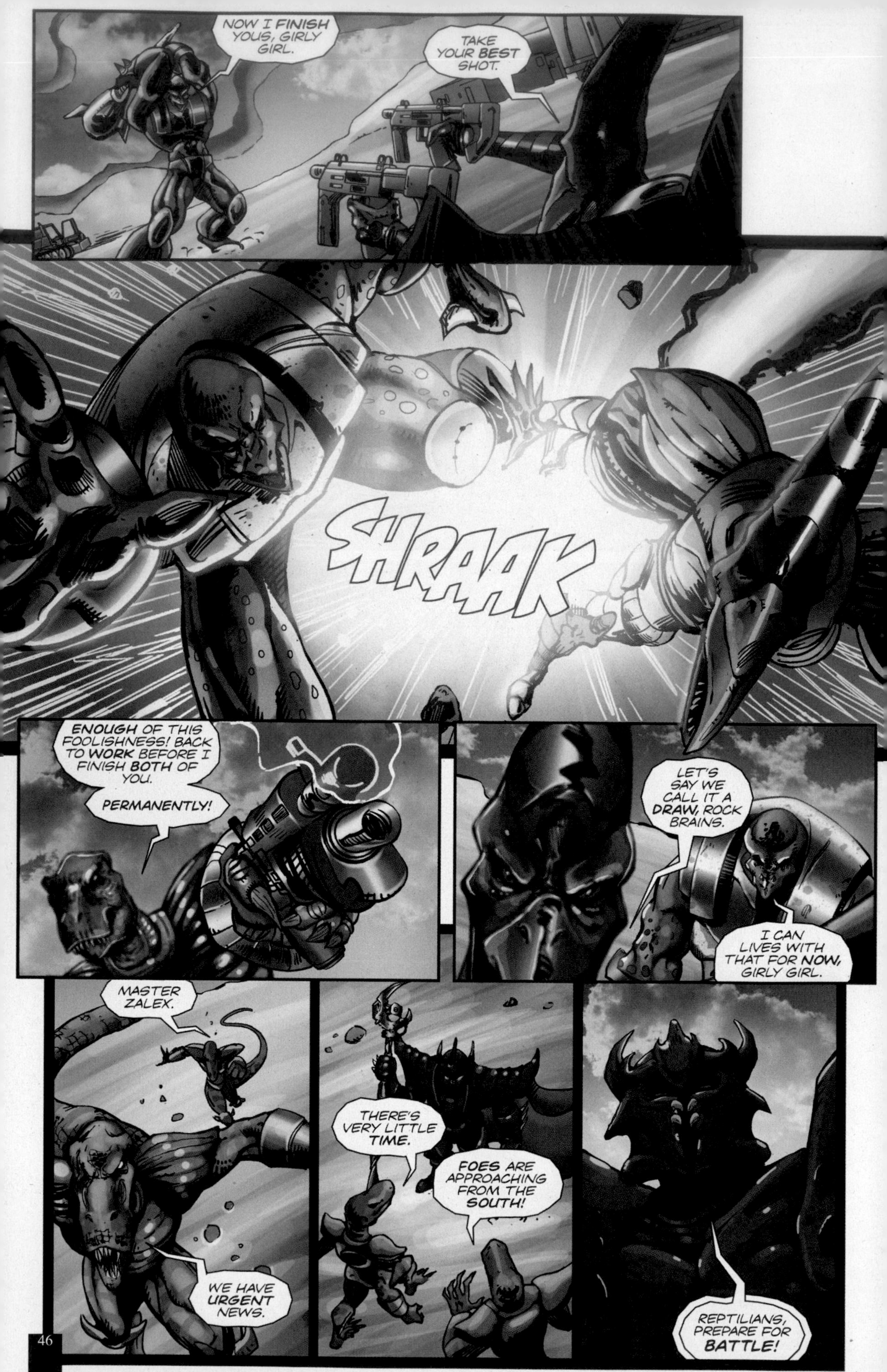
NOW I FINISH YOUS, GIRLY GIRL.
TAKE YOUR BEST SHOT.
SHRAAK
ENOUGH OF THIS FOOLISHNESS! BACK TO WORK BEFORE I FINISH BOTH OF YOU.
PERMANENTLY!
LET'S SAY WE CALL IT A DRAW, ROCK BRAINS.
I CAN LIVES WITH THAT FOR NOW, GIRLY GIRL.
MASTER ZALEX.
WE HAVE URGENT NEWS.
THERE'S VERY LITTLE TIME.
FOES ARE APPROACHING FROM THE SOUTH!
REPTILIANS, PREPARE FOR BATTLE!

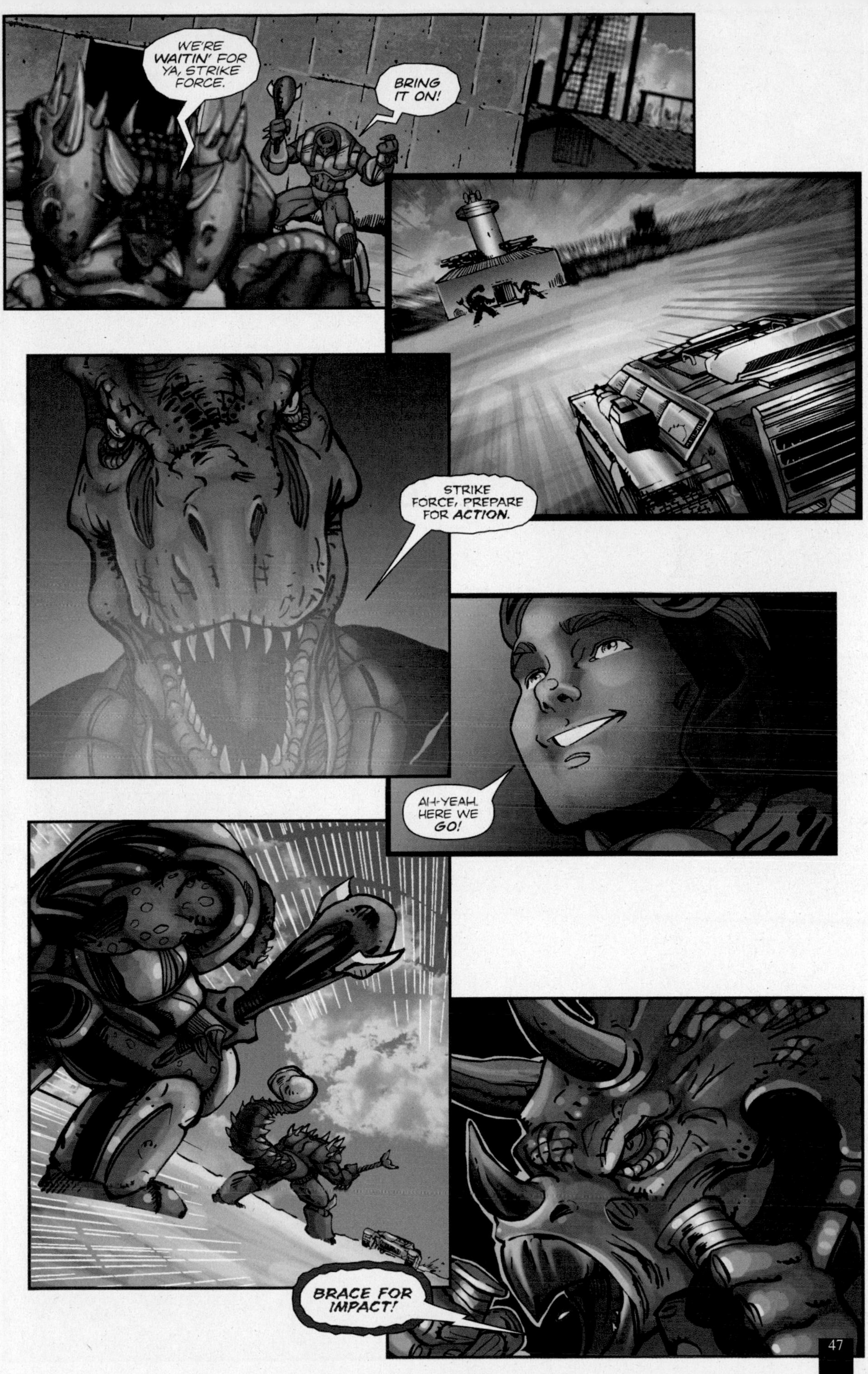
WE'RE WAITIN' FOR YA, STRIKE FORCE.
BRING IT ON!
STRIKE FORCE, PREPARE FOR ACTION.
AH-YEAH. HERE WE GO!
BRACE FOR IMPACT!

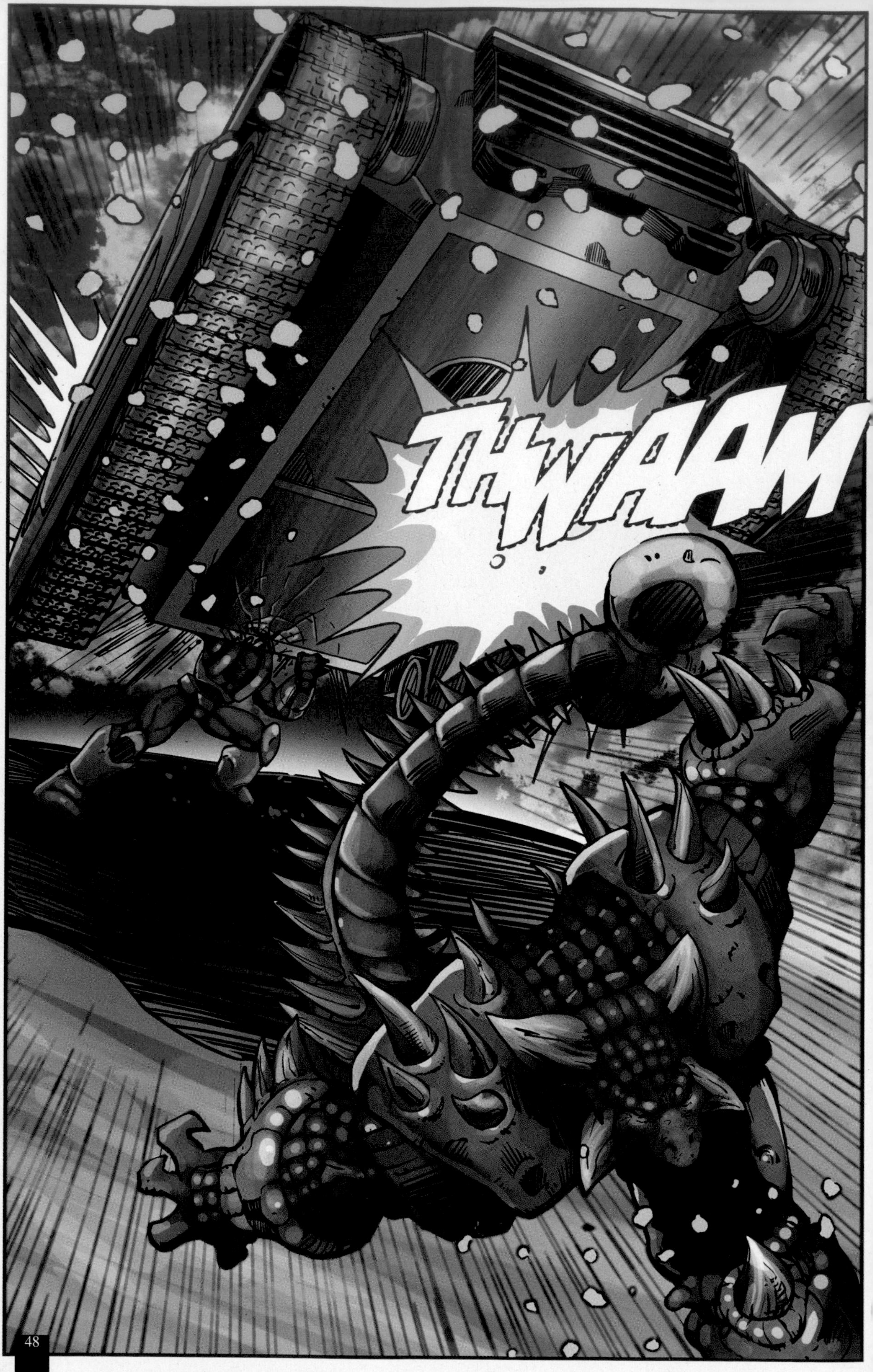
THWAAM

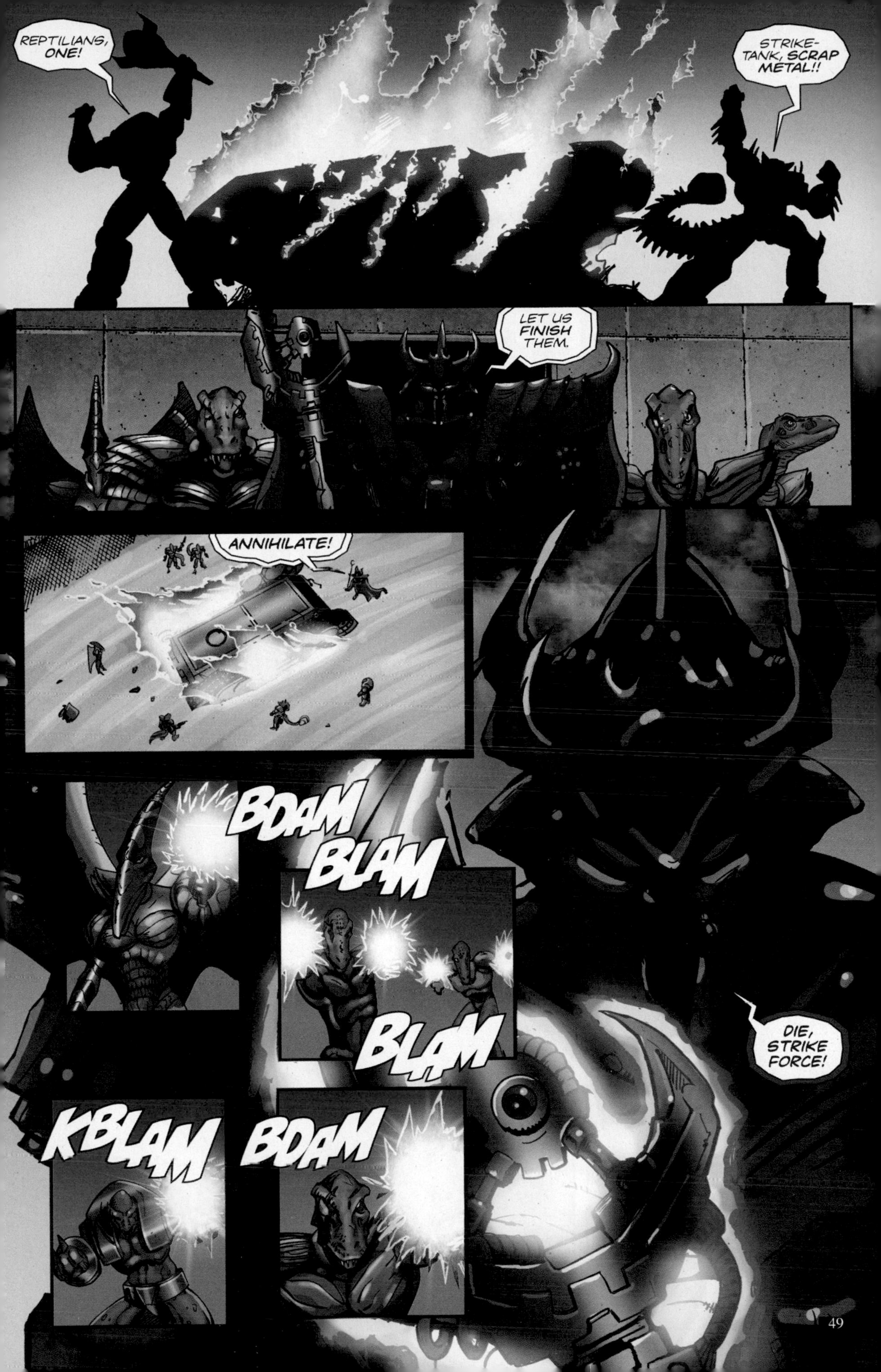
REPTILIANS, ONE!
STRIKE-TANK, SCRAP METAL!!
LET US FINISH THEM.
ANNIHILATE!
BDAM
BLAM
BLAM
DIE, STRIKE FORCE!
KBLAM
BDAM

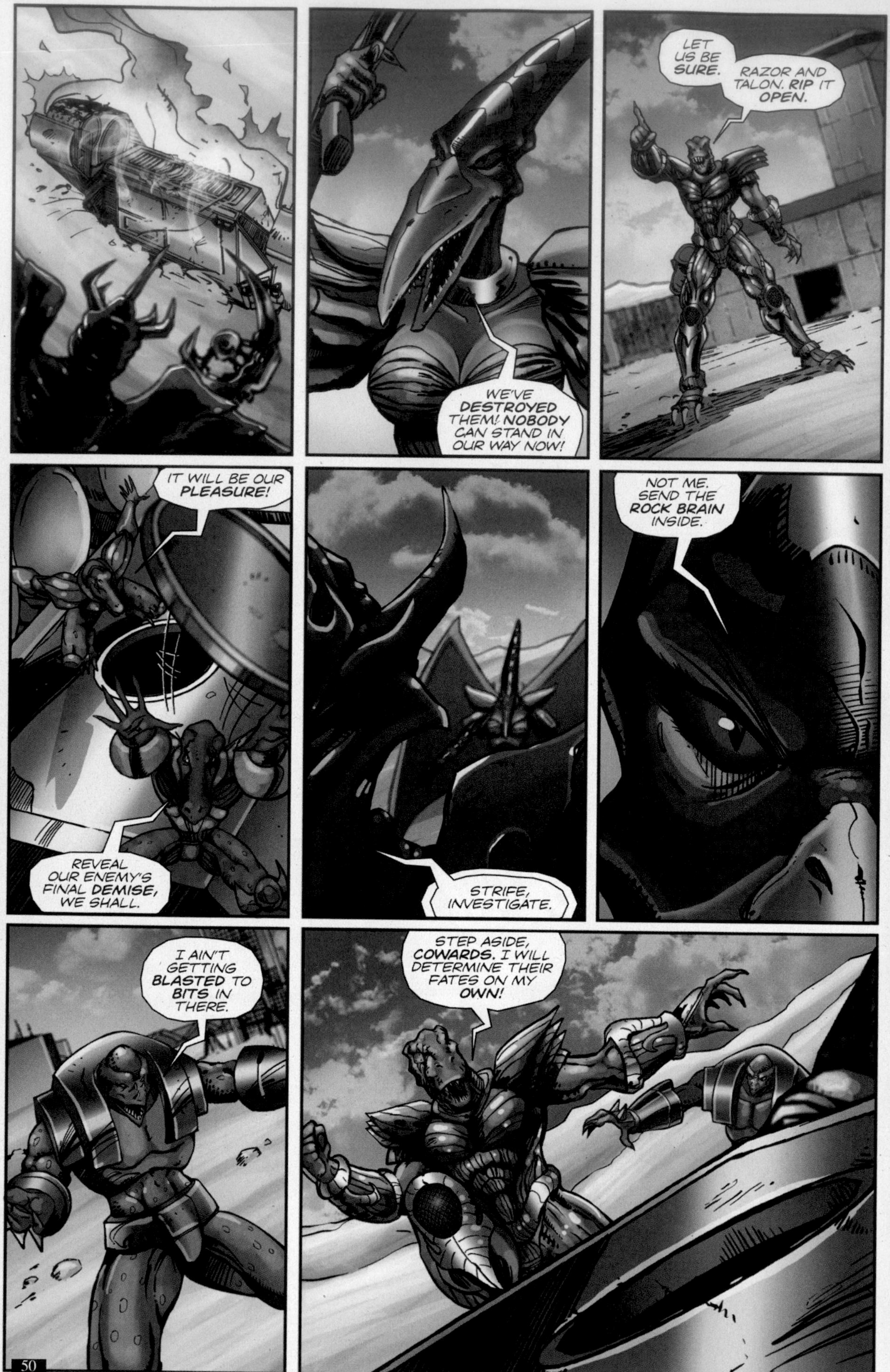

WE'VE DESTROYED THEM! NOBODY CAN STAND IN OUR WAY NOW!
LET US BE SURE.
RAZOR AND TALON. RIP IT OPEN.
IT WILL BE OUR PLEASURE!
REVEAL OUR ENEMY'S FINAL DEMISE, WE SHALL.
STRIFE, INVESTIGATE.
NOT ME. SEND THE ROCK BRAIN INSIDE.
I AIN'T GETTING BLASTED TO BITS IN THERE.
STEP ASIDE, COWARDS. I WILL DETERMINE THEIR FATES ON MY OWN!

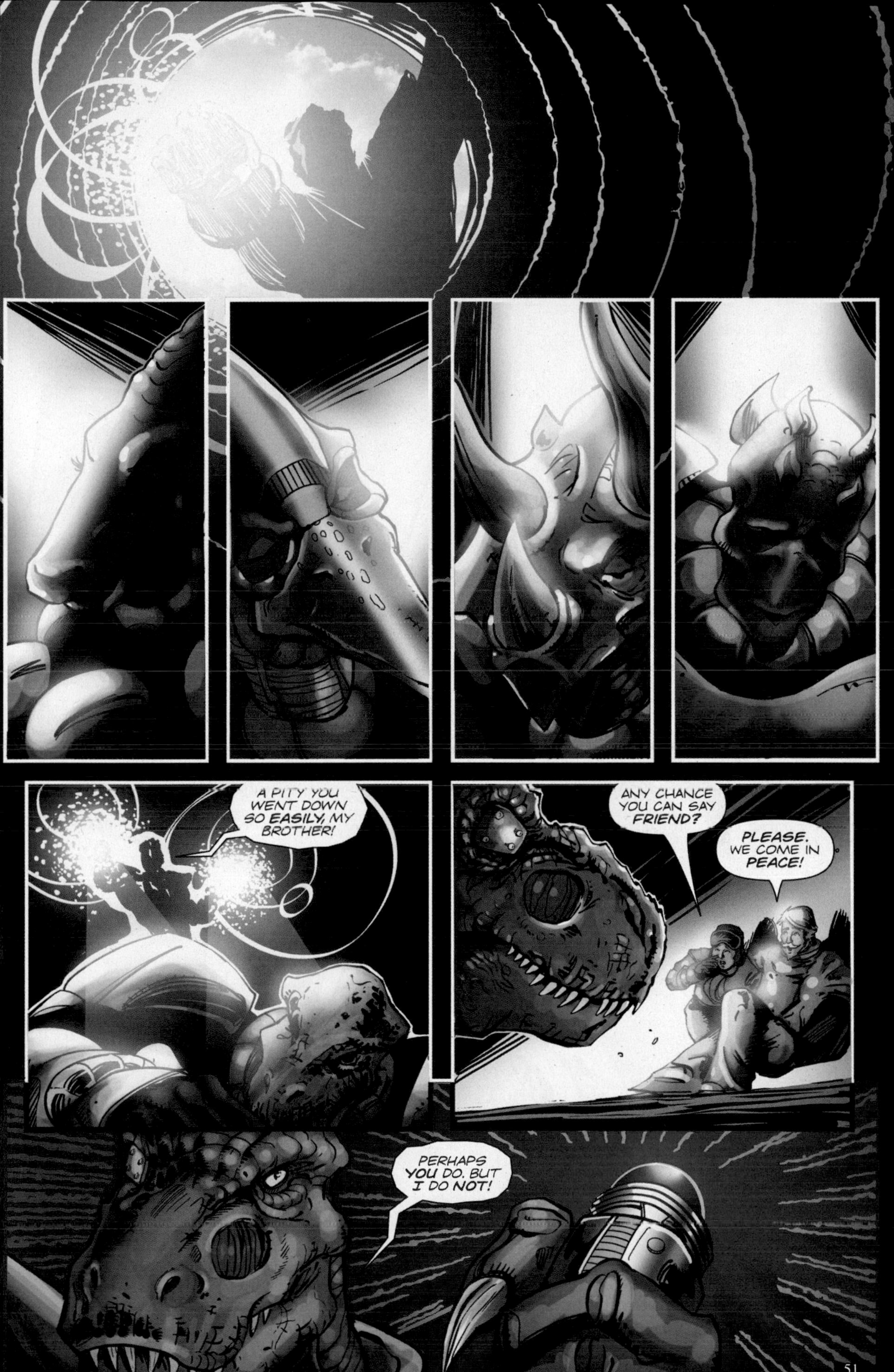
A PITY YOU WENT DOWN SO EASILY, MY BROTHER!
ANY CHANCE YOU CAN SAY FRIEND?
PLEASE. WE COME IN PEACE!
PERHAPS YOU DO. BUT I DO NOT!

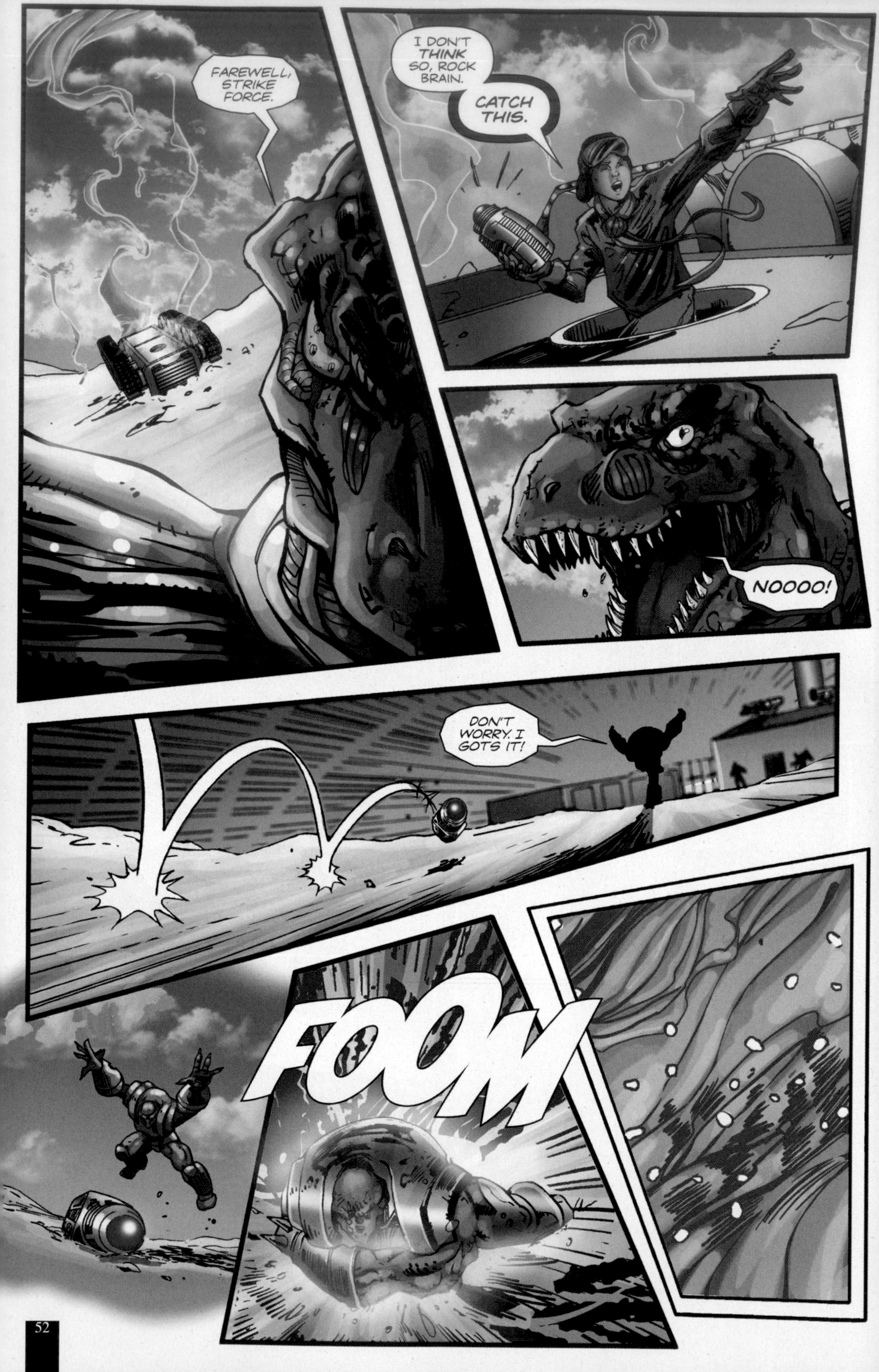
FAREWELL, STRIKE FORCE.
I DON'T THINK SO, ROCK BRAIN.
CATCH THIS.
NOOOO!
DON'T WORRY. I GOTS IT!
FOOM

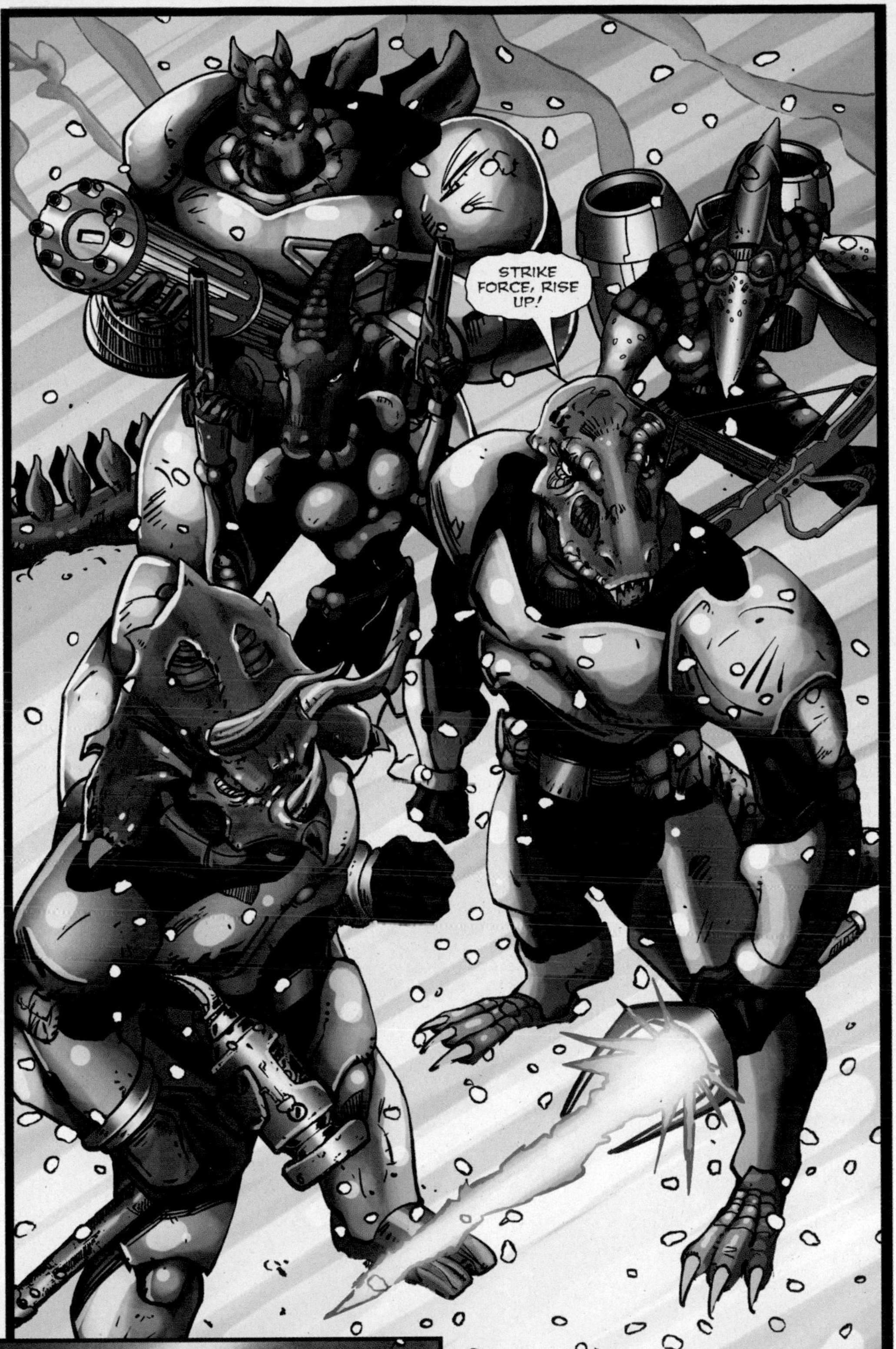
STRIKE FORCE, RISE UP!

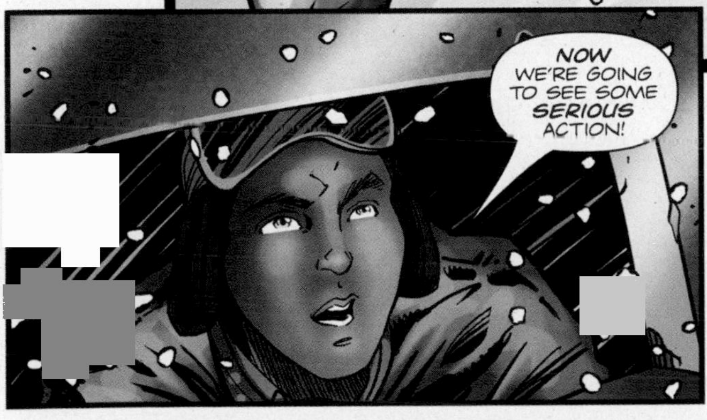
NOW WE'RE GOING TO SEE SOME SERIOUS ACTION!

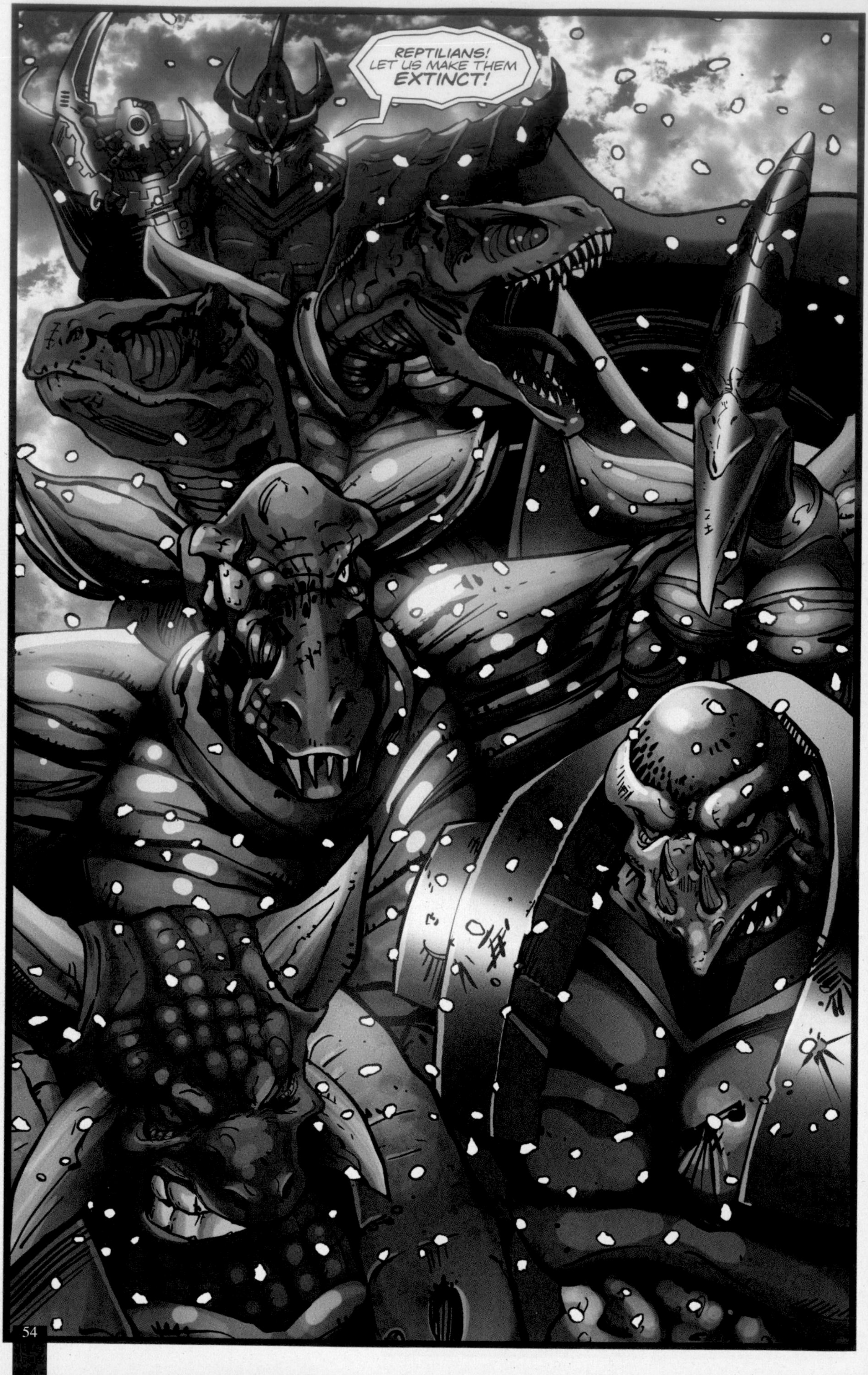
REPTILIANS! LET US MAKE THEM EXTINCT!

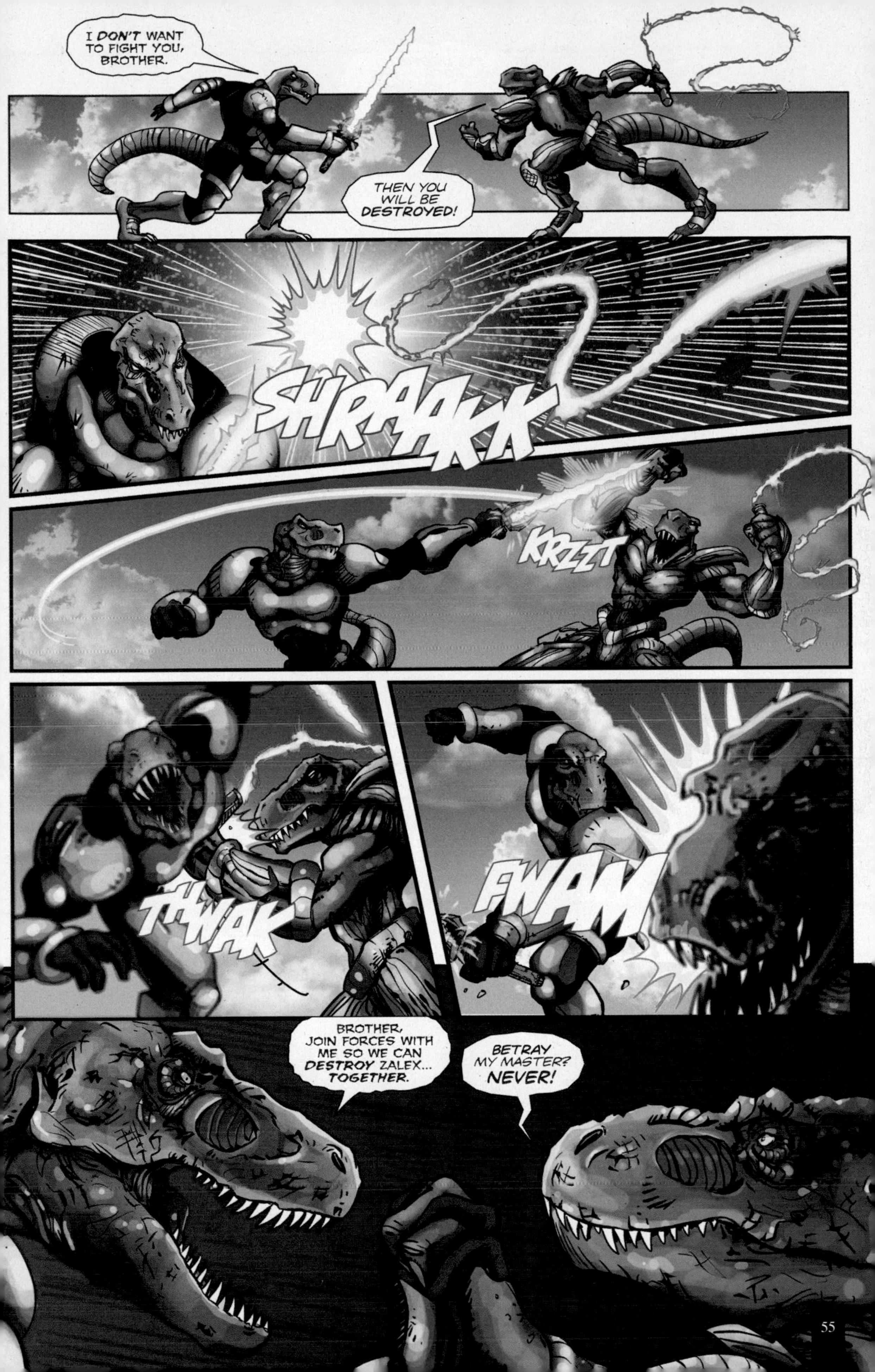
I DON'T WANT TO FIGHT YOU, BROTHER.
THEN YOU WILL BE DESTROYED!
SHRAAKK
KRZZT
THWAK
FWAM
BROTHER, JOIN FORCES WITH ME SO WE CAN DESTROY ZALEX... TOGETHER.
BETRAY MY MASTER? NEVER!

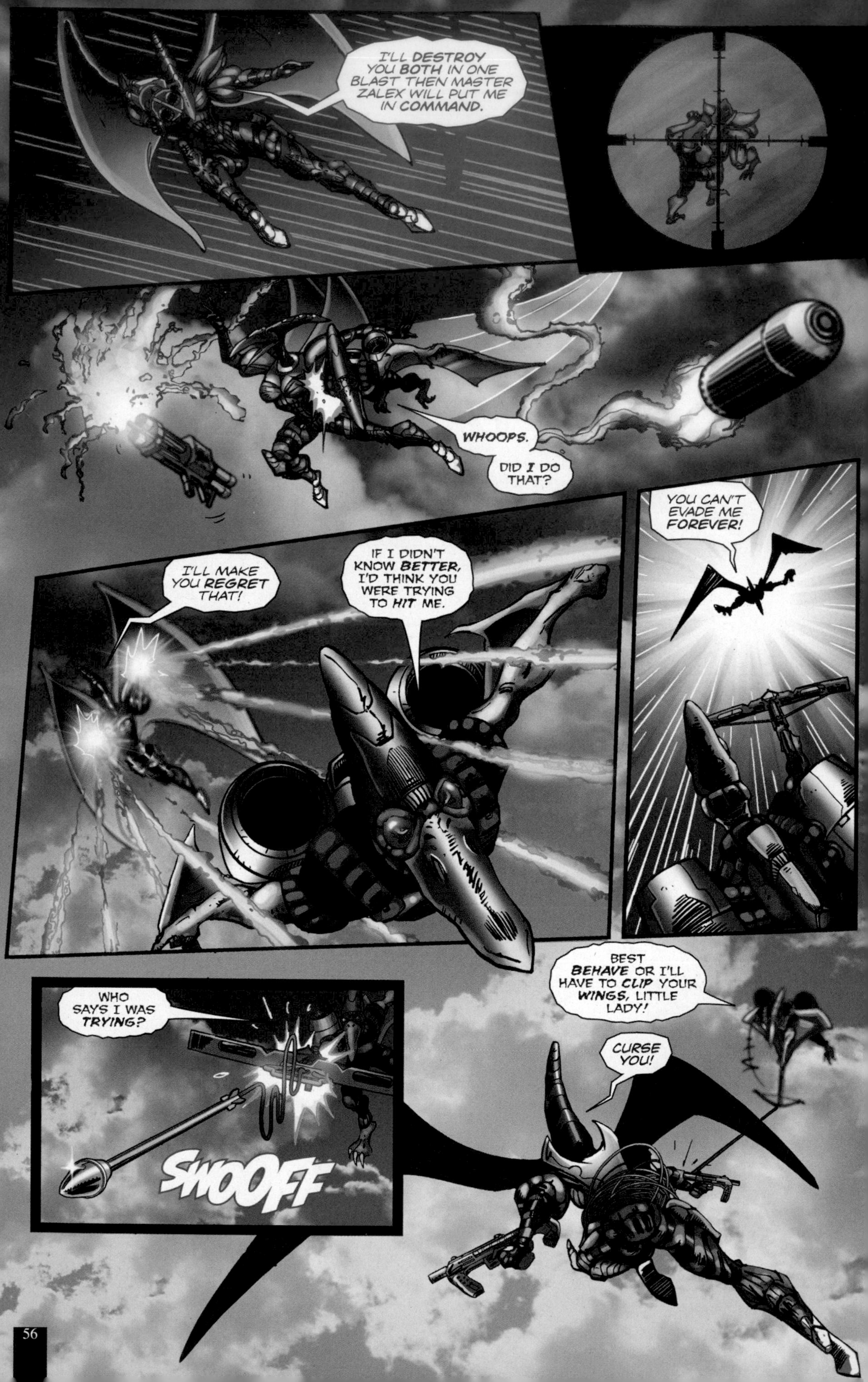
I'LL DESTROY YOU BOTH IN ONE BLAST THEN MASTER ZALEX WILL PUT ME IN COMMAND.
WHOOPS.
DID I DO THAT?
I'LL MAKE YOU REGRET THAT!
IF I DIDN'T KNOW BETTER, I'D THINK YOU WERE TRYING TO HIT ME.
YOU CAN'T EVADE ME FOREVER!
WHO SAYS I WAS TRYING?
SWOOFF
BEST BEHAVE OR I'LL HAVE TO CLIP YOUR WINGS, LITTLE LADY!
CURSE YOU!

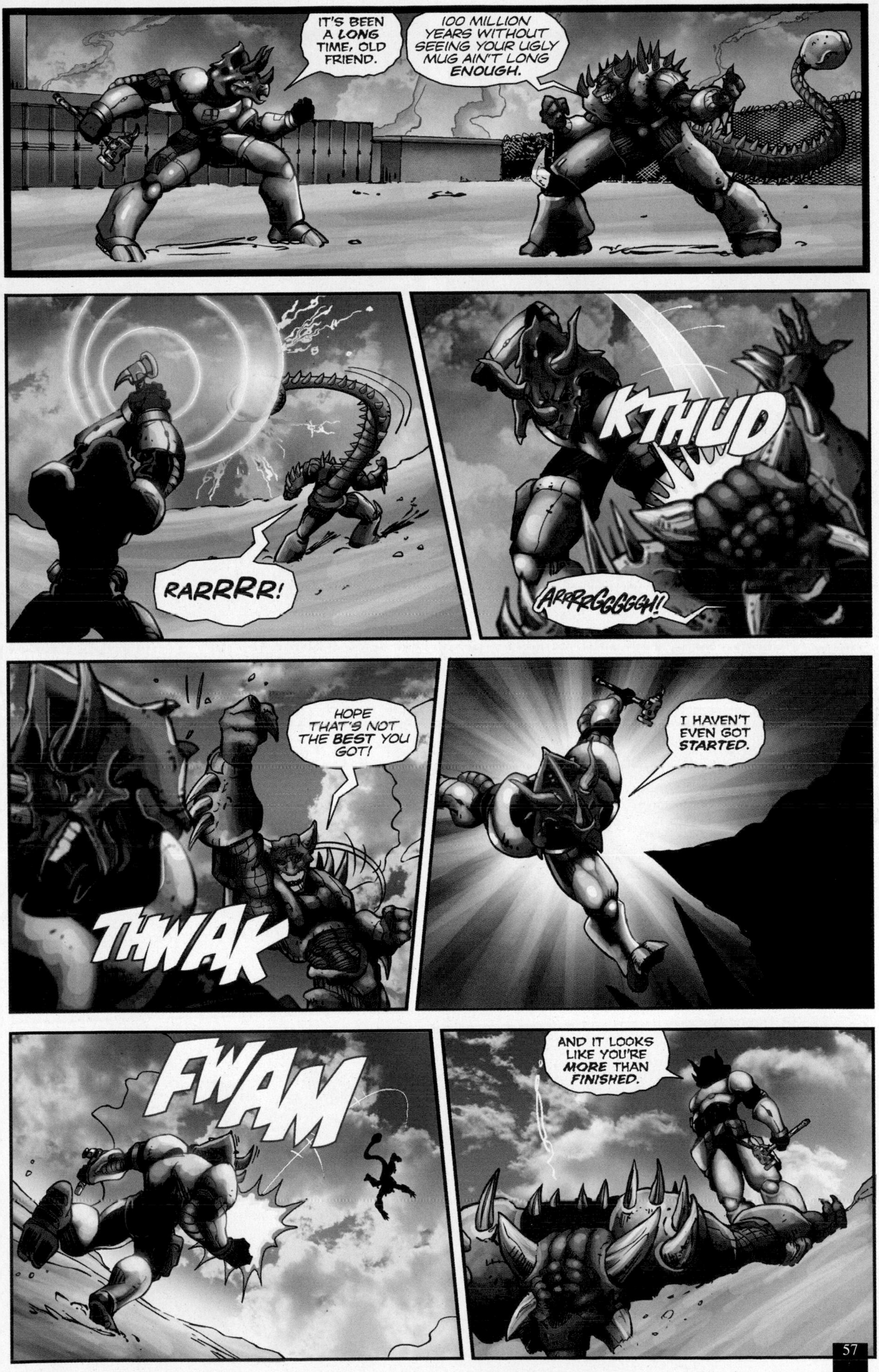
IT'S BEEN A LONG TIME, OLD FRIEND.
100 MILLION YEARS WITHOUT SEEING YOUR UGLY MUG AIN'T LONG ENOUGH.
RARRRR!
KTHUD
ARRRRGGGGGH!
HOPE THAT'S NOT THE BEST YOU GOT!
THWAK
I HAVEN'T EVEN GOT STARTED.
FWAM
AND IT LOOKS LIKE YOU'RE MORE THAN FINISHED.

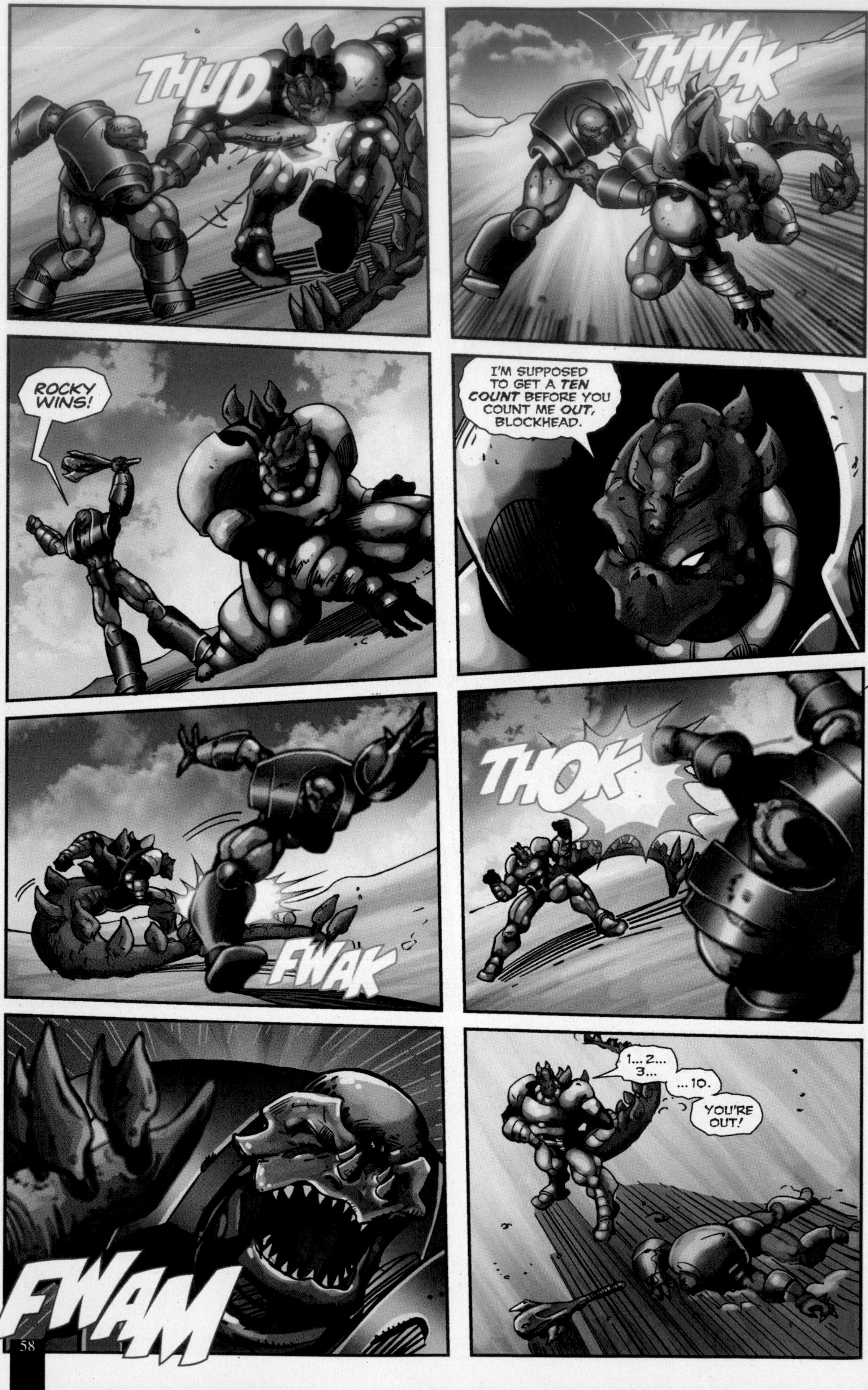
THUD
THWAK
ROCKY WINS!
I'M SUPPOSED TO GET A TEN COUNT BEFORE YOU COUNT ME OUT, BLOCKHEAD.
FWAK
THOK
FWAM
1... 2... 3...
... 10.
YOU'RE OUT!

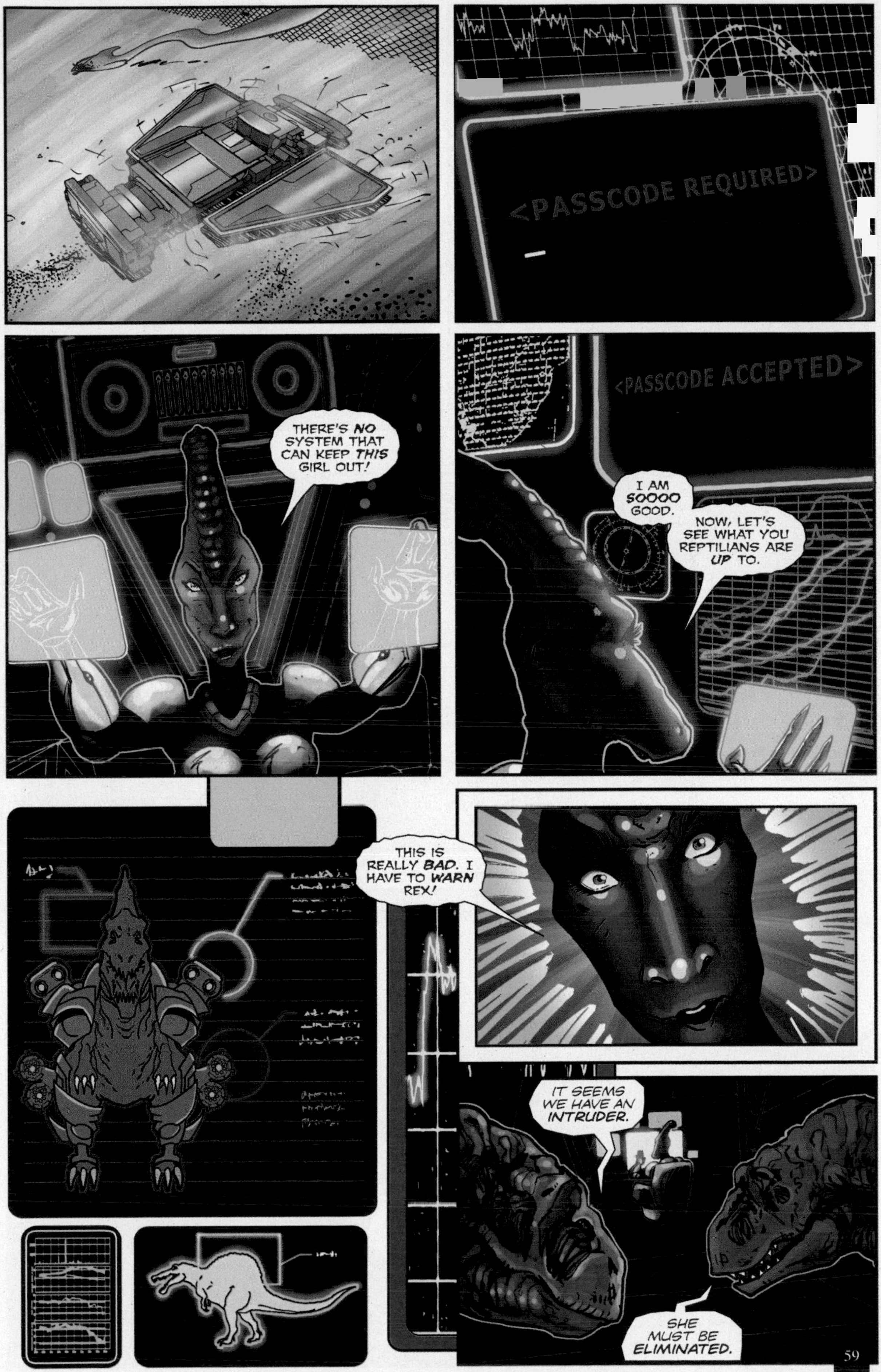
<PASSCODE REQUIRED>
THERE'S NO SYSTEM THAT CAN KEEP THIS GIRL OUT!
<PASSCODE ACCEPTED>
I AM SOOOO GOOD.
NOW, LET'S SEE WHAT YOU REPTILIANS ARE UP TO.
THIS IS REALLY BAD. I HAVE TO WARN REX!
IT SEEMS WE HAVE AN INTRUDER.
SHE MUST BE ELIMINATED.

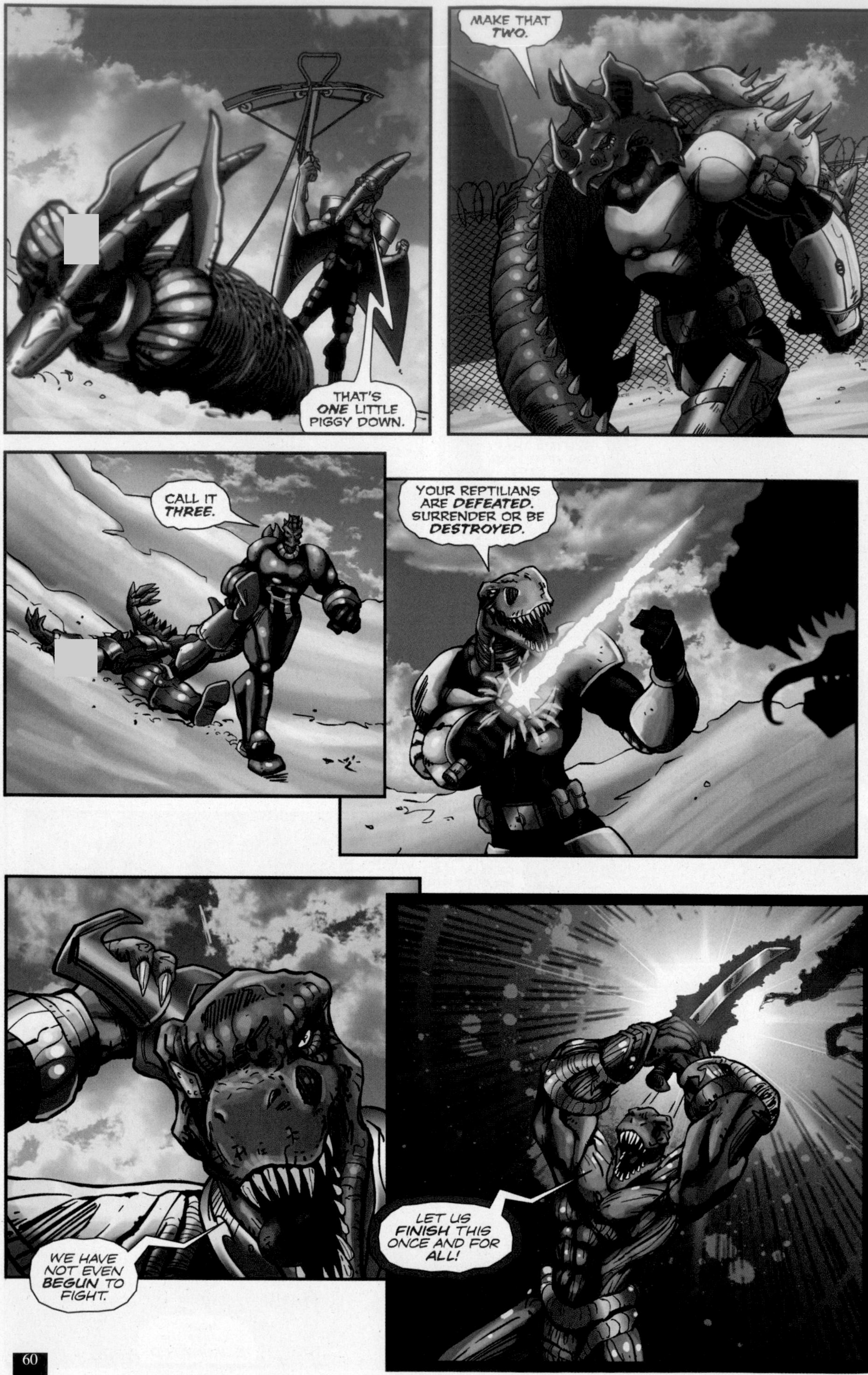
THAT'S ONE LITTLE PIGGY DOWN.
MAKE THAT TWO.
CALL IT THREE.
YOUR REPTILIANS ARE DEFEATED. SURRENDER OR BE DESTROYED.
WE HAVE NOT EVEN BEGUN TO FIGHT.
LET US FINISH THIS ONCE AND FOR ALL!

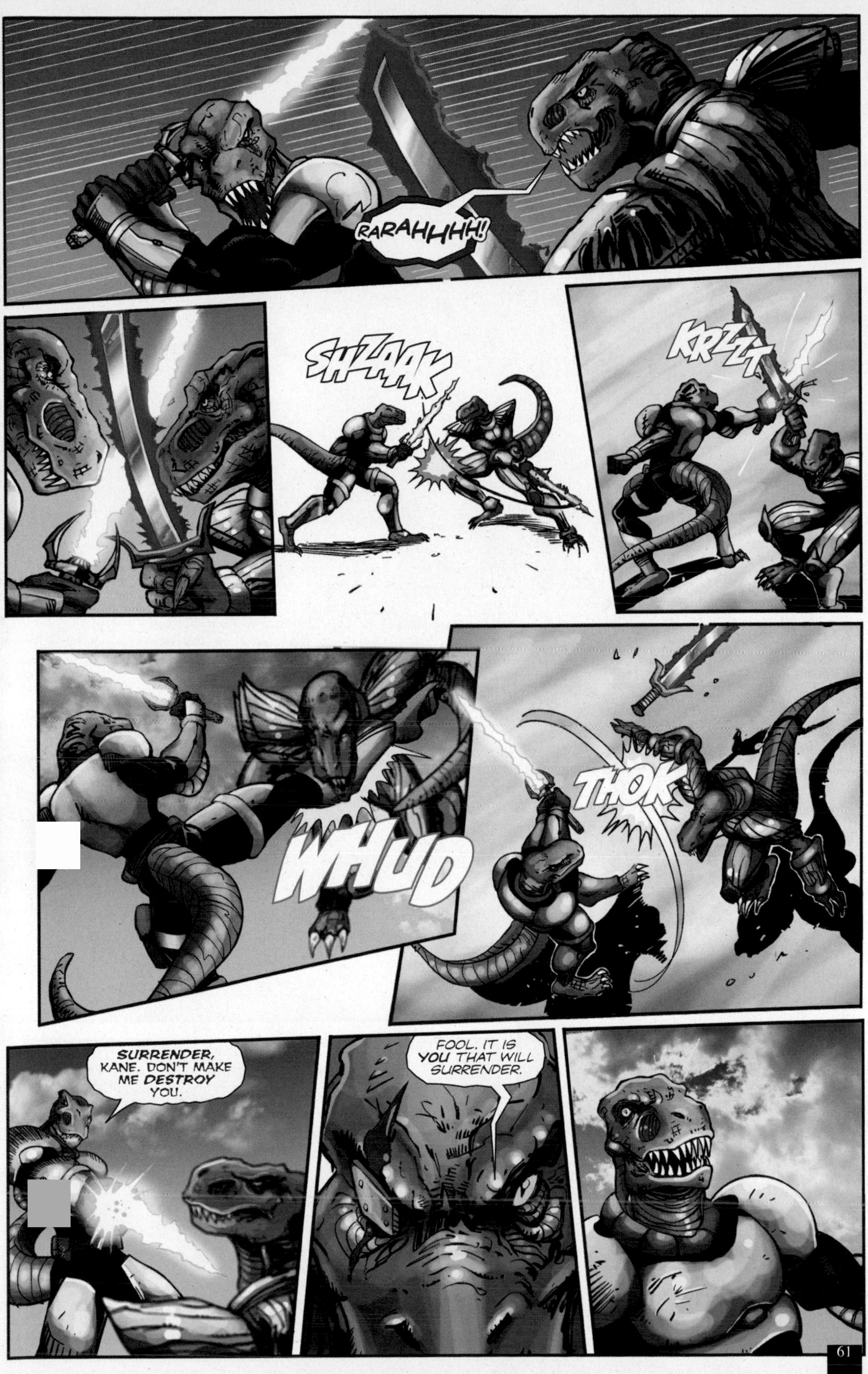
RARAHHHH!
SHZAAK
KRZZT
THOK
WHUD
SURRENDER, KANE. DON'T MAKE ME DESTROY YOU.
FOOL. IT IS YOU THAT WILL SURRENDER.

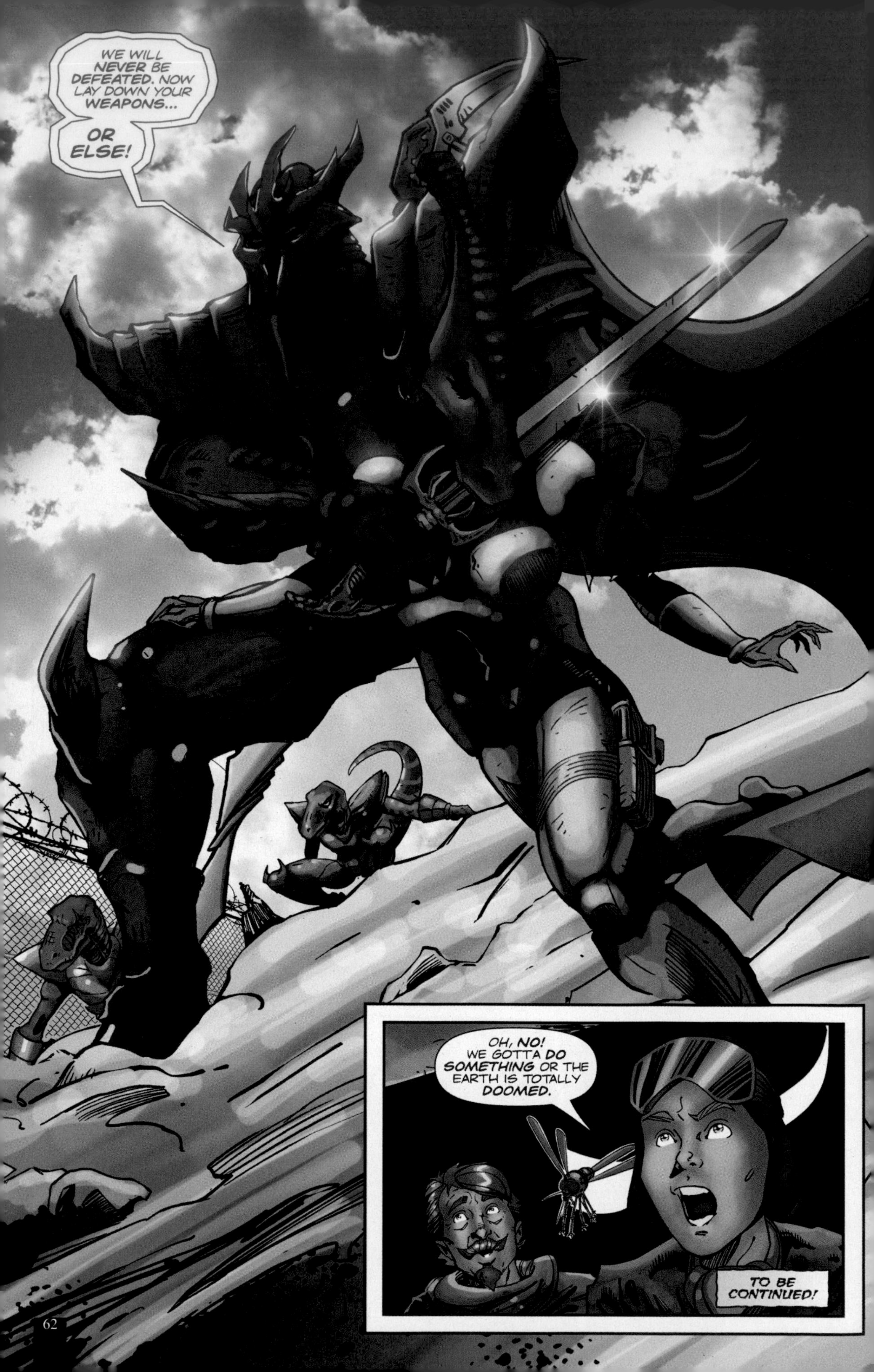
WE WILL NEVER BE DEFEATED. NOW LAY DOWN YOUR WEAPONS...
OR ELSE!
OH, NO! WE GOTTA DO SOMETHING OR THE EARTH IS TOTALLY DOOMED.
TO BE CONTINUED!

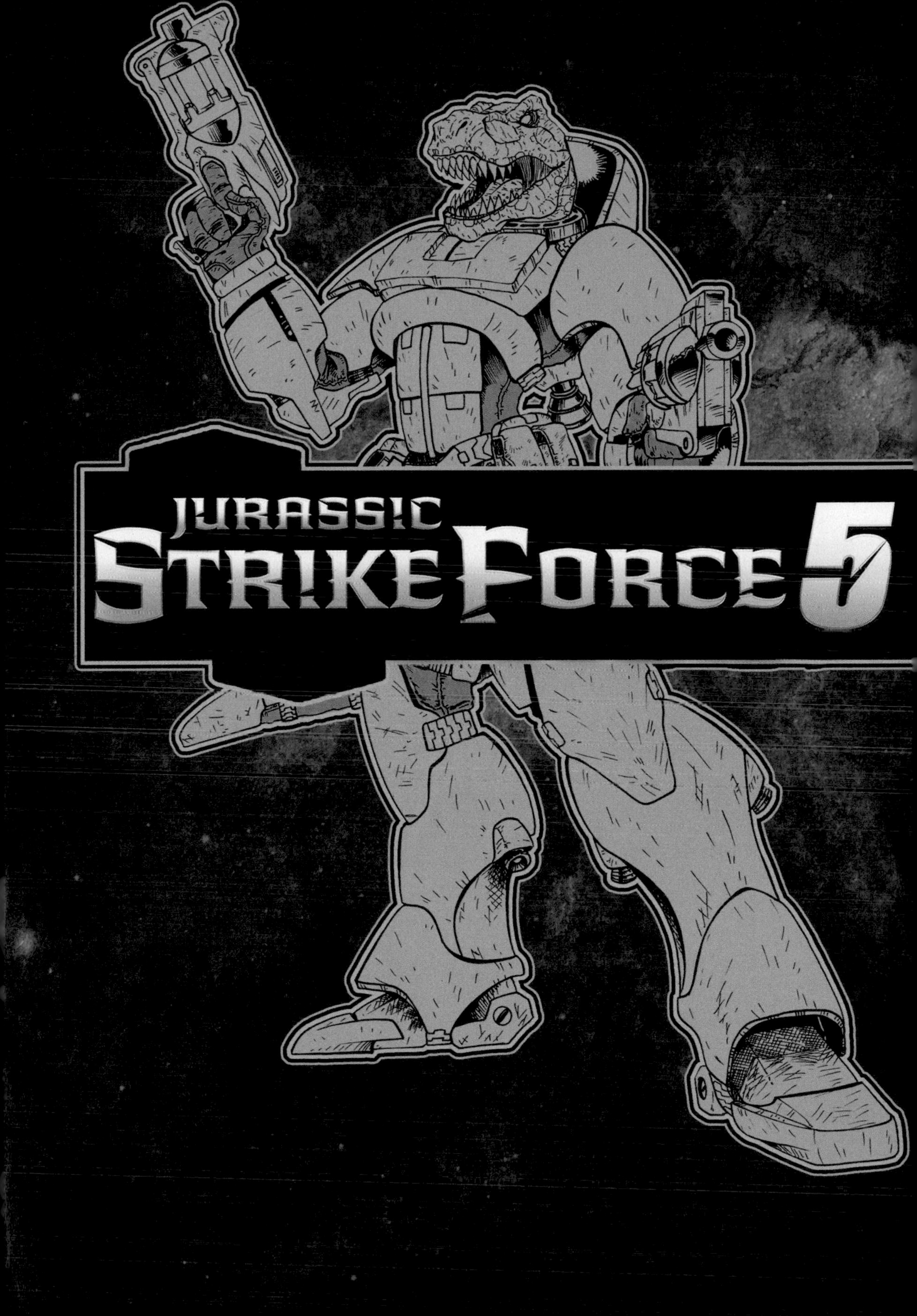
JURASSIC
STRIKE FORCE 5

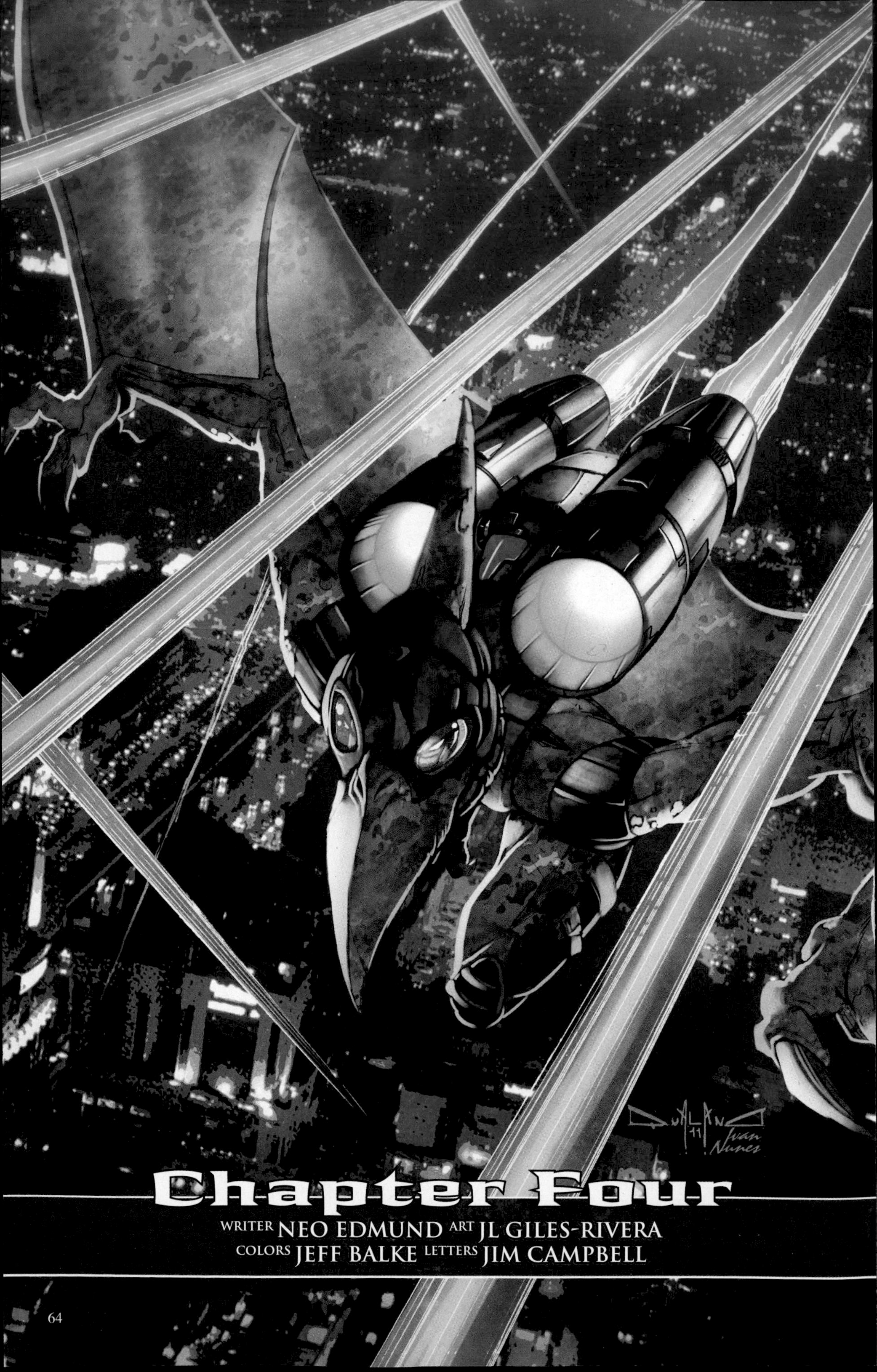
Chapter Four
WRITER NEO EDMUND ART JL GILES-RIVERA
COLORS JEFF BALKE LETTERS JIM CAMPBELL

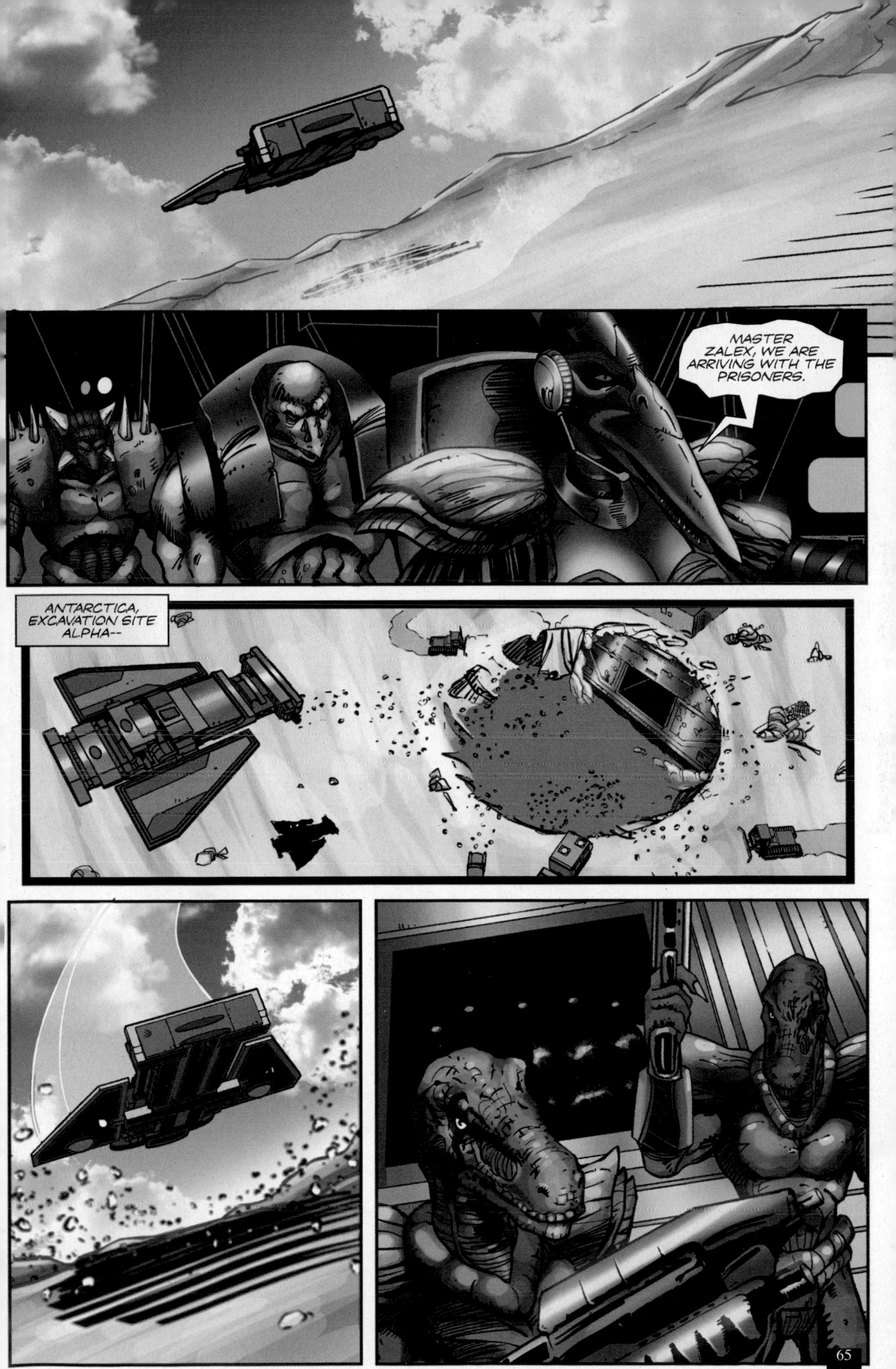
MASTER ZALEX, WE ARE ARRIVING WITH THE PRISONERS.
ANTARCTICA, EXCAVATION SITE ALPHA--

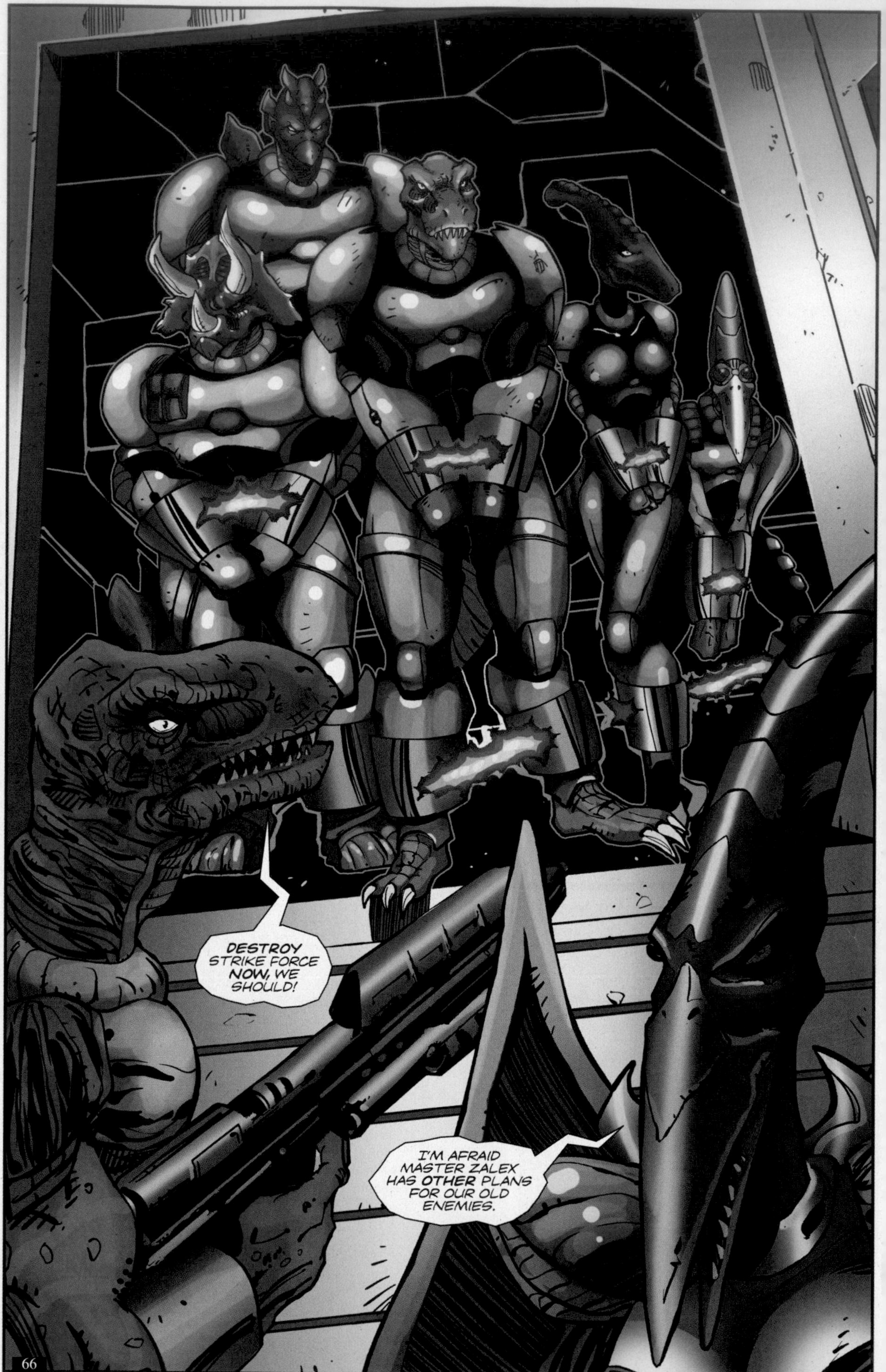
DESTROY STRIKE FORCE NOW, WE SHOULD!
I'M AFRAID MASTER ZALEX HAS OTHER PLANS FOR OUR OLD ENEMIES.

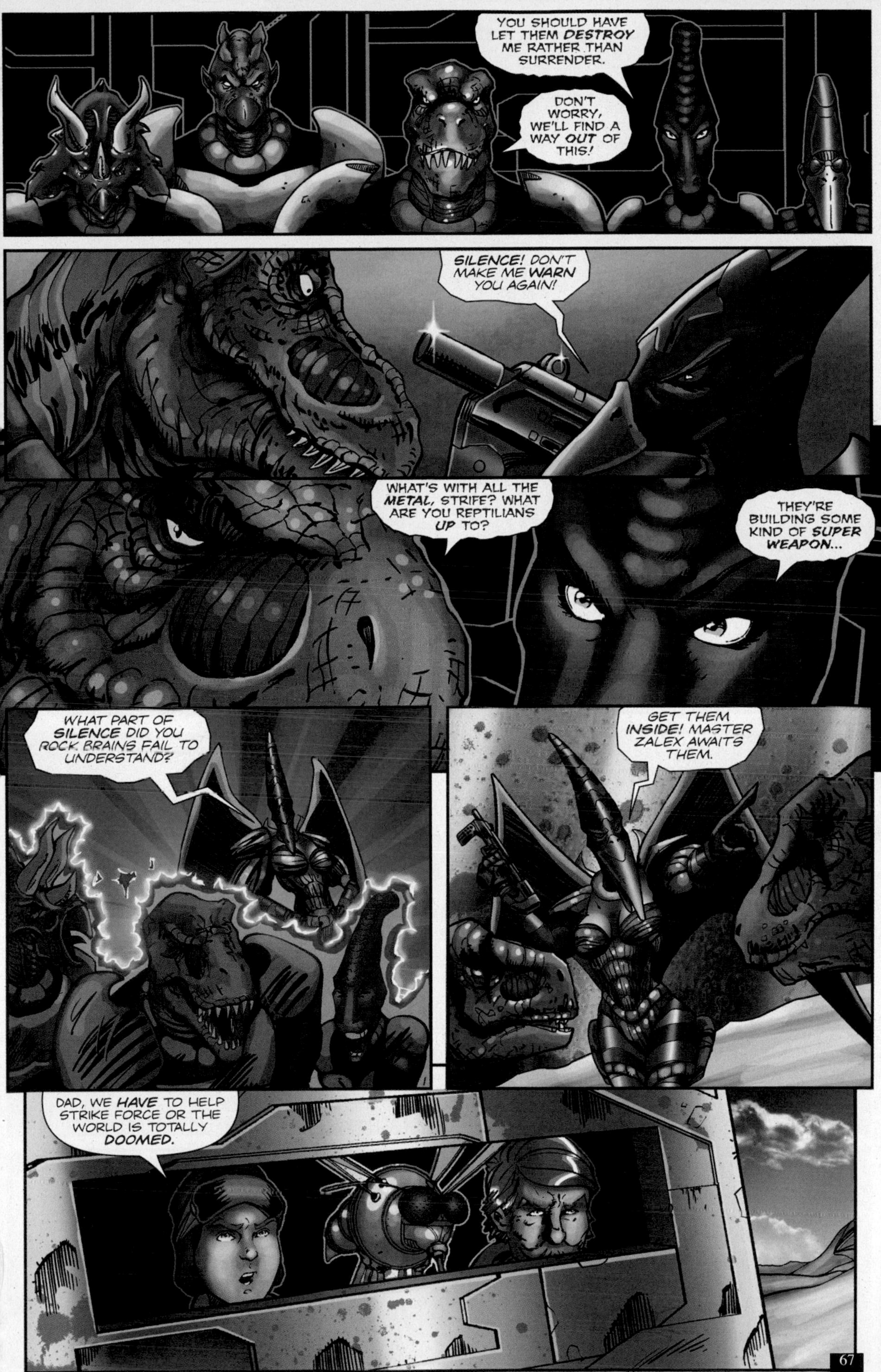
YOU SHOULD HAVE LET THEM DESTROY ME RATHER THAN SURRENDER.
DON'T WORRY, WE'LL FIND A WAY OUT OF THIS!
SILENCE! DON'T MAKE ME WARN YOU AGAIN!
WHAT'S WITH ALL THE METAL, STRIFE? WHAT ARE YOU REPTILIANS UP TO?
THEY'RE BUILDING SOME KIND OF SUPER WEAPON...
WHAT PART OF SILENCE DID YOU ROCK BRAINS FAIL TO UNDERSTAND?
GET THEM INSIDE! MASTER ZALEX AWAITS THEM.
DAD, WE HAVE TO HELP STRIKE FORCE OR THE WORLD IS TOTALLY DOOMED.

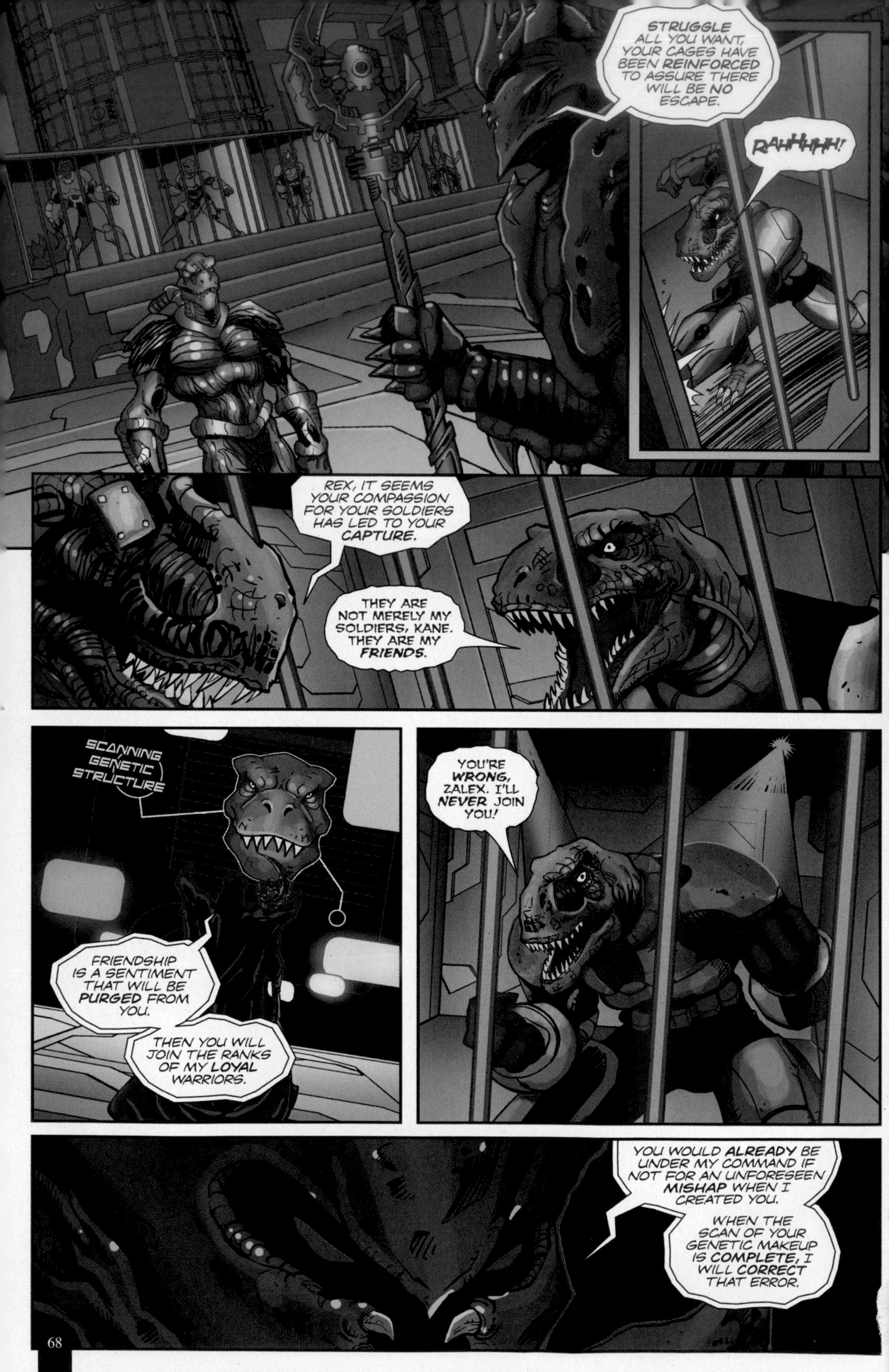

STRUGGLE ALL YOU WANT, YOUR CAGES HAVE BEEN REINFORCED TO ASSURE THERE WILL BE NO ESCAPE.
RAHHHHH!
REX, IT SEEMS YOUR COMPASSION FOR YOUR SOLDIERS HAS LED TO YOUR CAPTURE.
THEY ARE NOT MERELY MY SOLDIERS, KANE. THEY ARE MY FRIENDS.
SCANNING GENETIC STRUCTURE
FRIENDSHIP IS A SENTIMENT THAT WILL BE PURGED FROM YOU.
THEN YOU WILL JOIN THE RANKS OF MY LOYAL WARRIORS.
YOU'RE WRONG, ZALEX. I'LL NEVER JOIN YOU!
YOU WOULD ALREADY BE UNDER MY COMMAND IF NOT FOR AN UNFORESEEN MISHAP WHEN I CREATED YOU.
WHEN THE SCAN OF YOUR GENETIC MAKEUP IS COMPLETE, I WILL CORRECT THAT ERROR.

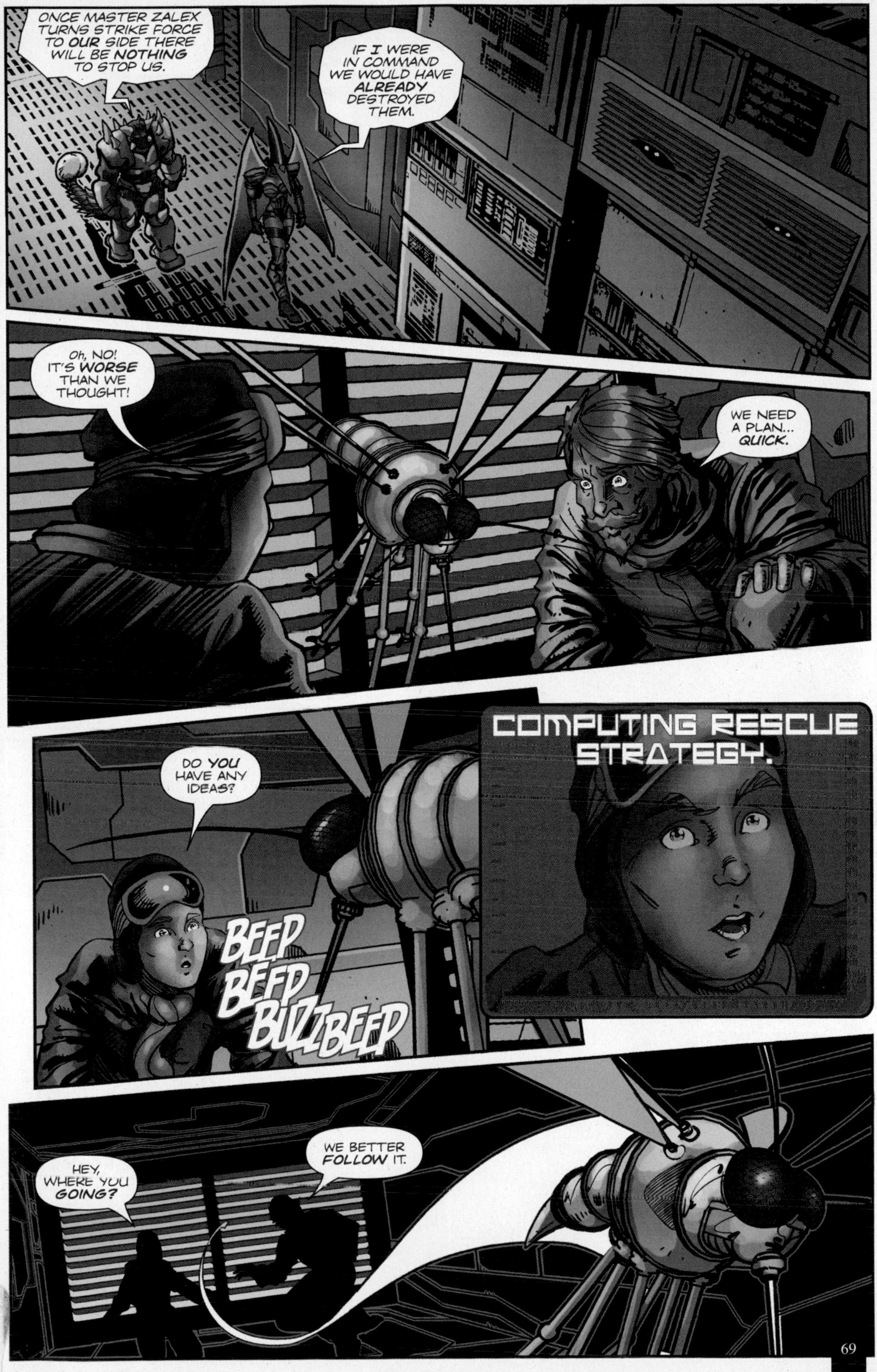

ONCE MASTER ZALEX TURNS STRIKE FORCE TO OUR SIDE THERE WILL BE NOTHING TO STOP US.
IF I WERE IN COMMAND WE WOULD HAVE ALREADY DESTROYED THEM.
Oh, NO! IT'S WORSE THAN WE THOUGHT!
WE NEED A PLAN... QUICK.
DO YOU HAVE ANY IDEAS?
BEEP BEEP BUZZBEEP
COMPUTING RESCUE STRATEGY.
HEY, WHERE YOU GOING?
WE BETTER FOLLOW IT.

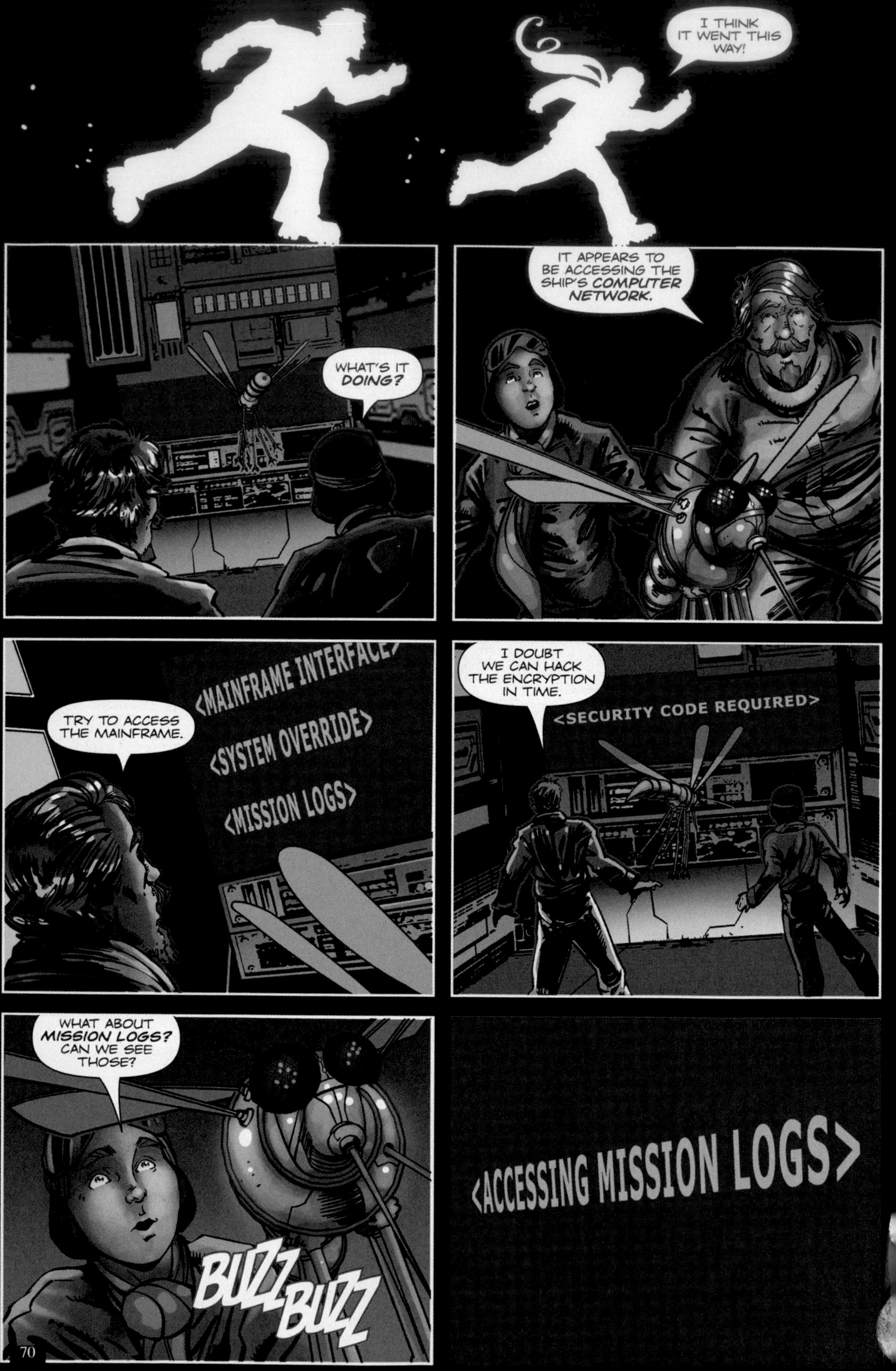
I THINK IT WENT THIS WAY!
WHAT'S IT DOING?
IT APPEARS TO BE ACCESSING THE SHIP'S COMPUTER NETWORK.
TRY TO ACCESS THE MAINFRAME.
<MAINFRAME INTERFACE>
<SYSTEM OVERRIDE>
<MISSION LOGS>
I DOUBT WE CAN HACK THE ENCRYPTION IN TIME.
<SECURITY CODE REQUIRED>
WHAT ABOUT MISSION LOGS? CAN WE SEE THOSE?
BUZZ BUZZ
<ACCESSING MISSION LOGS>

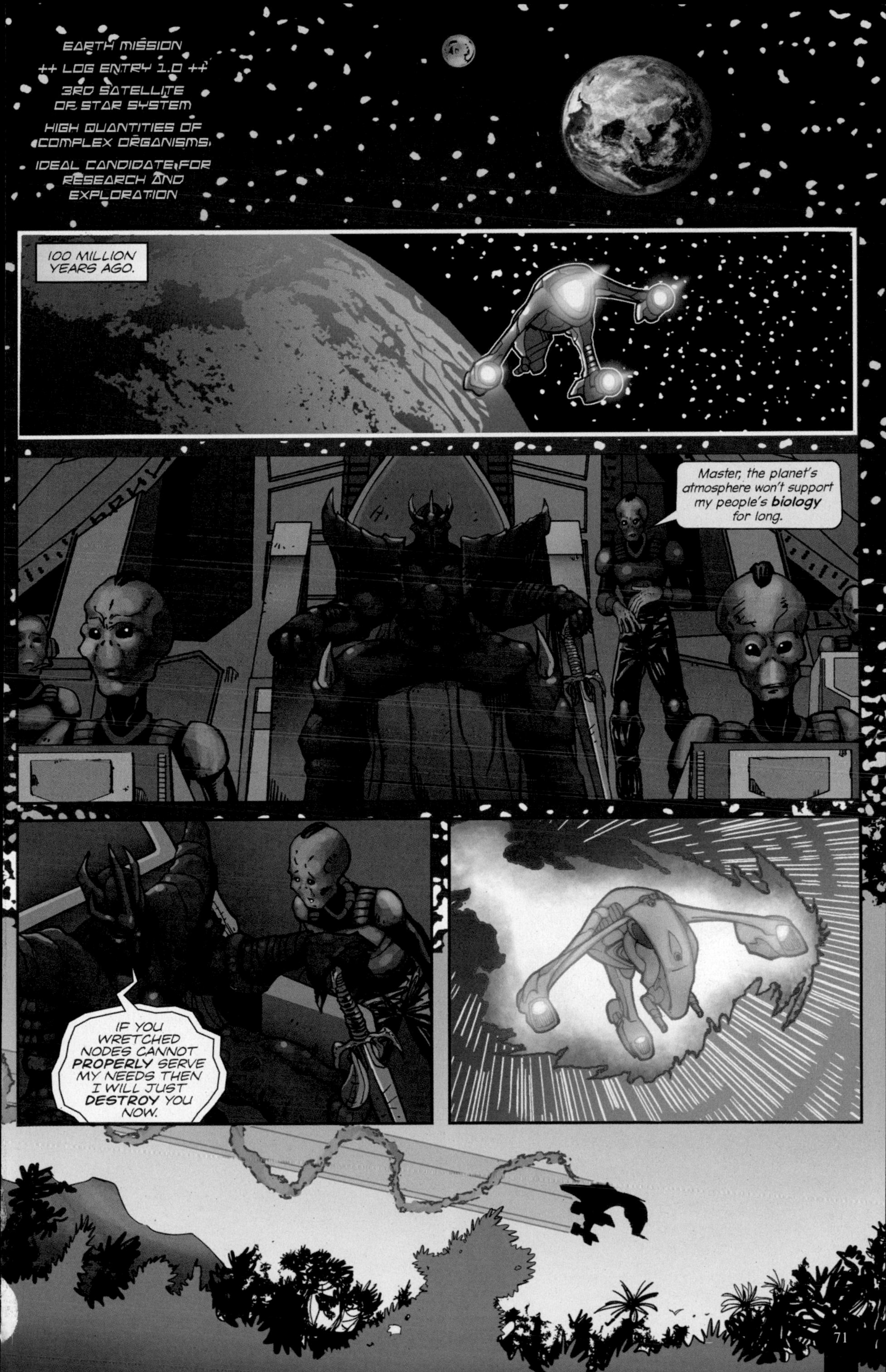
EARTH MISSION
++ LOG ENTRY 1.0 ++
3RD SATELLITE OF STAR SYSTEM
HIGH QUANTITIES OF COMPLEX ORGANISMS
IDEAL CANDIDATE FOR RESEARCH AND EXPLORATION
100 MILLION YEARS AGO.
Master, the planet's atmosphere won't support my people's biology for long.
IF YOU WRETCHED NODES CANNOT PROPERLY SERVE MY NEEDS THEN I WILL JUST DESTROY YOU NOW.

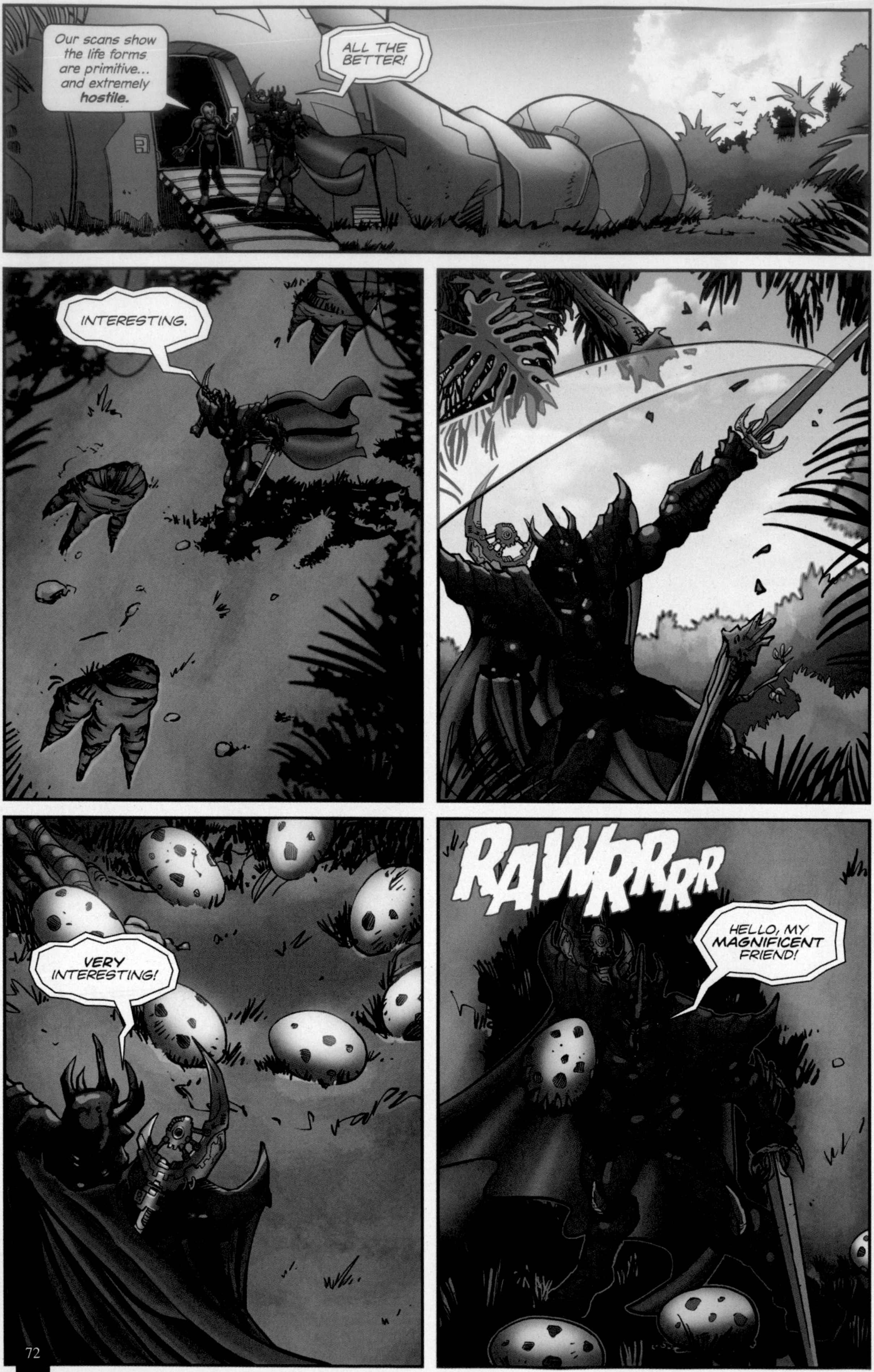
Our scans show the life forms are primitive... and extremely **hostile.**
ALL THE BETTER!
INTERESTING.
VERY INTERESTING!
RAWRRRR
HELLO, MY MAGNIFICENT FRIEND!

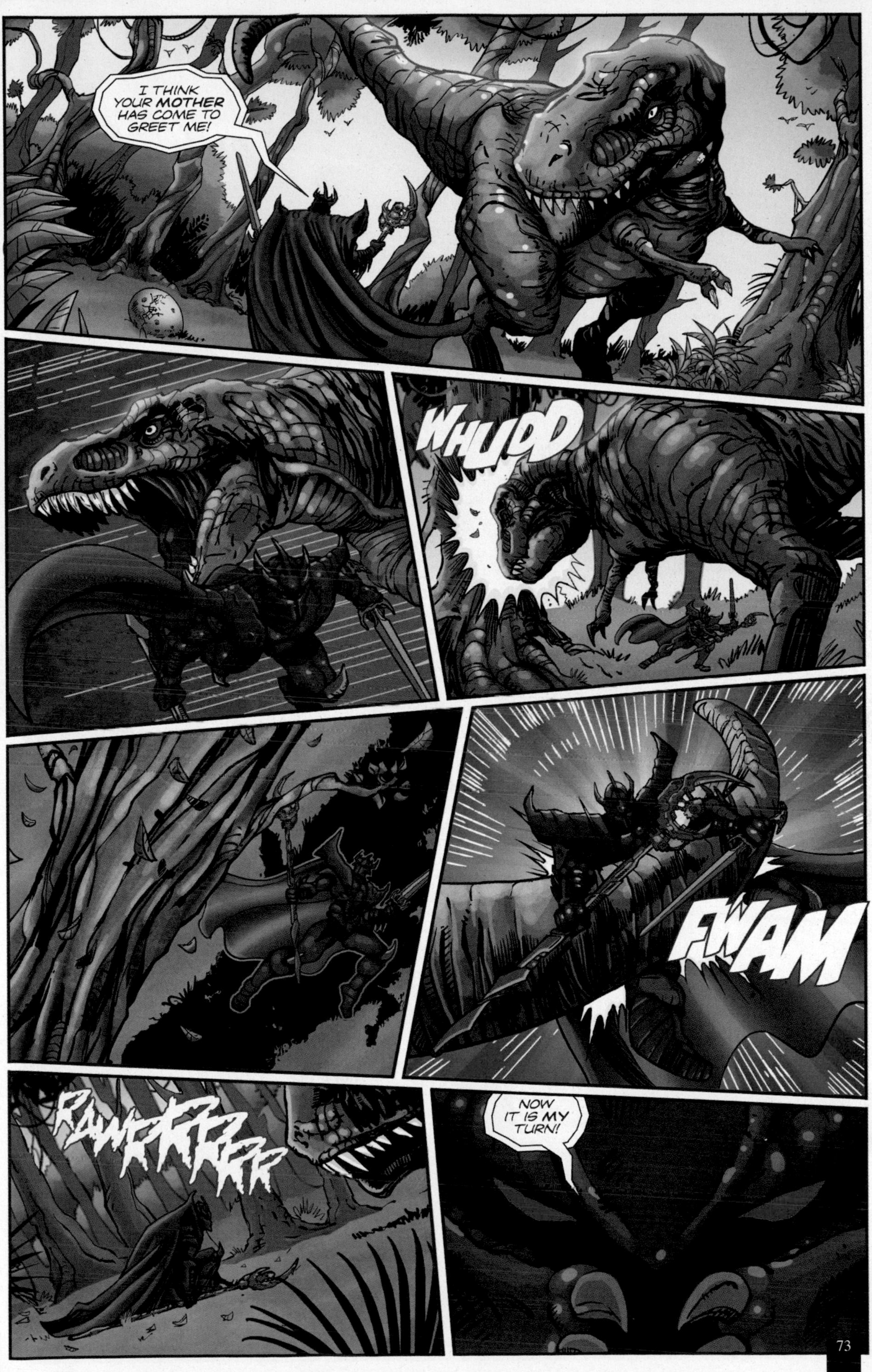
I THINK YOUR MOTHER HAS COME TO GREET ME!
WHUDD
FWAM
RAWRRRR
NOW IT IS MY TURN!

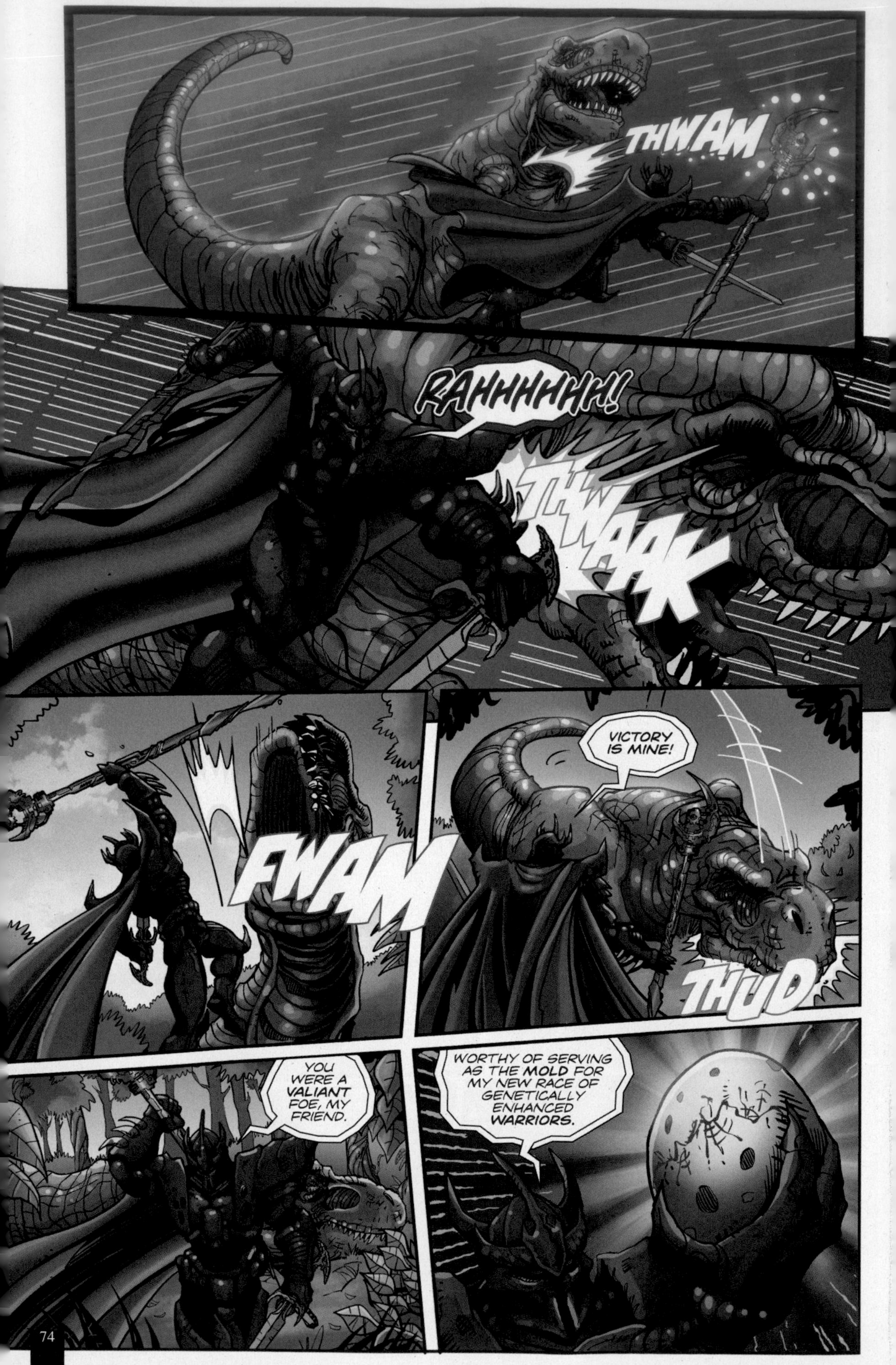
THWAM
RAHHHHHH!
THWAAK
FWAM
VICTORY IS MINE!
THUD
YOU WERE A VALIANT FOE, MY FRIEND.
WORTHY OF SERVING AS THE MOLD FOR MY NEW RACE OF GENETICALLY ENHANCED WARRIORS.

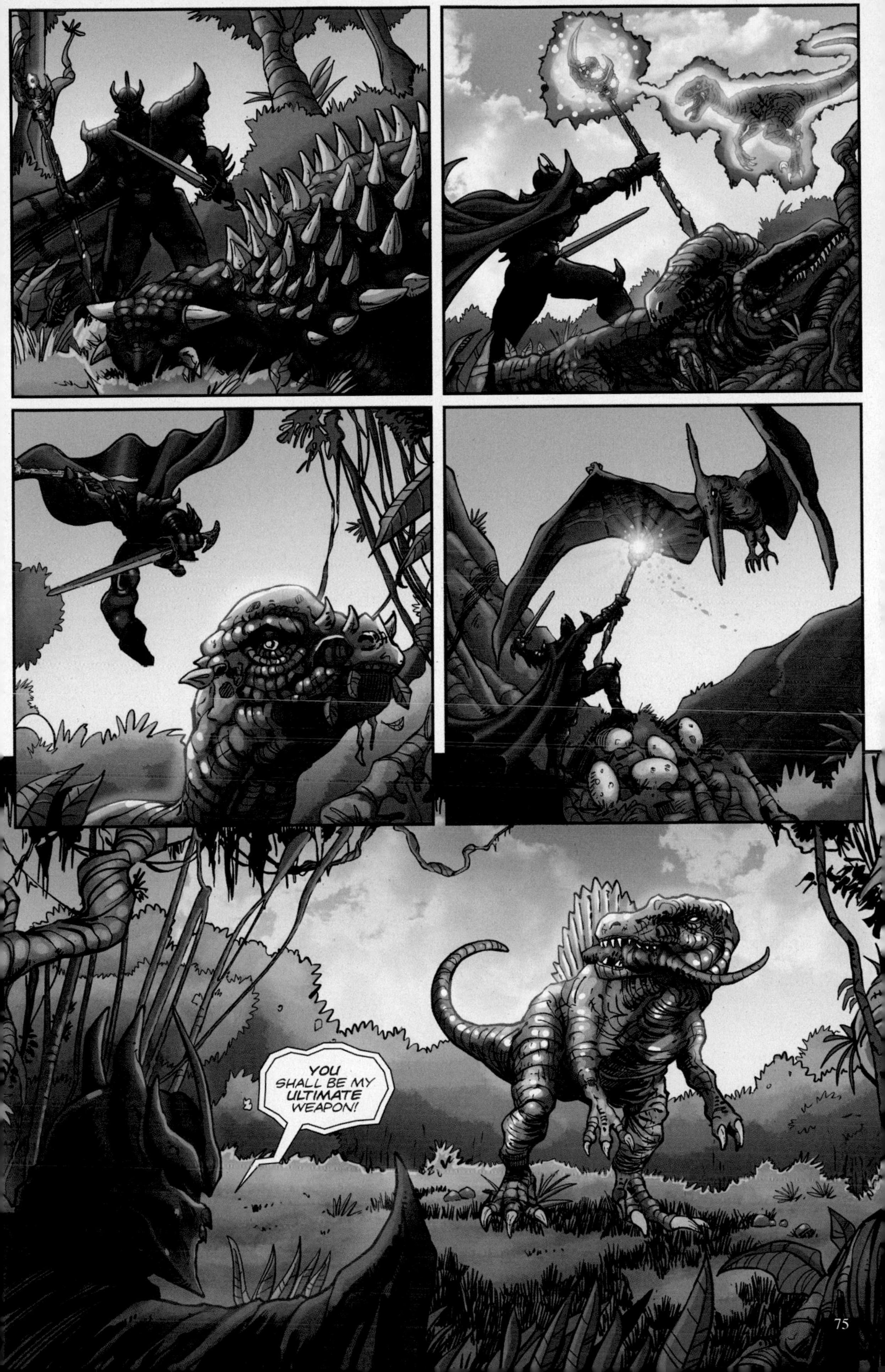
YOU SHALL BE MY ULTIMATE WEAPON!

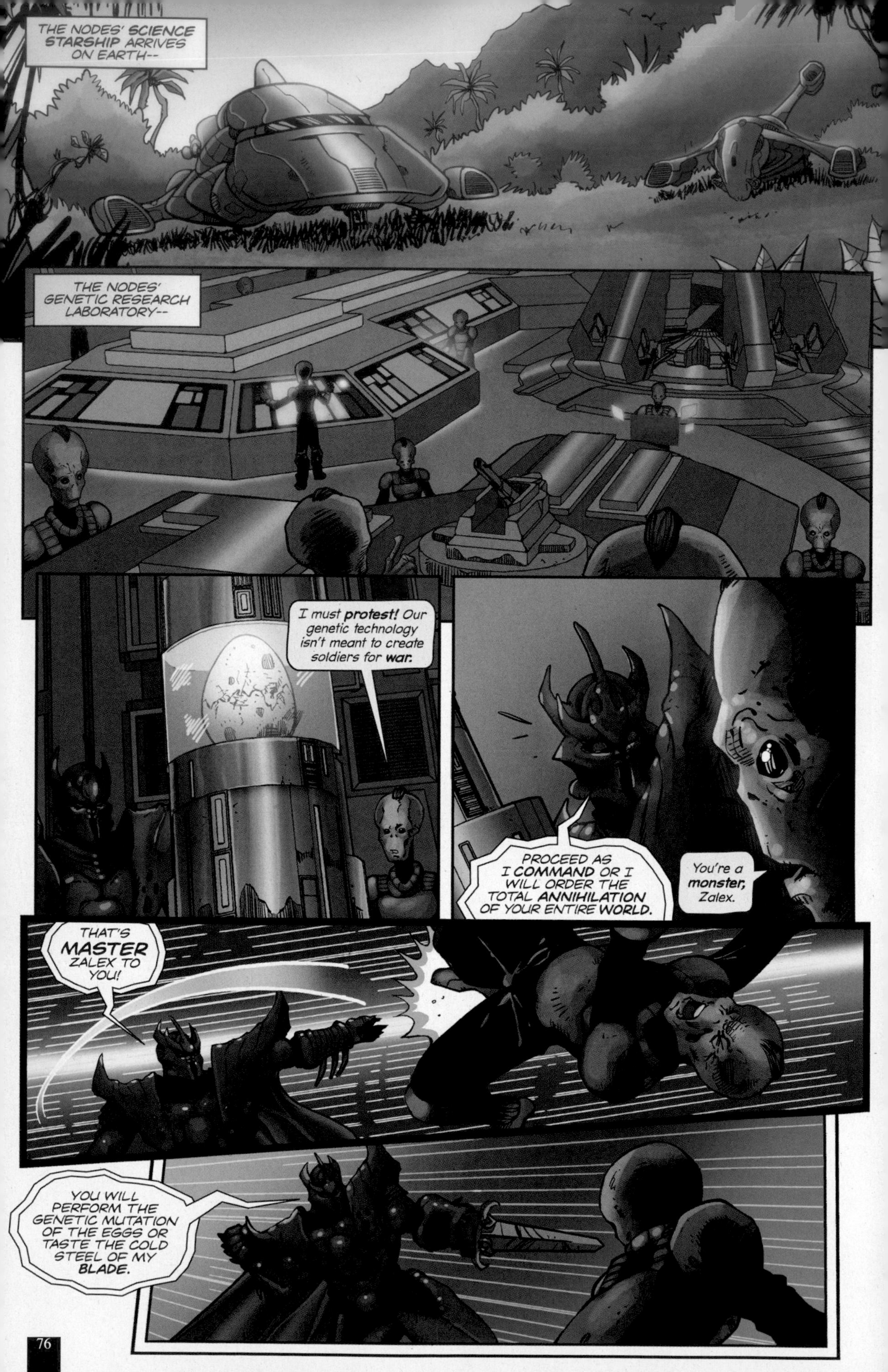

THE NODES' SCIENCE STARSHIP ARRIVES ON EARTH--
THE NODES' GENETIC RESEARCH LABORATORY--
I must protest! Our genetic technology isn't meant to create soldiers for war.
PROCEED AS I COMMAND OR I WILL ORDER THE TOTAL ANNIHILATION OF YOUR ENTIRE WORLD.
You're a monster, Zalex.
THAT'S MASTER ZALEX TO YOU!
YOU WILL PERFORM THE GENETIC MUTATION OF THE EGGS OR TASTE THE COLD STEEL OF MY BLADE.

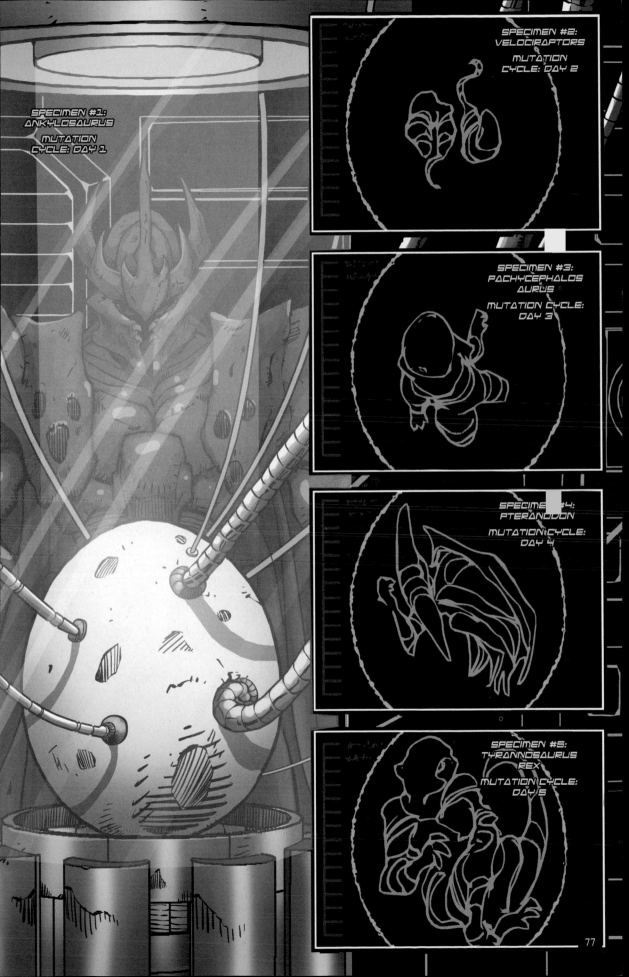

SPECIMEN #1:
ANKYLOSAURUS

MUTATION
CYCLE: DAY 1

SPECIMEN #2:
VELOCIRAPTORS

MUTATION
CYCLE: DAY 2

SPECIMEN #3:
PACHYCEPHALOS
AURUS

MUTATION CYCLE:
DAY 3

SPECIMEN #4:
PTERANODON

MUTATION CYCLE:
DAY 4

SPECIMEN #5:
TYRANNOSAURUS
REX

MUTATION CYCLE:
DAY 5

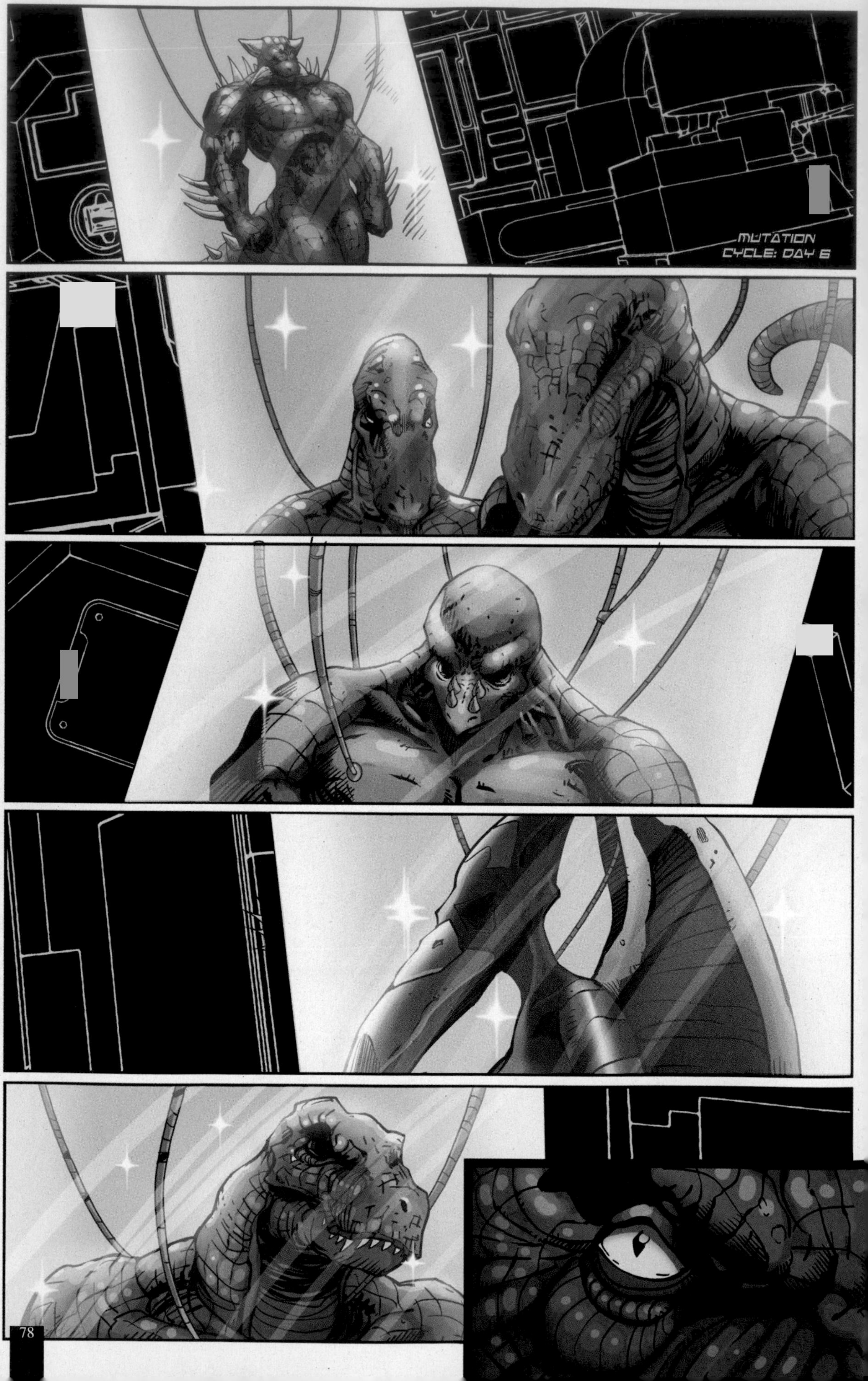
MUTATION
CYCLE: DAY 6

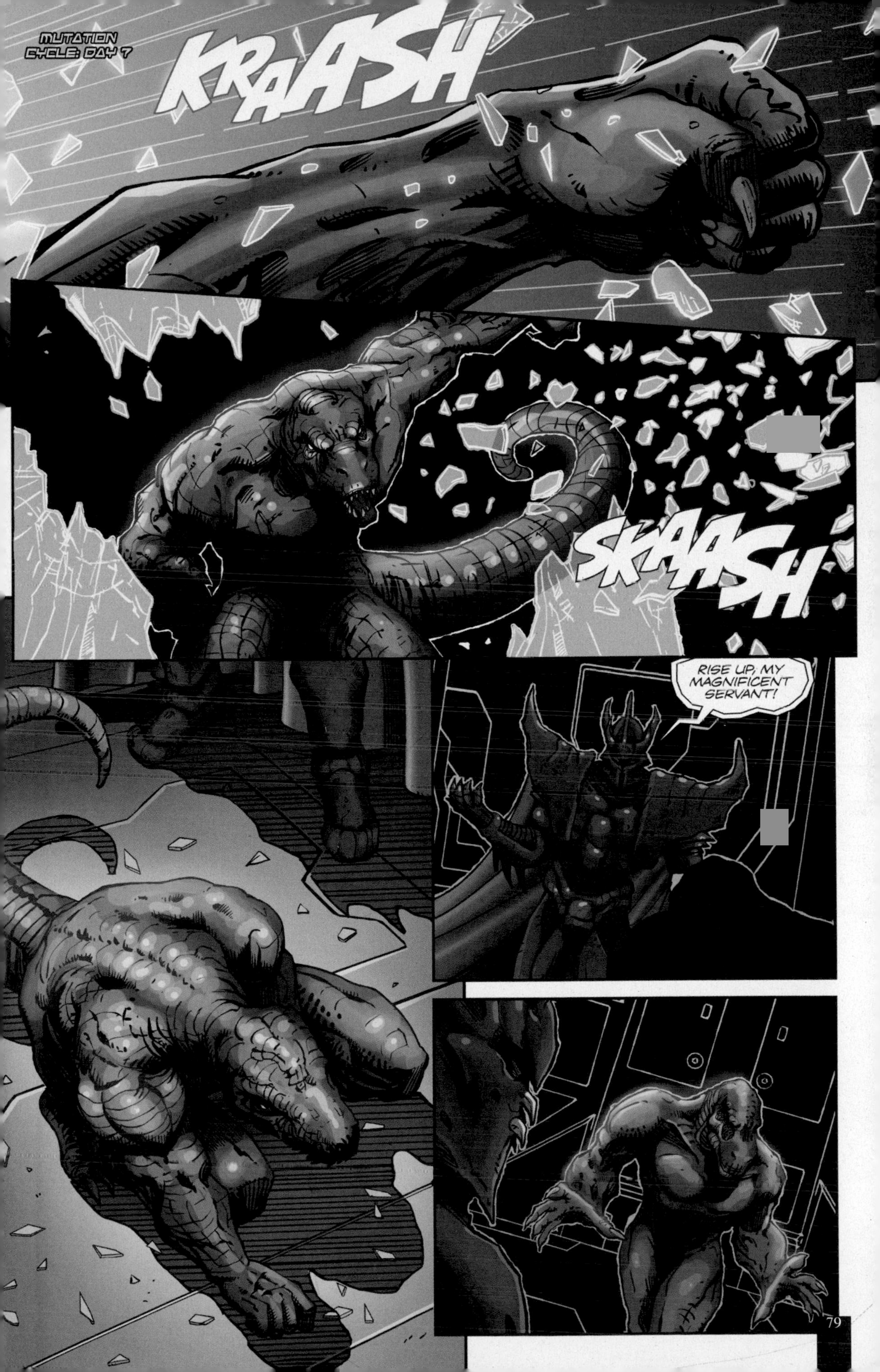
MUTATION CYCLE: DAY 7
KRAASH
SKAASH
RISE UP, MY MAGNIFICENT SERVANT!

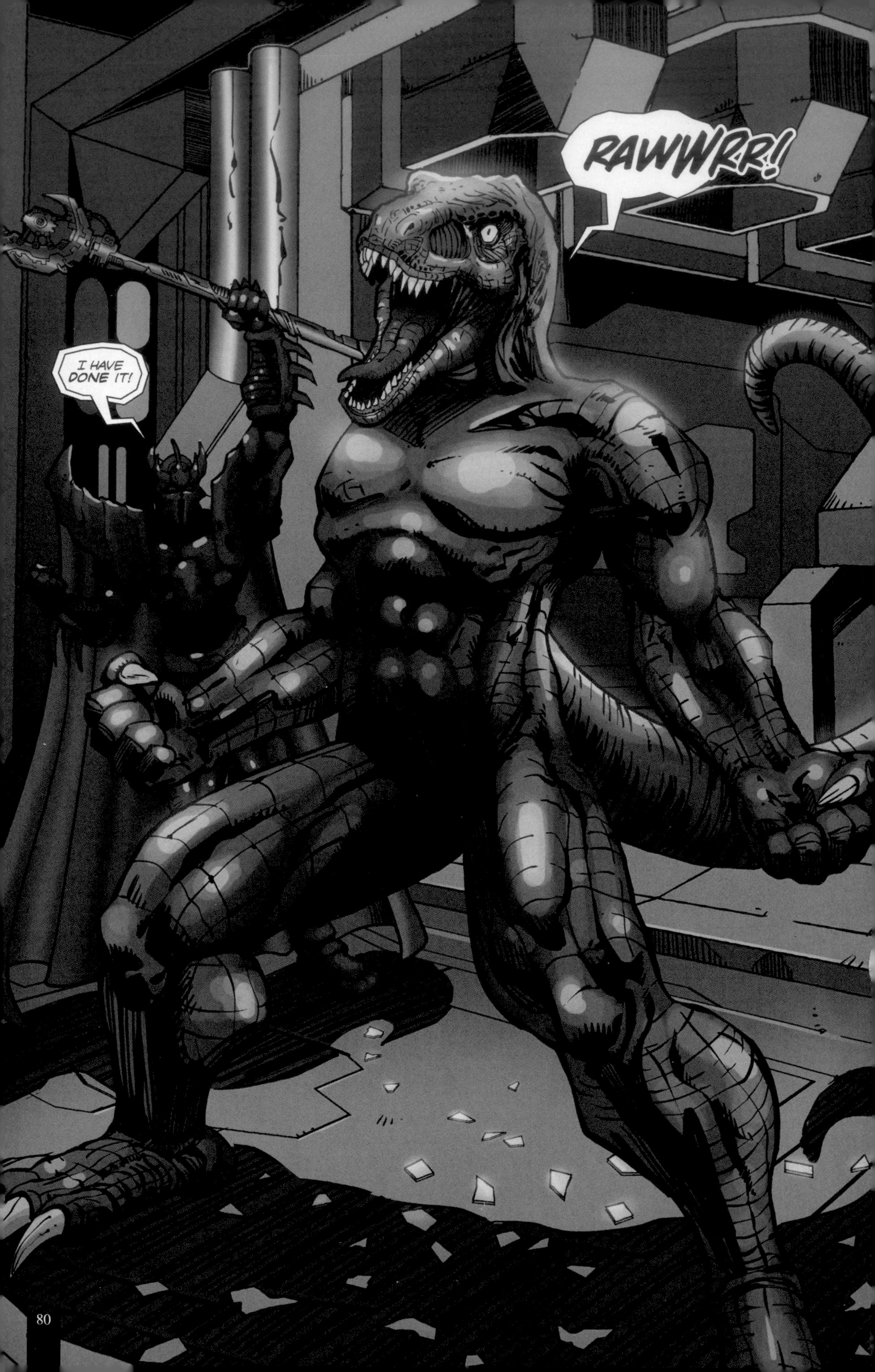
I HAVE DONE IT!
RAWWRR!

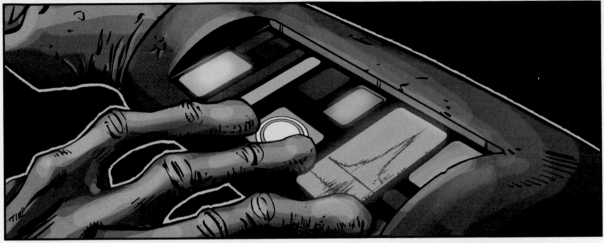

MUTATION CYCLE: DAY 5

You are the galaxy's **only** hope.

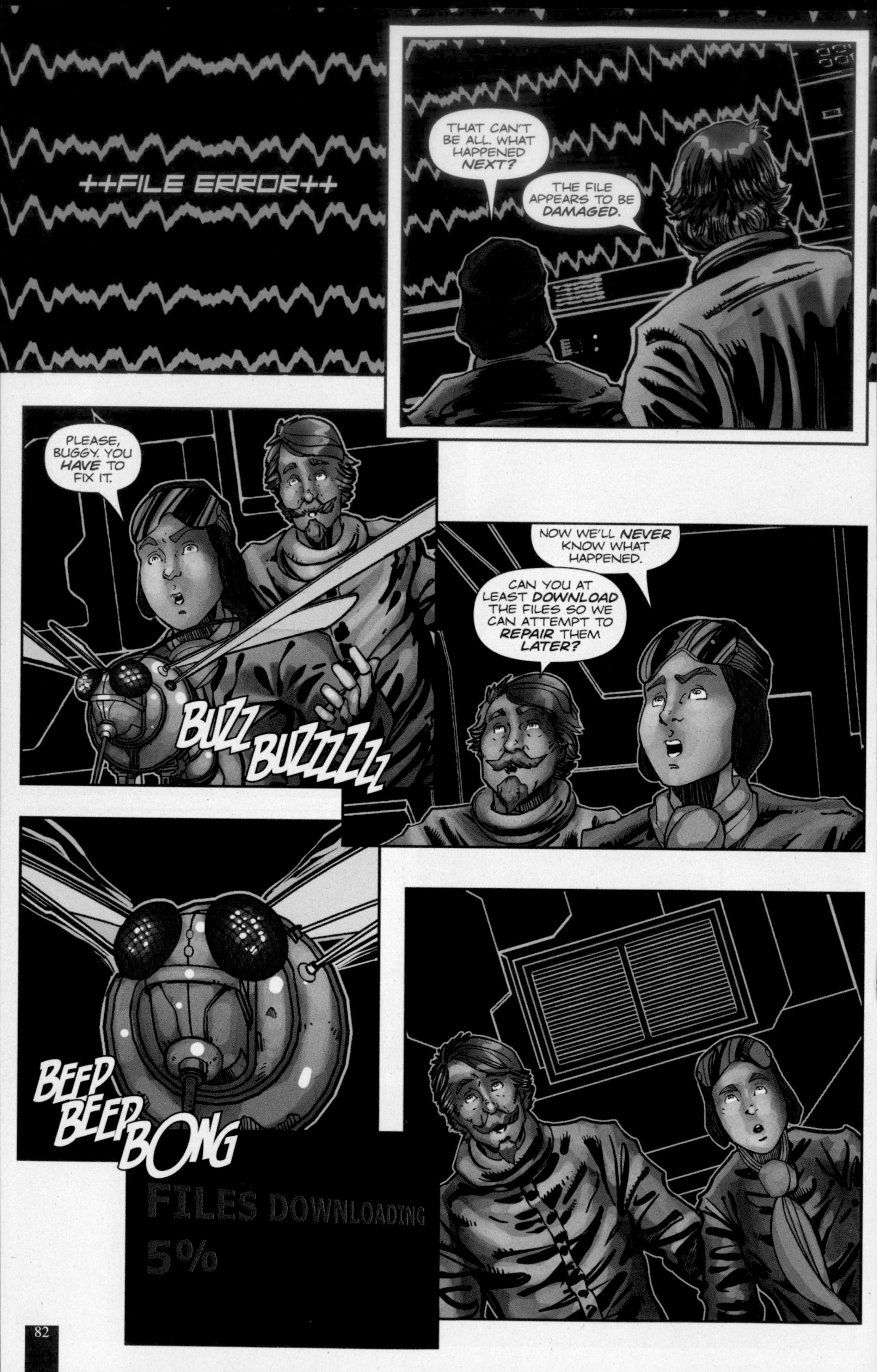

++FILE ERROR++
THAT CAN'T BE ALL. WHAT HAPPENED NEXT?
THE FILE APPEARS TO BE DAMAGED.
PLEASE, BUGGY. YOU HAVE TO FIX IT.
BUZZ BUZZZZZZ
NOW WE'LL NEVER KNOW WHAT HAPPENED.
CAN YOU AT LEAST DOWNLOAD THE FILES SO WE CAN ATTEMPT TO REPAIR THEM LATER?
BEEP BEEP BONG
FILES DOWNLOADING
5%

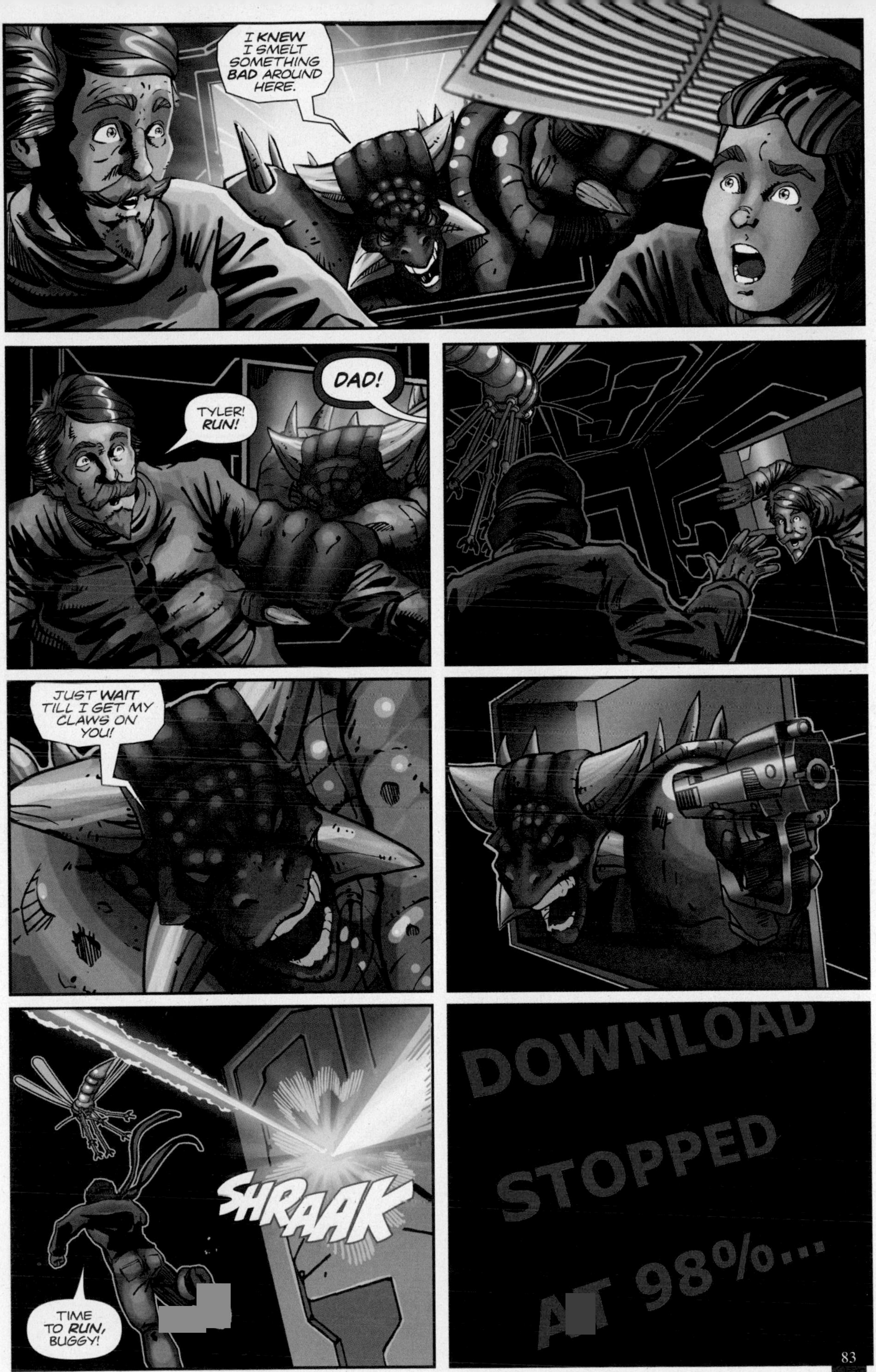
I KNEW I SMELT SOMETHING BAD AROUND HERE.
TYLER! RUN!
DAD!
JUST WAIT TILL I GET MY CLAWS ON YOU!
SHRAAK
TIME TO RUN, BUGGY!
DOWNLOAD STOPPED AT 98%...

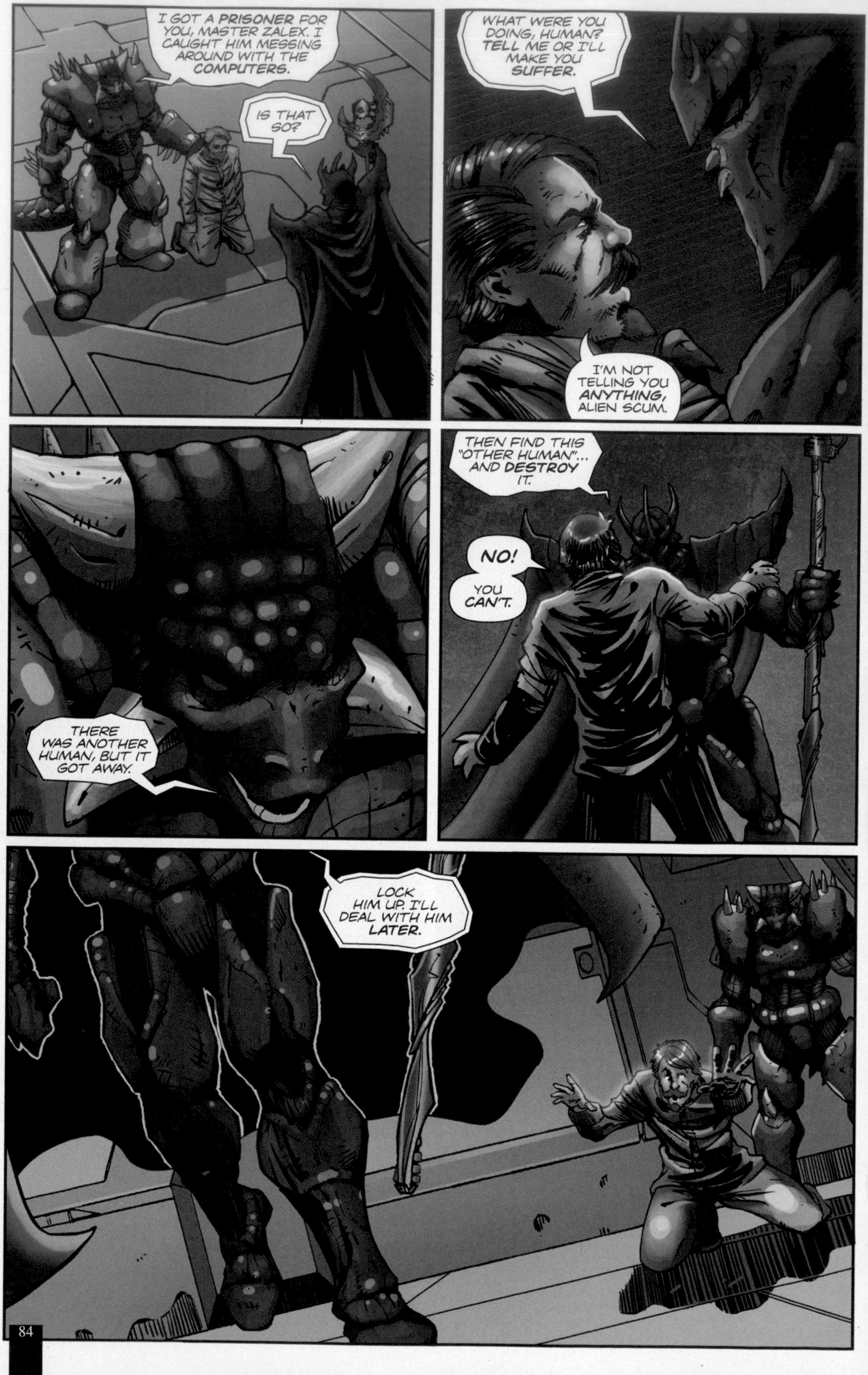
I GOT A PRISONER FOR YOU, MASTER ZALEX. I CAUGHT HIM MESSING AROUND WITH THE COMPUTERS.
IS THAT SO?
WHAT WERE YOU DOING, HUMAN? TELL ME OR I'LL MAKE YOU SUFFER.
I'M NOT TELLING YOU ANYTHING, ALIEN SCUM.
THERE WAS ANOTHER HUMAN, BUT IT GOT AWAY.
THEN FIND THIS "OTHER HUMAN"... AND DESTROY IT.
NO!
YOU CAN'T.
LOCK HIM UP. I'LL DEAL WITH HIM LATER.

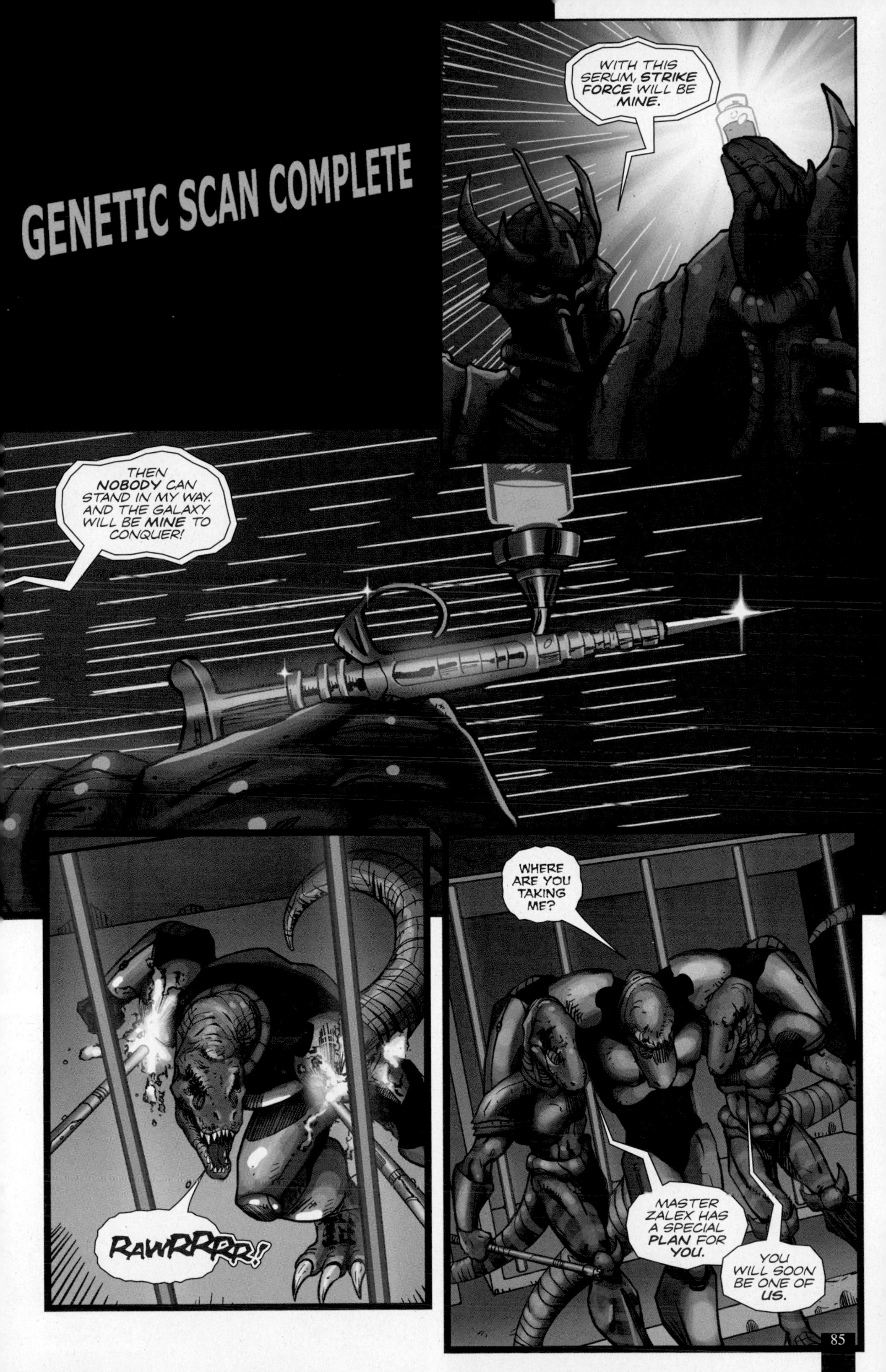
GENETIC SCAN COMPLETE
WITH THIS SERUM, STRIKE FORCE WILL BE MINE.
THEN NOBODY CAN STAND IN MY WAY. AND THE GALAXY WILL BE MINE TO CONQUER!
RAWRRRR!
WHERE ARE YOU TAKING ME?
MASTER ZALEX HAS A SPECIAL PLAN FOR YOU.
YOU WILL SOON BE ONE OF US.

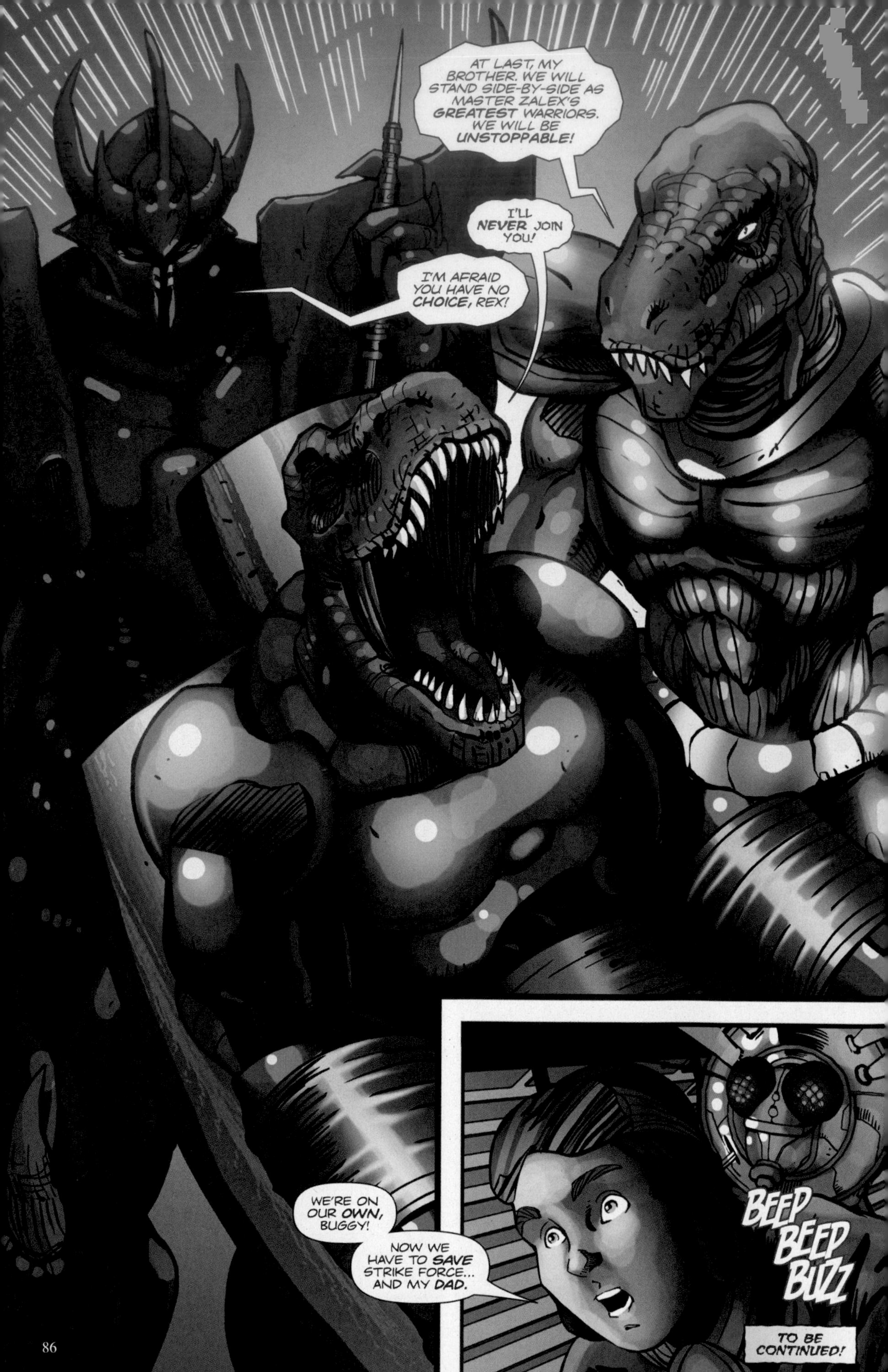
AT LAST, MY BROTHER. WE WILL STAND SIDE-BY-SIDE AS MASTER ZALEX'S GREATEST WARRIORS. WE WILL BE UNSTOPPABLE!
I'LL NEVER JOIN YOU!
I'M AFRAID YOU HAVE NO CHOICE, REX!
WE'RE ON OUR OWN, BUGGY!
NOW WE HAVE TO SAVE STRIKE FORCE... AND MY DAD.
BEEP BEEP BUZZ
TO BE CONTINUED!

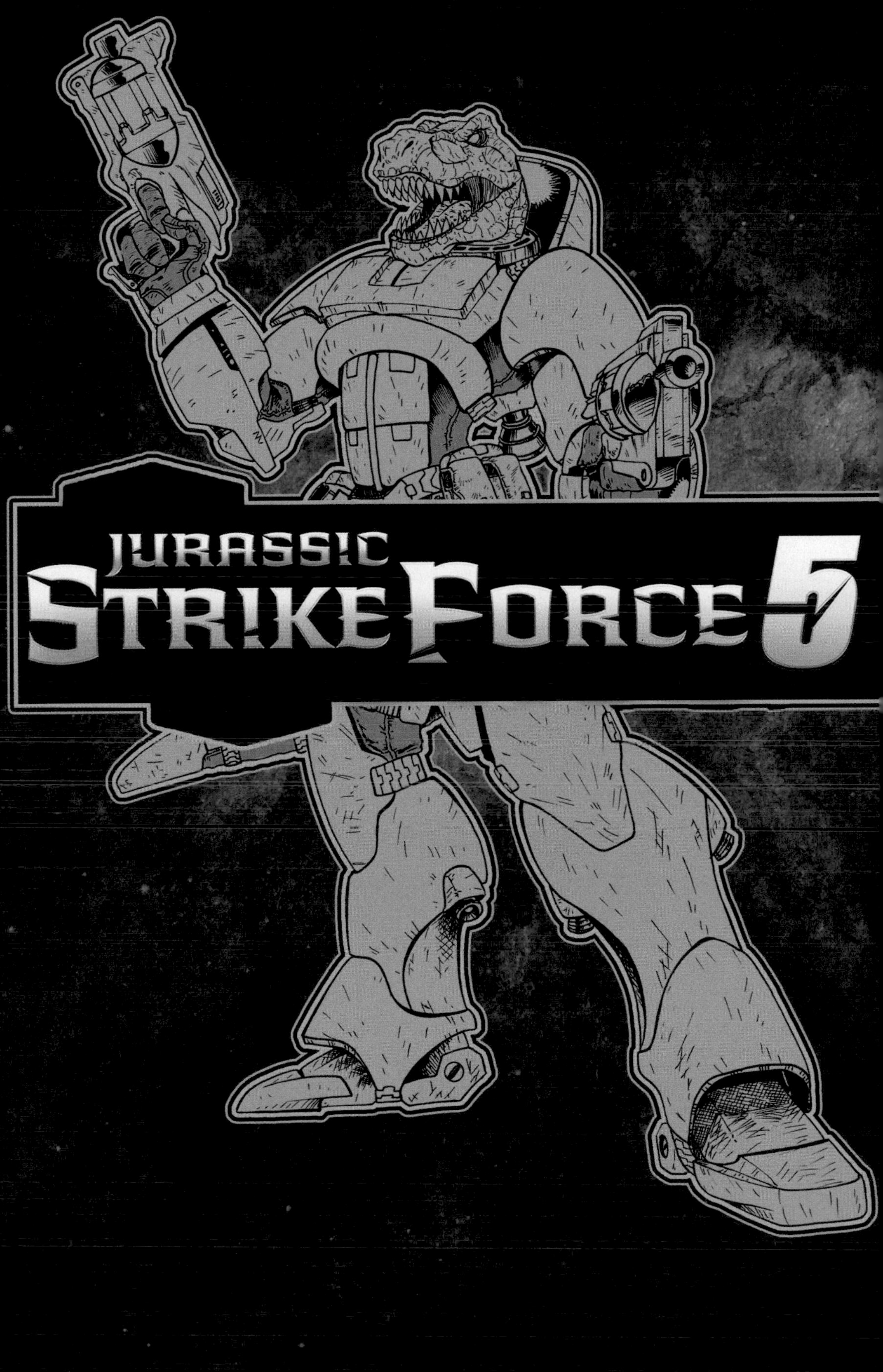
JURASSIC
STRIKE FORCE 5

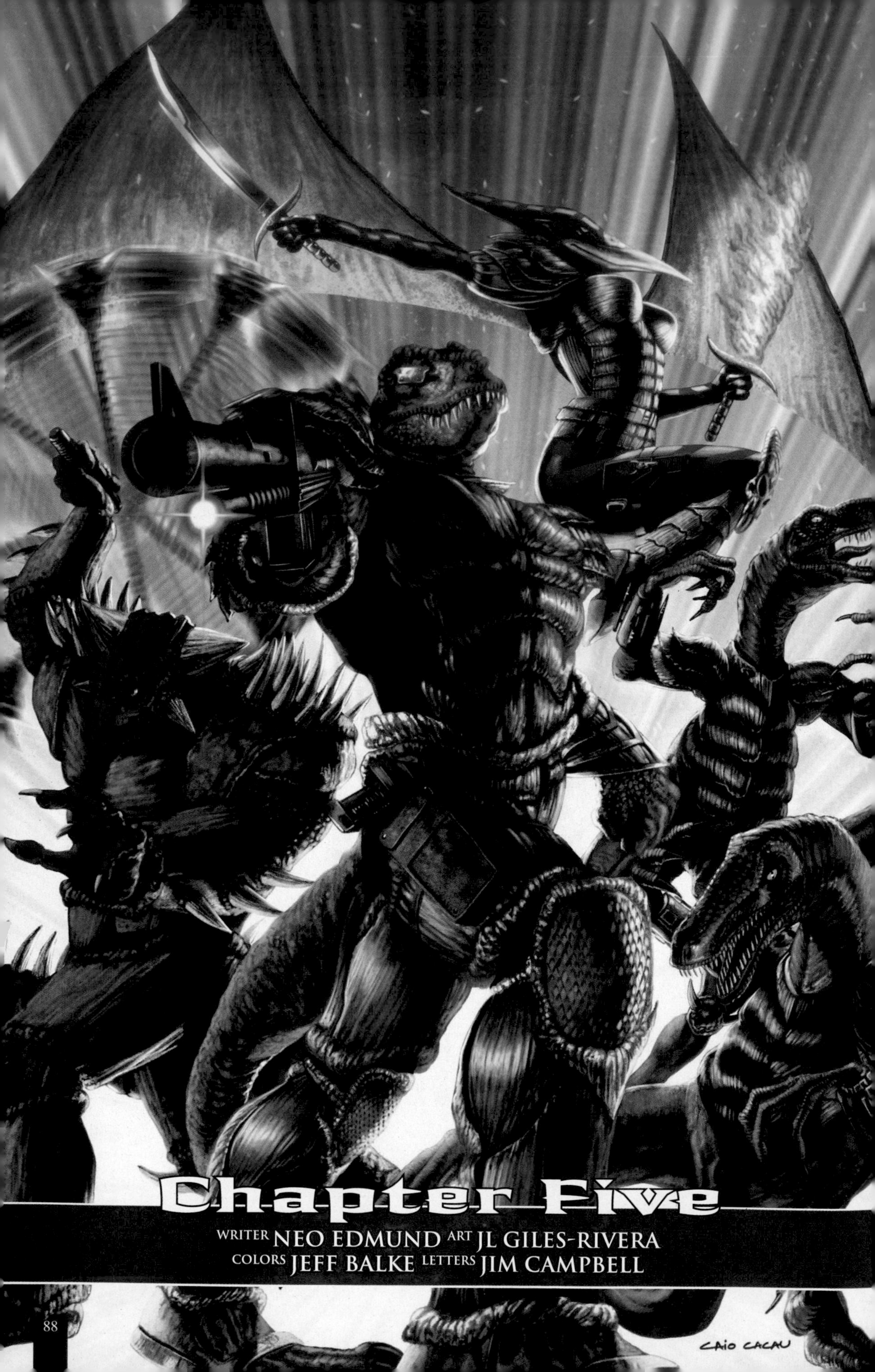
CAIO CACAU

Chapter Five

WRITER NEO EDMUND ART JL GILES-RIVERA
COLORS JEFF BALKE LETTERS JIM CAMPBELL

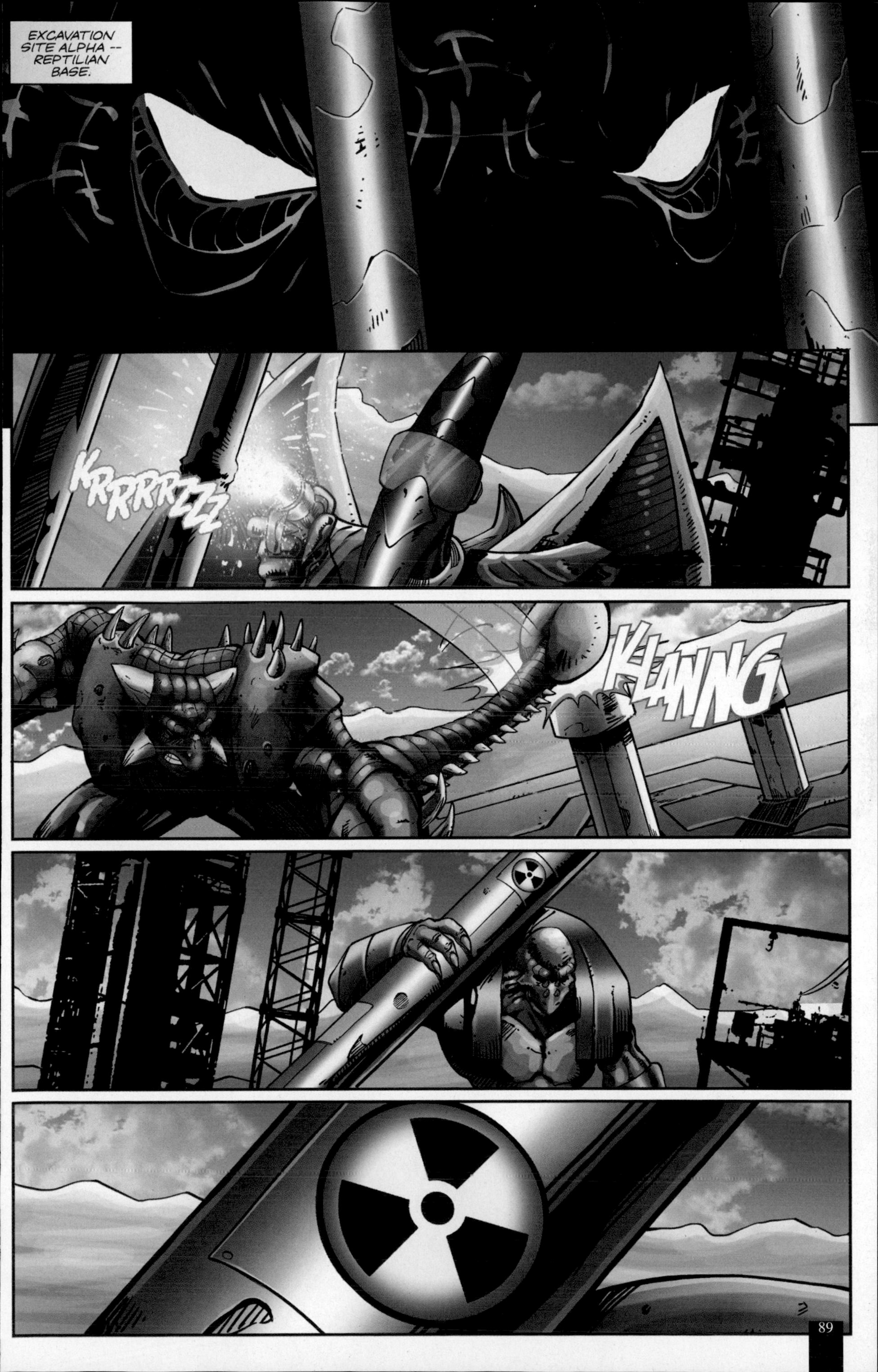
EXCAVATION SITE ALPHA -- REPTILIAN BASE.
KRRRRZZZ
KLANNG

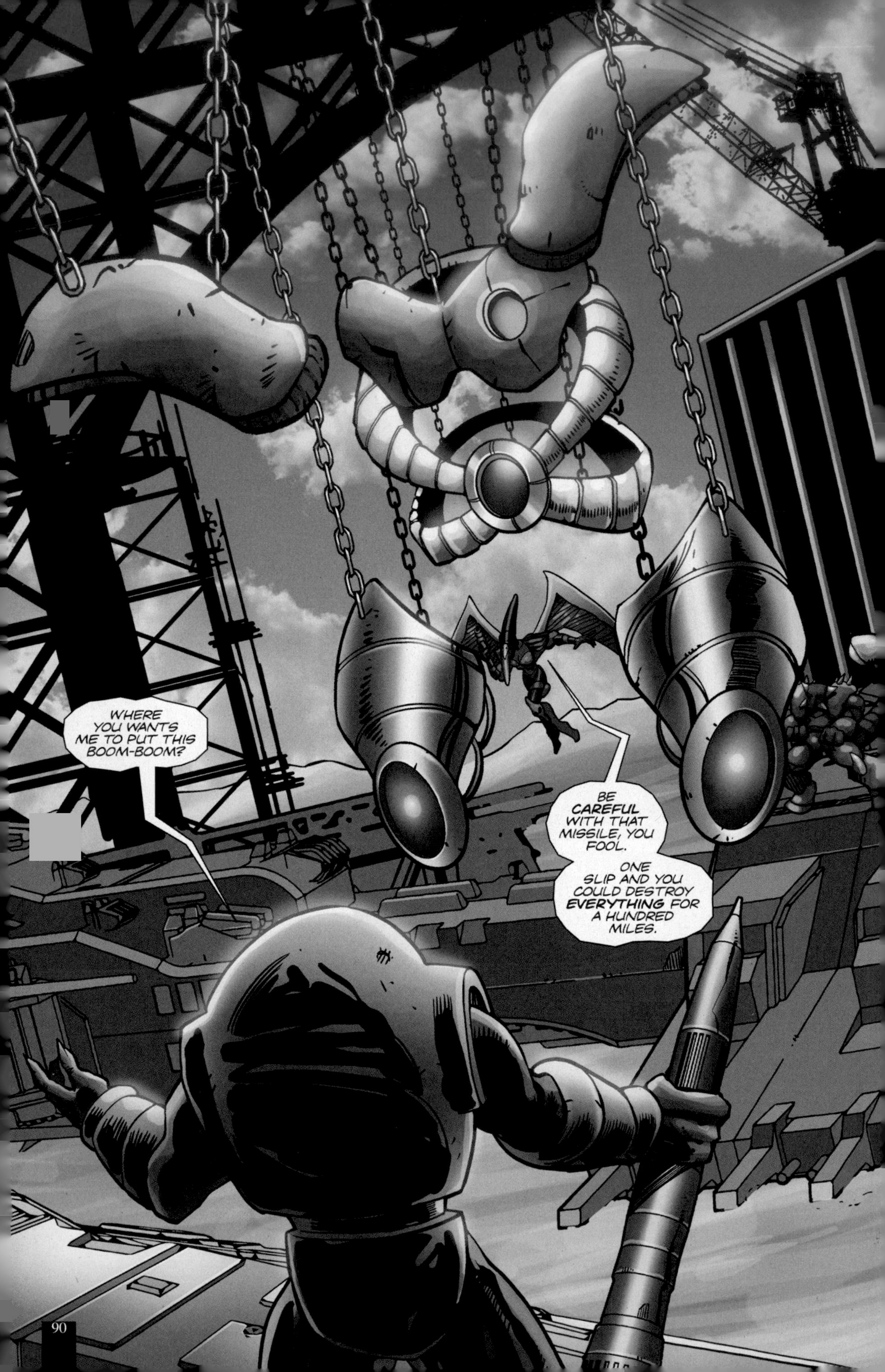
WHERE YOU WANTS ME TO PUT THIS BOOM-BOOM?
BE CAREFUL WITH THAT MISSILE, YOU FOOL.
ONE SLIP AND YOU COULD DESTROY EVERYTHING FOR A HUNDRED MILES.

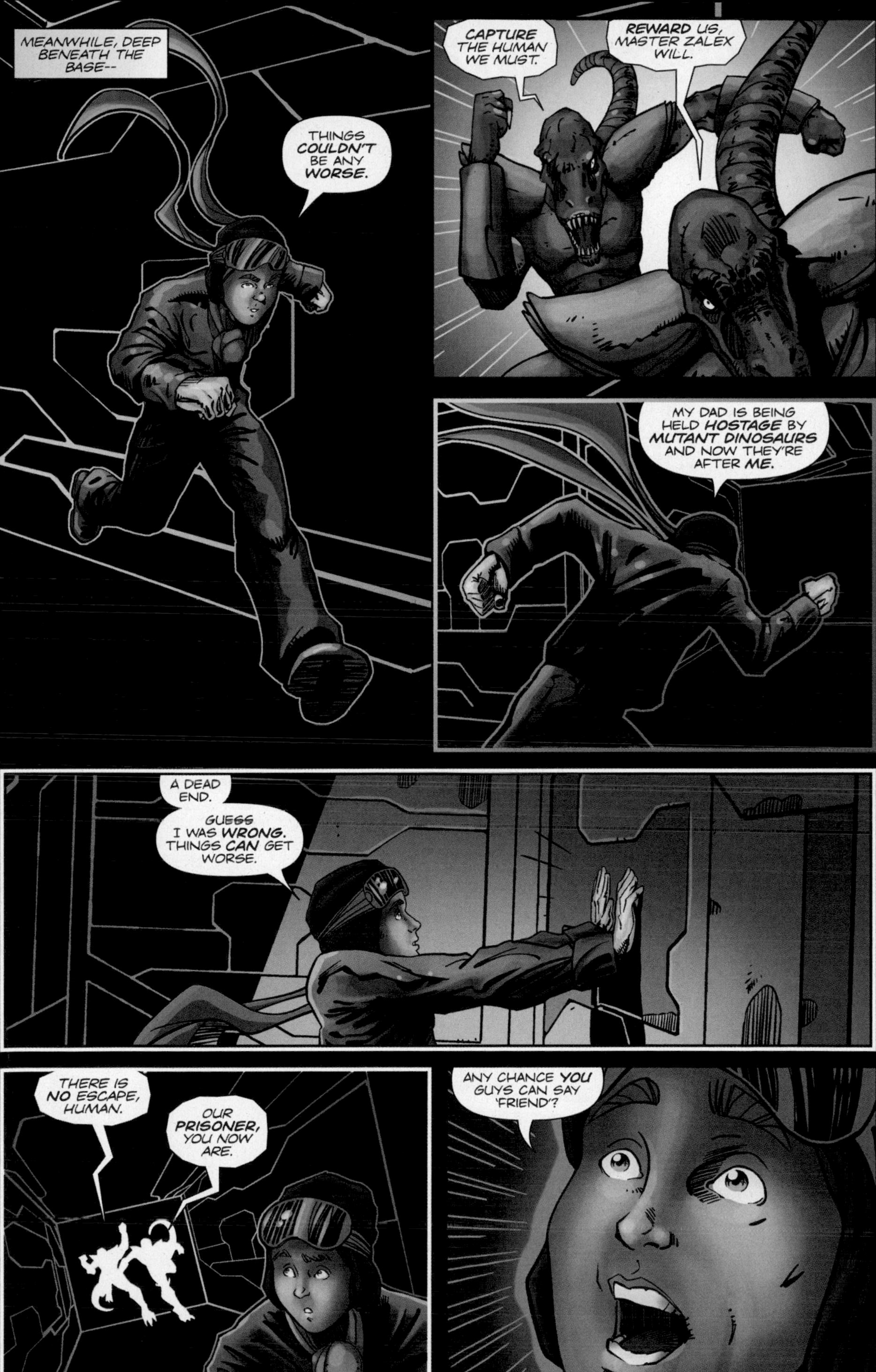
MEANWHILE, DEEP BENEATH THE BASE--
THINGS COULDN'T BE ANY WORSE.
CAPTURE THE HUMAN WE MUST.
REWARD US, MASTER ZALEX WILL.
MY DAD IS BEING HELD HOSTAGE BY MUTANT DINOSAURS AND NOW THEY'RE AFTER ME.
A DEAD END.
GUESS I WAS WRONG. THINGS CAN GET WORSE.
THERE IS NO ESCAPE, HUMAN.
OUR PRISONER, YOU NOW ARE.
ANY CHANCE YOU GUYS CAN SAY 'FRIEND'?

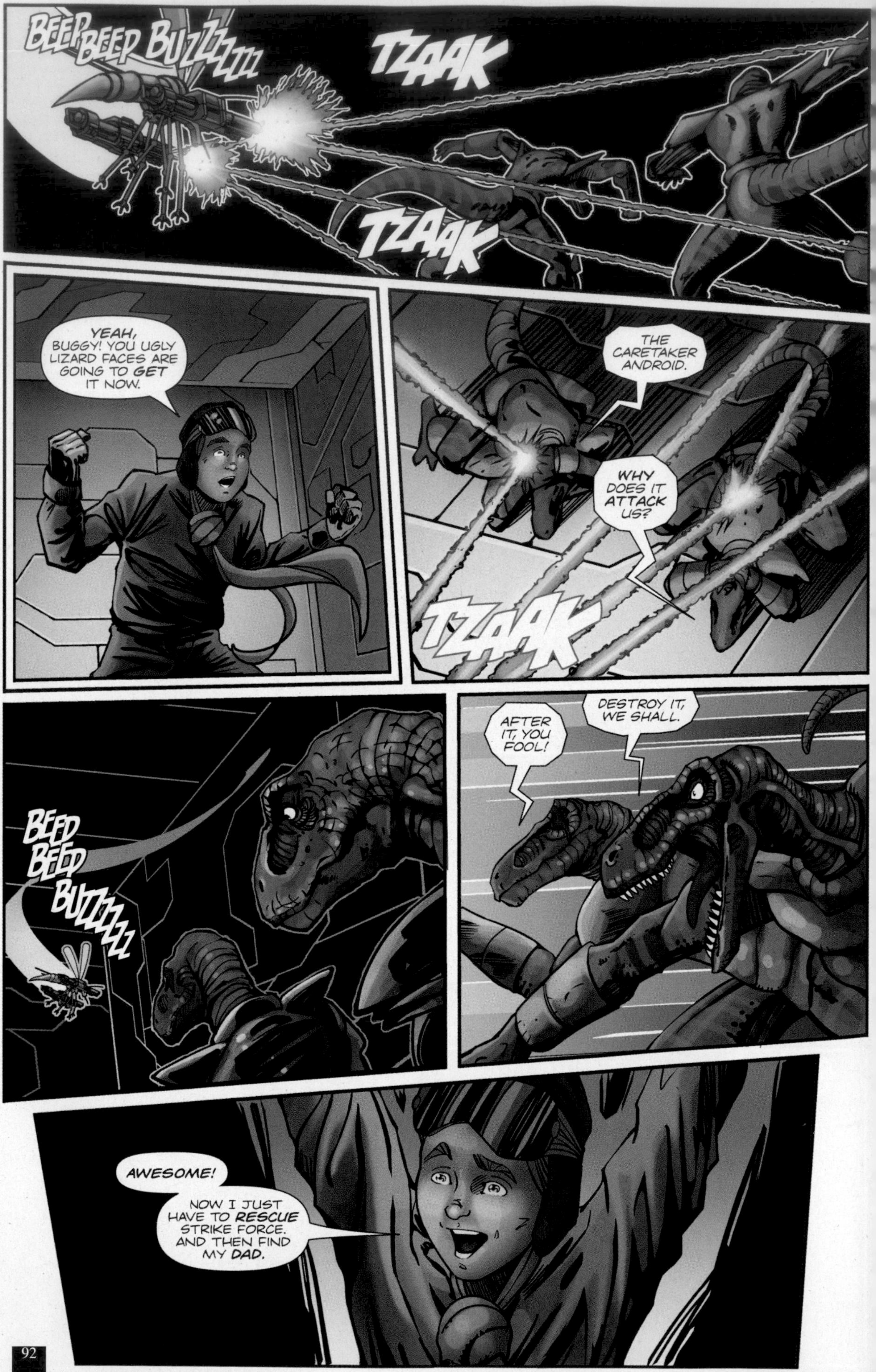
BEEP BEEP BUZZZZZZZ
TZAAK
TZAAK
YEAH, BUGGY! YOU UGLY LIZARD FACES ARE GOING TO GET IT NOW.
THE CARETAKER ANDROID.
WHY DOES IT ATTACK US?
TZAAK
BEEP BEEP BUZZZZZZZ
DESTROY IT, WE SHALL.
AFTER IT, YOU FOOL!
AWESOME!
NOW I JUST HAVE TO RESCUE STRIKE FORCE. AND THEN FIND MY DAD.

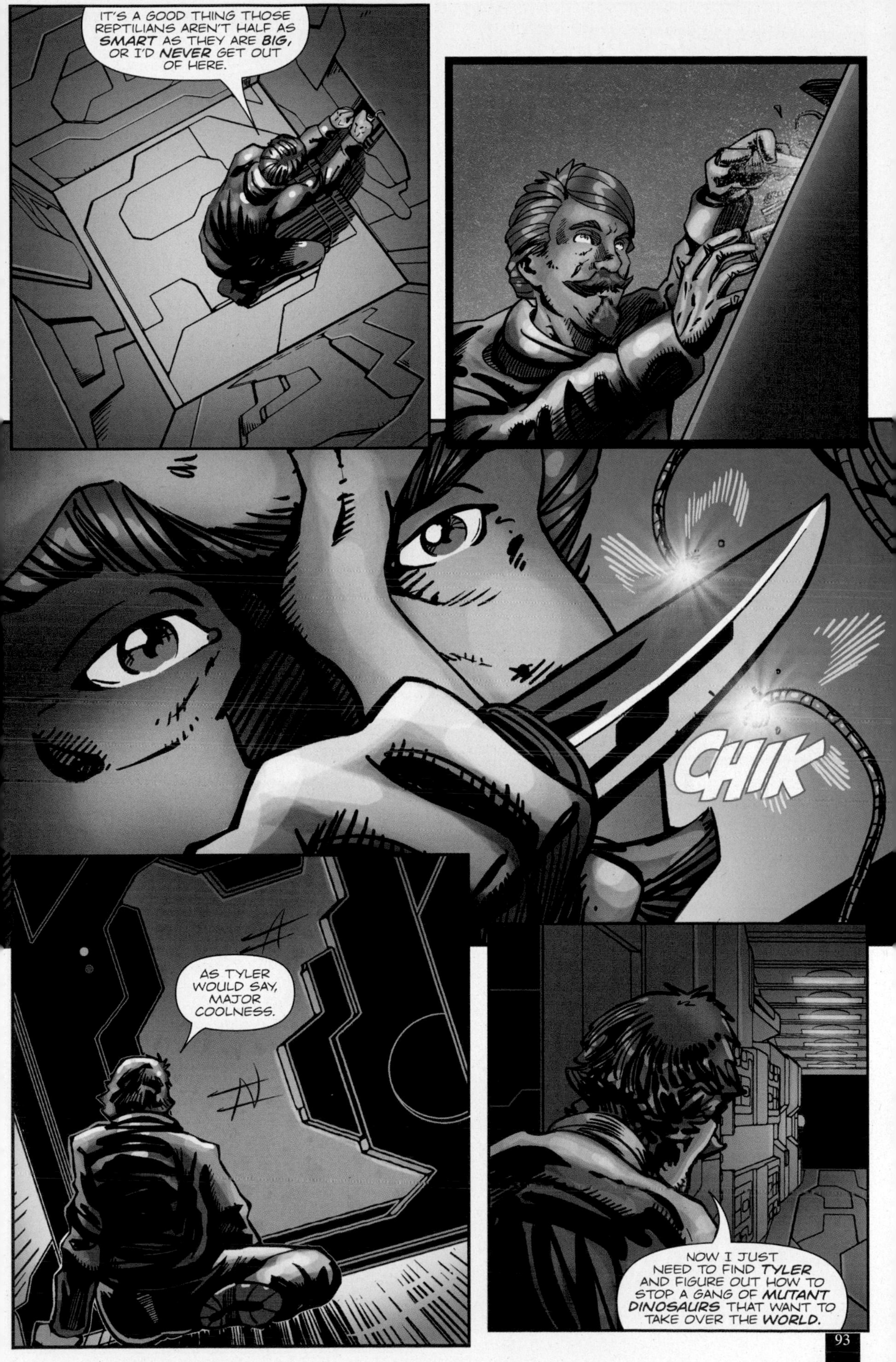
IT'S A GOOD THING THOSE REPTILIANS AREN'T HALF AS SMART AS THEY ARE BIG, OR I'D NEVER GET OUT OF HERE.
CHIK
AS TYLER WOULD SAY, MAJOR COOLNESS.
NOW I JUST NEED TO FIND TYLER AND FIGURE OUT HOW TO STOP A GANG OF MUTANT DINOSAURS THAT WANT TO TAKE OVER THE WORLD.

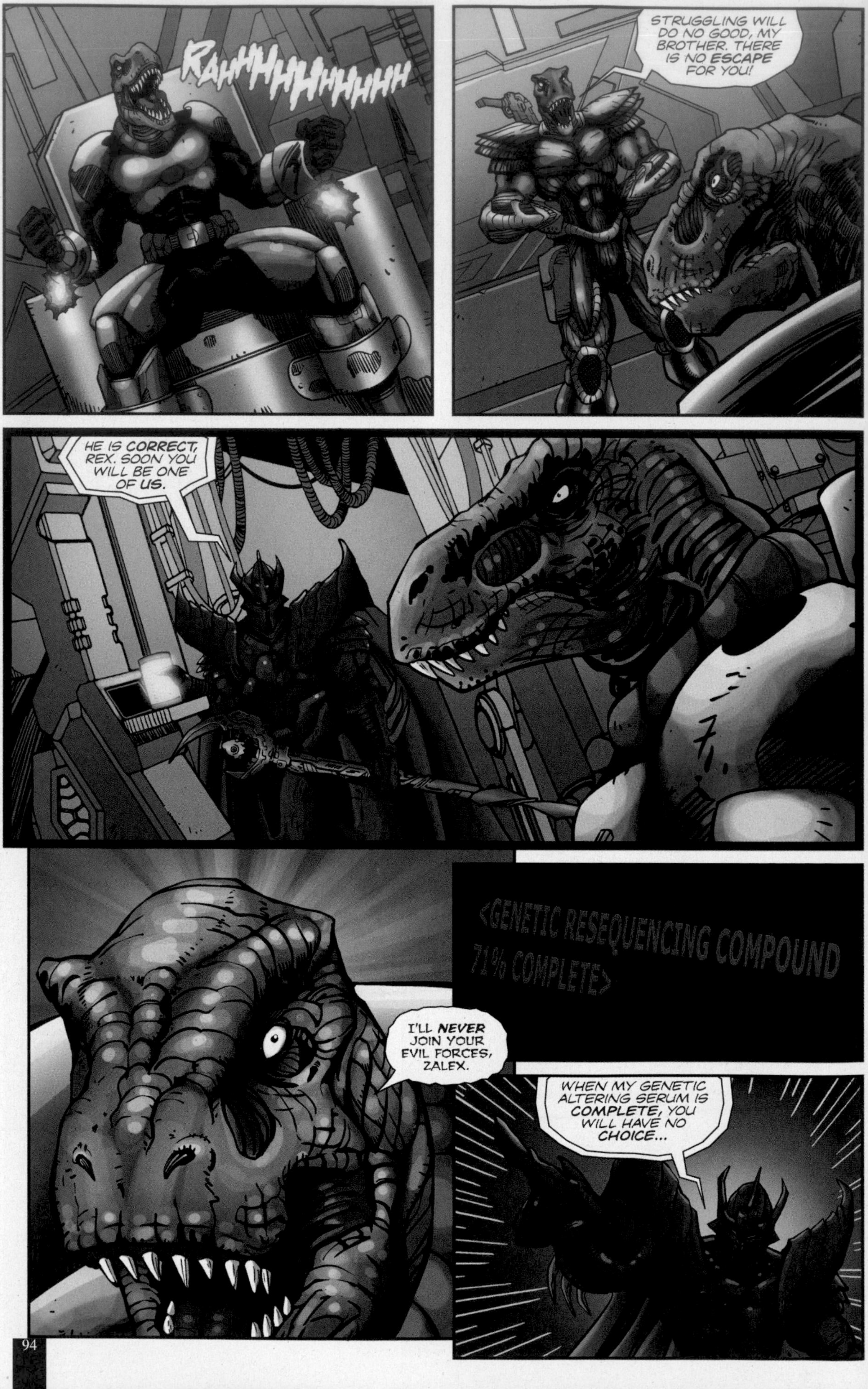
RAHHHHHHHHHH
STRUGGLING WILL DO NO GOOD, MY BROTHER. THERE IS NO ESCAPE FOR YOU!
HE IS CORRECT, REX. SOON YOU WILL BE ONE OF US.
<GENETIC RESEQUENCING COMPOUND 71% COMPLETE>
I'LL NEVER JOIN YOUR EVIL FORCES, ZALEX.
WHEN MY GENETIC ALTERING SERUM IS COMPLETE, YOU WILL HAVE NO CHOICE...

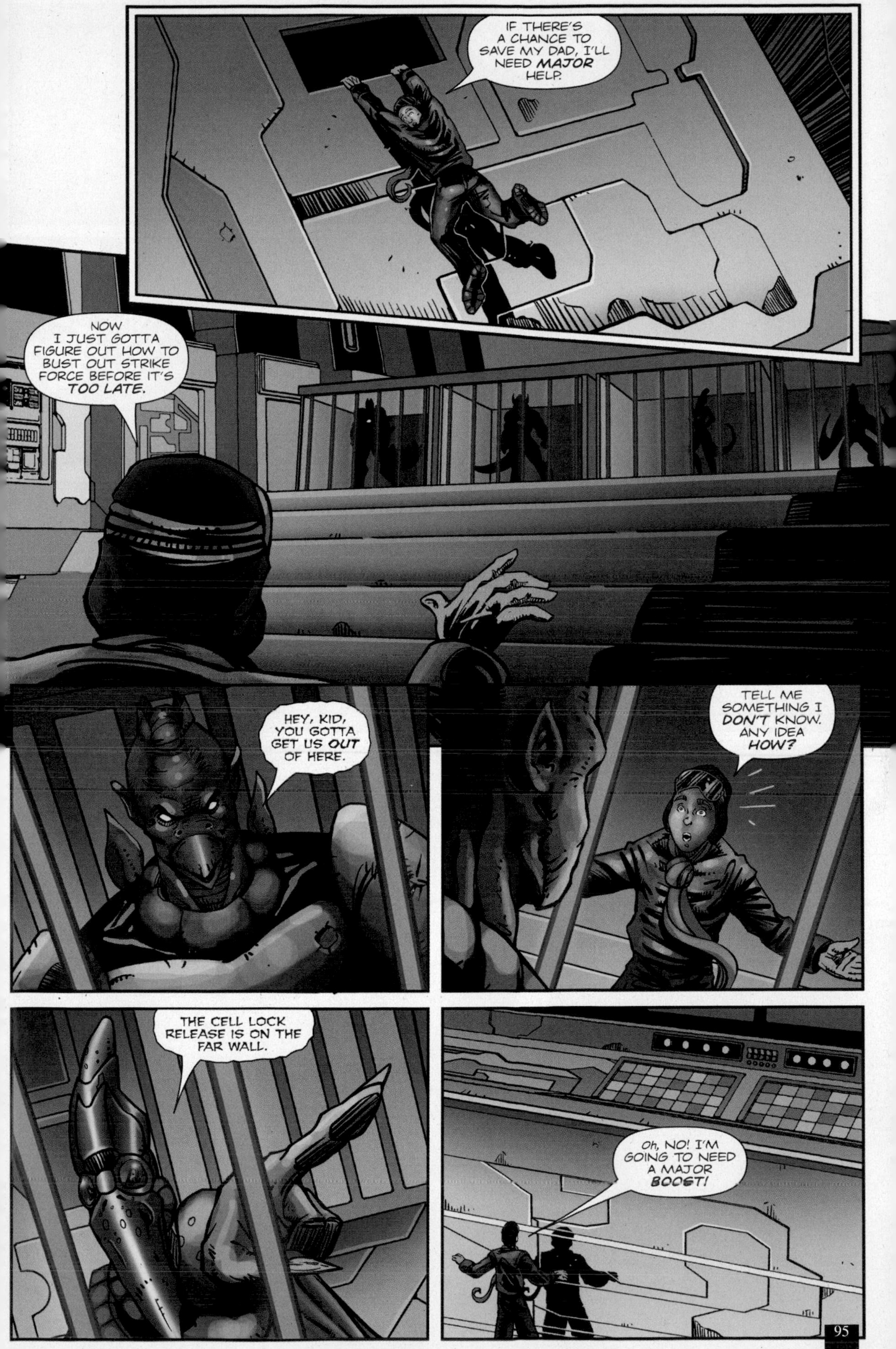
IF THERE'S A CHANCE TO SAVE MY DAD, I'LL NEED MAJOR HELP.
NOW I JUST GOTTA FIGURE OUT HOW TO BUST OUT STRIKE FORCE BEFORE IT'S TOO LATE.
HEY, KID, YOU GOTTA GET US OUT OF HERE.
TELL ME SOMETHING I DON'T KNOW. ANY IDEA HOW?
THE CELL LOCK RELEASE IS ON THE FAR WALL.
Oh, NO! I'M GOING TO NEED A MAJOR BOOST!

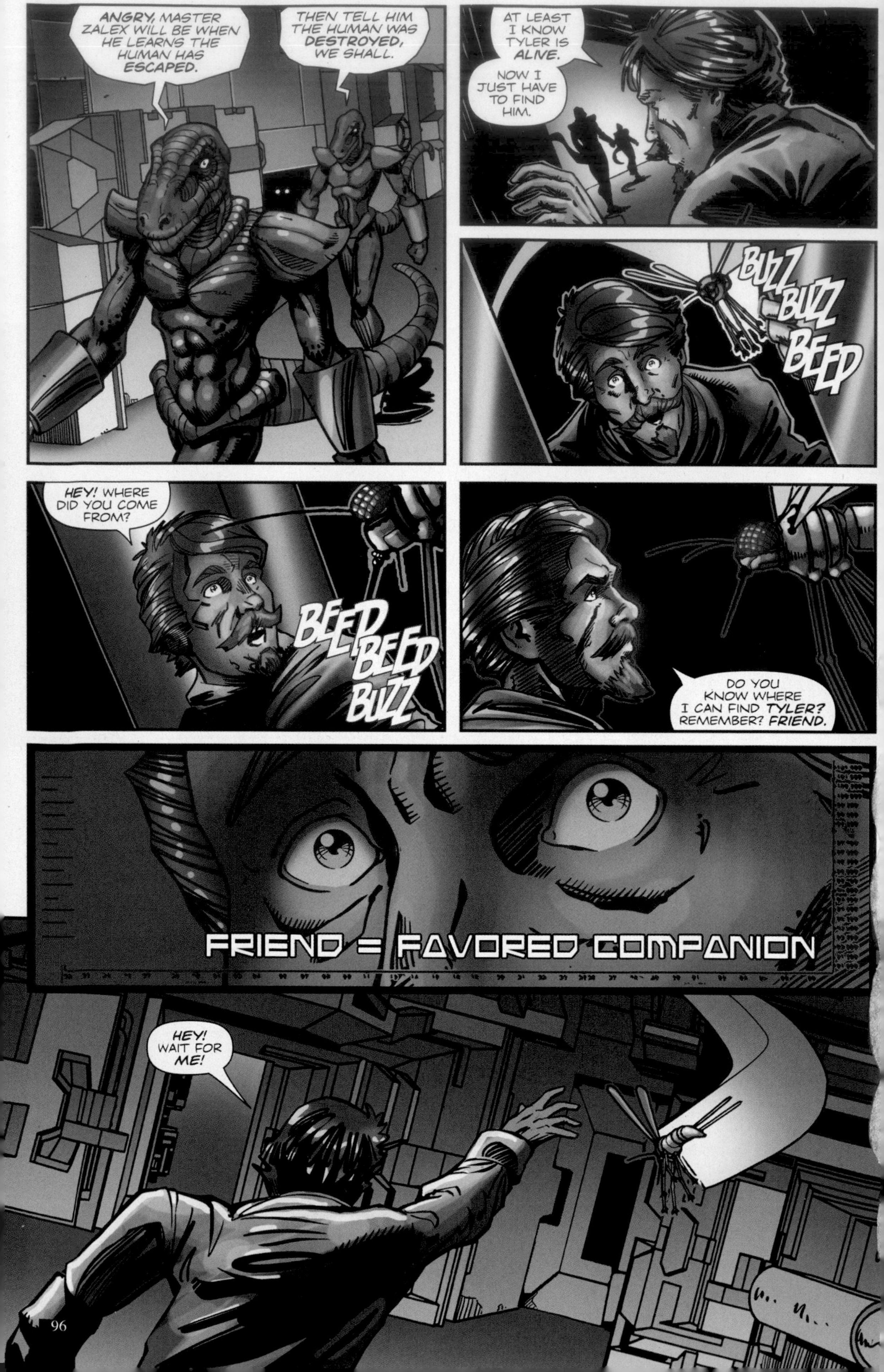
ANGRY, MASTER ZALEX WILL BE WHEN HE LEARNS THE HUMAN HAS ESCAPED.
THEN TELL HIM THE HUMAN WAS DESTROYED, WE SHALL.
AT LEAST I KNOW TYLER IS ALIVE.
NOW I JUST HAVE TO FIND HIM.
BUZZ BUZZ BEEP
HEY! WHERE DID YOU COME FROM?
BEEP BEEP BUZZ
DO YOU KNOW WHERE I CAN FIND TYLER? REMEMBER? FRIEND.
FRIEND = FAVORED COMPANION
HEY! WAIT FOR ME!

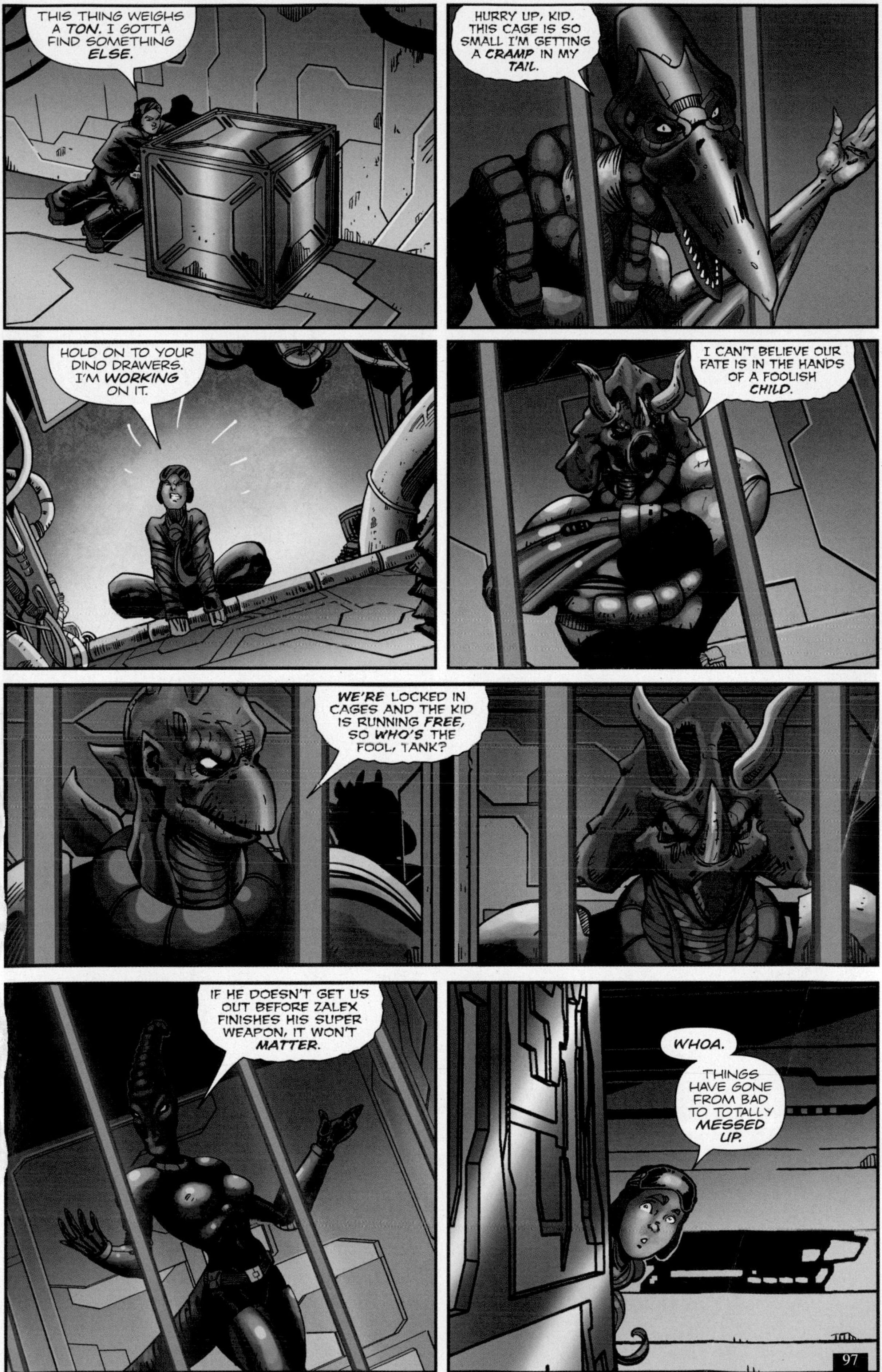
THIS THING WEIGHS A TON. I GOTTA FIND SOMETHING ELSE.
HURRY UP, KID. THIS CAGE IS SO SMALL I'M GETTING A CRAMP IN MY TAIL.
HOLD ON TO YOUR DINO DRAWERS. I'M WORKING ON IT.
I CAN'T BELIEVE OUR FATE IS IN THE HANDS OF A FOOLISH CHILD.
WE'RE LOCKED IN CAGES AND THE KID IS RUNNING FREE, SO WHO'S THE FOOL, TANK?
IF HE DOESN'T GET US OUT BEFORE ZALEX FINISHES HIS SUPER WEAPON, IT WON'T MATTER.
WHOA.
THINGS HAVE GONE FROM BAD TO TOTALLY MESSED UP.

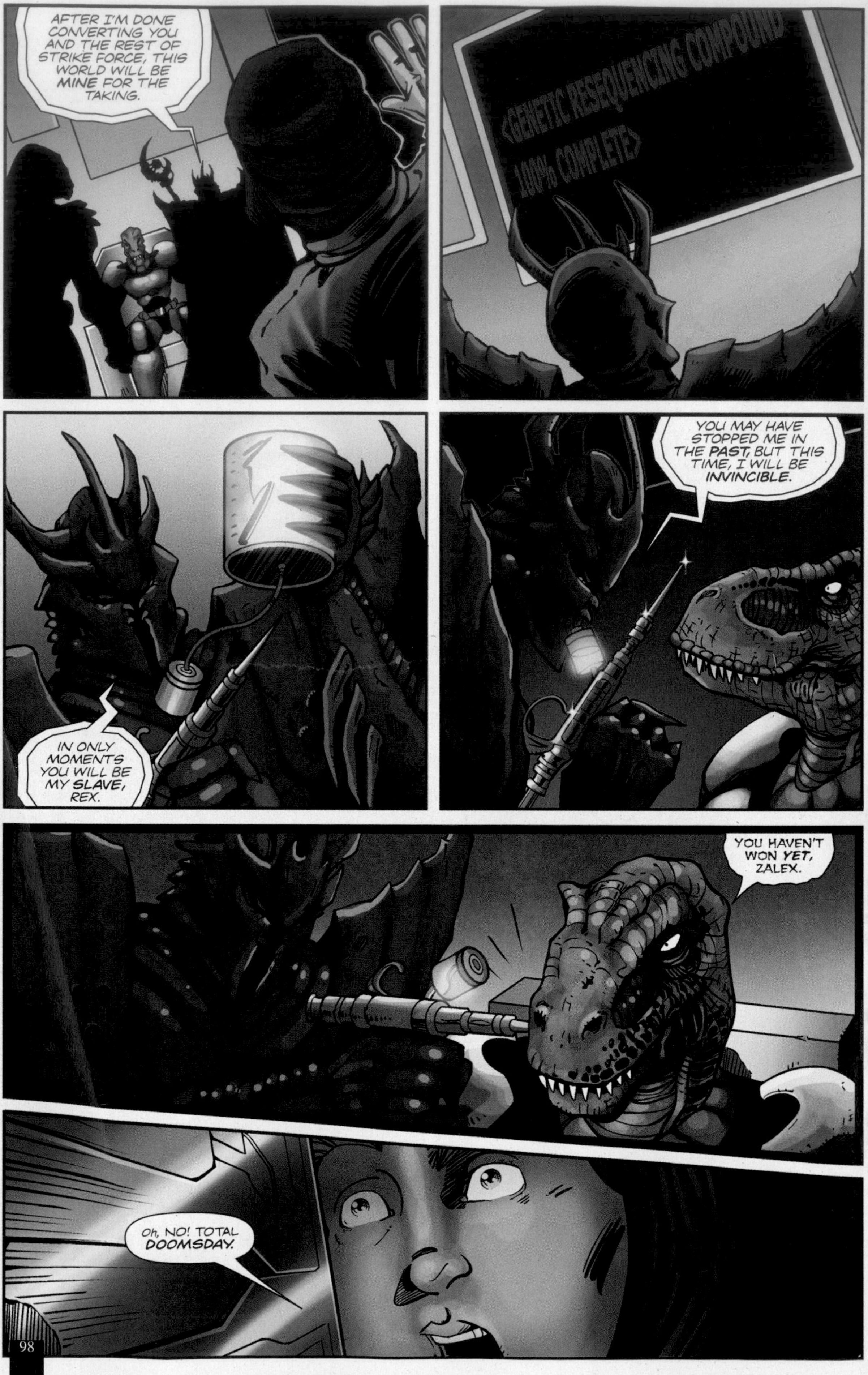
AFTER I'M DONE CONVERTING YOU AND THE REST OF STRIKE FORCE, THIS WORLD WILL BE MINE FOR THE TAKING.
<GENETIC RESEQUENCING COMPOUND 100% COMPLETE>
IN ONLY MOMENTS YOU WILL BE MY SLAVE, REX.
YOU MAY HAVE STOPPED ME IN THE PAST, BUT THIS TIME, I WILL BE INVINCIBLE.
YOU HAVEN'T WON YET, ZALEX.
Oh, NO! TOTAL DOOMSDAY.

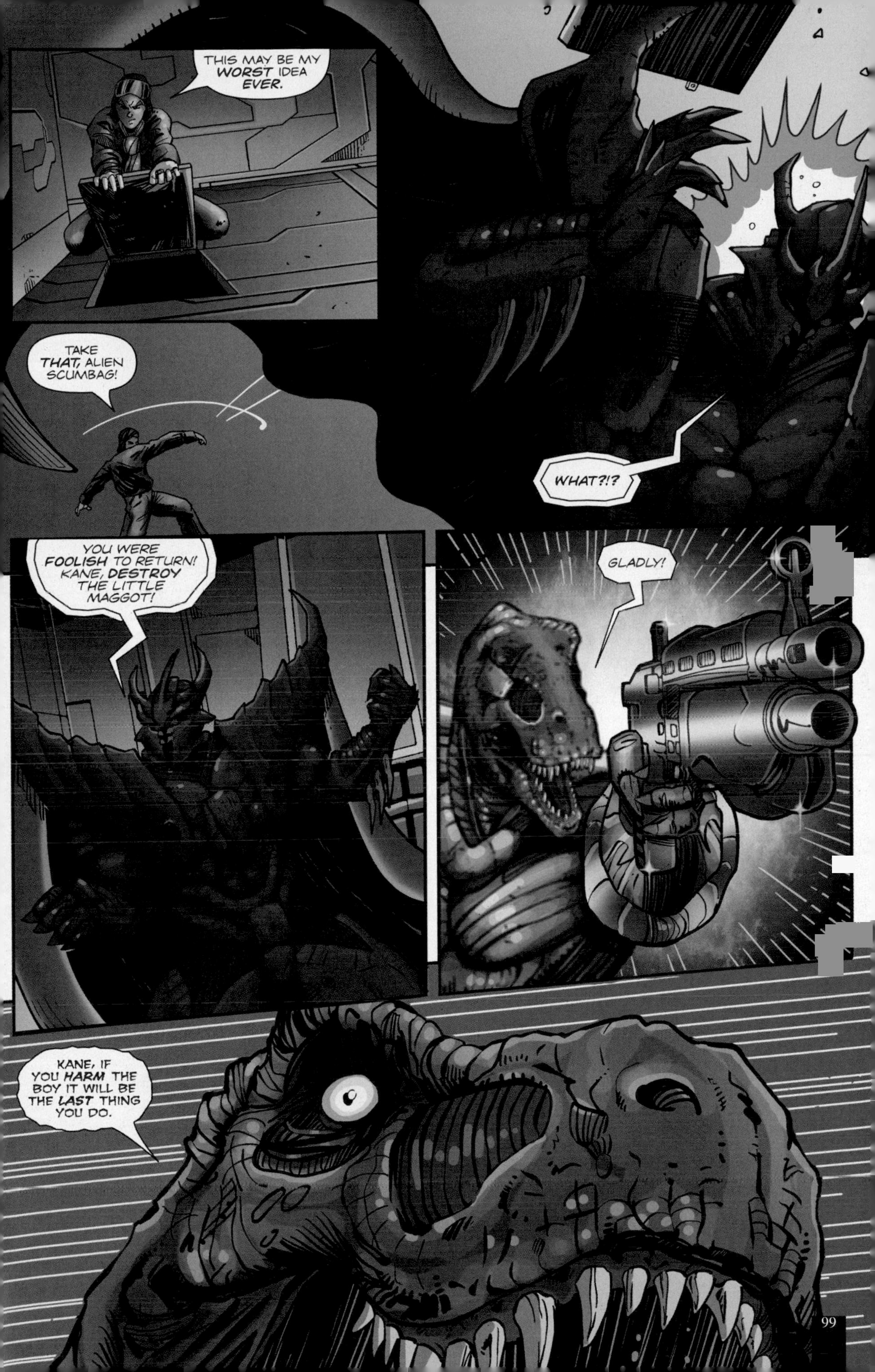

THIS MAY BE MY WORST IDEA EVER.
TAKE THAT, ALIEN SCUMBAG!
WHAT?!?
YOU WERE FOOLISH TO RETURN! KANE, DESTROY THE LITTLE MAGGOT!
GLADLY!
KANE, IF YOU HARM THE BOY IT WILL BE THE LAST THING YOU DO.

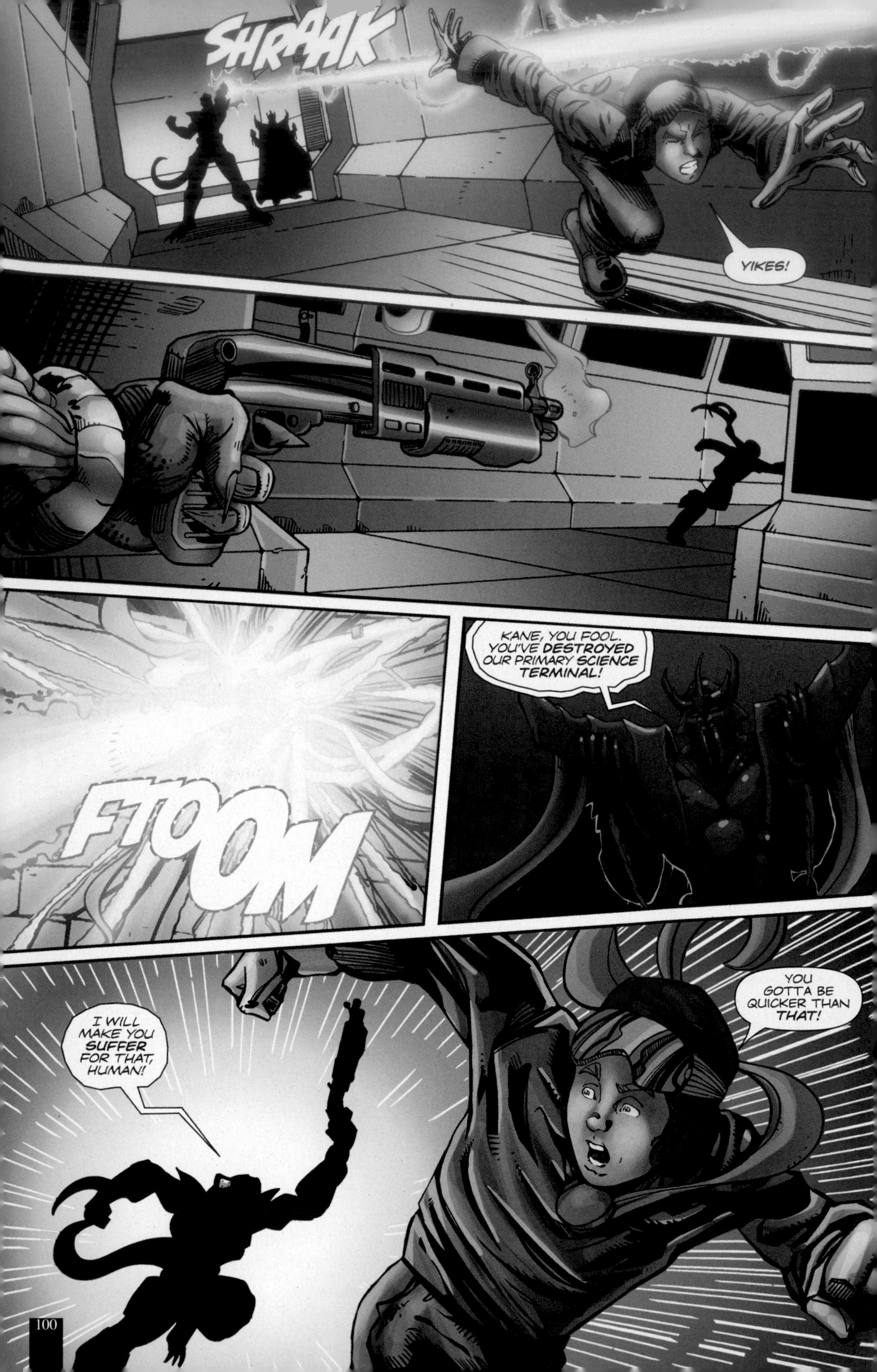

SHRAAK
YIKES!
FTOOM
KANE, YOU FOOL. YOU'VE DESTROYED OUR PRIMARY SCIENCE TERMINAL!
YOU GOTTA BE QUICKER THAN THAT!
I WILL MAKE YOU SUFFER FOR THAT, HUMAN!

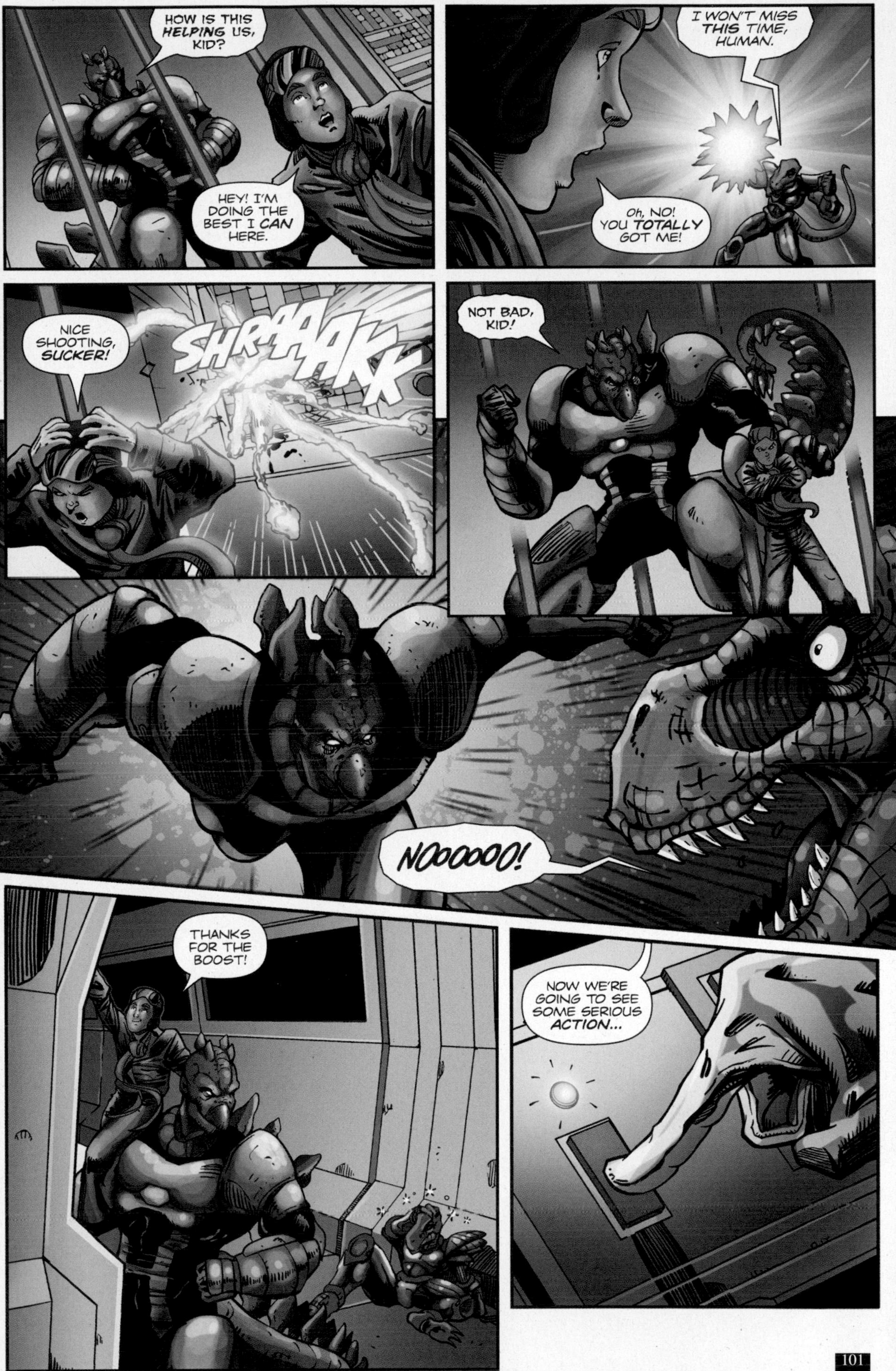
HOW IS THIS HELPING US, KID?
HEY! I'M DOING THE BEST I CAN HERE.
I WON'T MISS THIS TIME, HUMAN.
Oh, NO! YOU TOTALLY GOT ME!
NICE SHOOTING, SUCKER!
SHRAAAKK
NOT BAD, KID!
NOOOOOO!
THANKS FOR THE BOOST!
NOW WE'RE GOING TO SEE SOME SERIOUS ACTION...

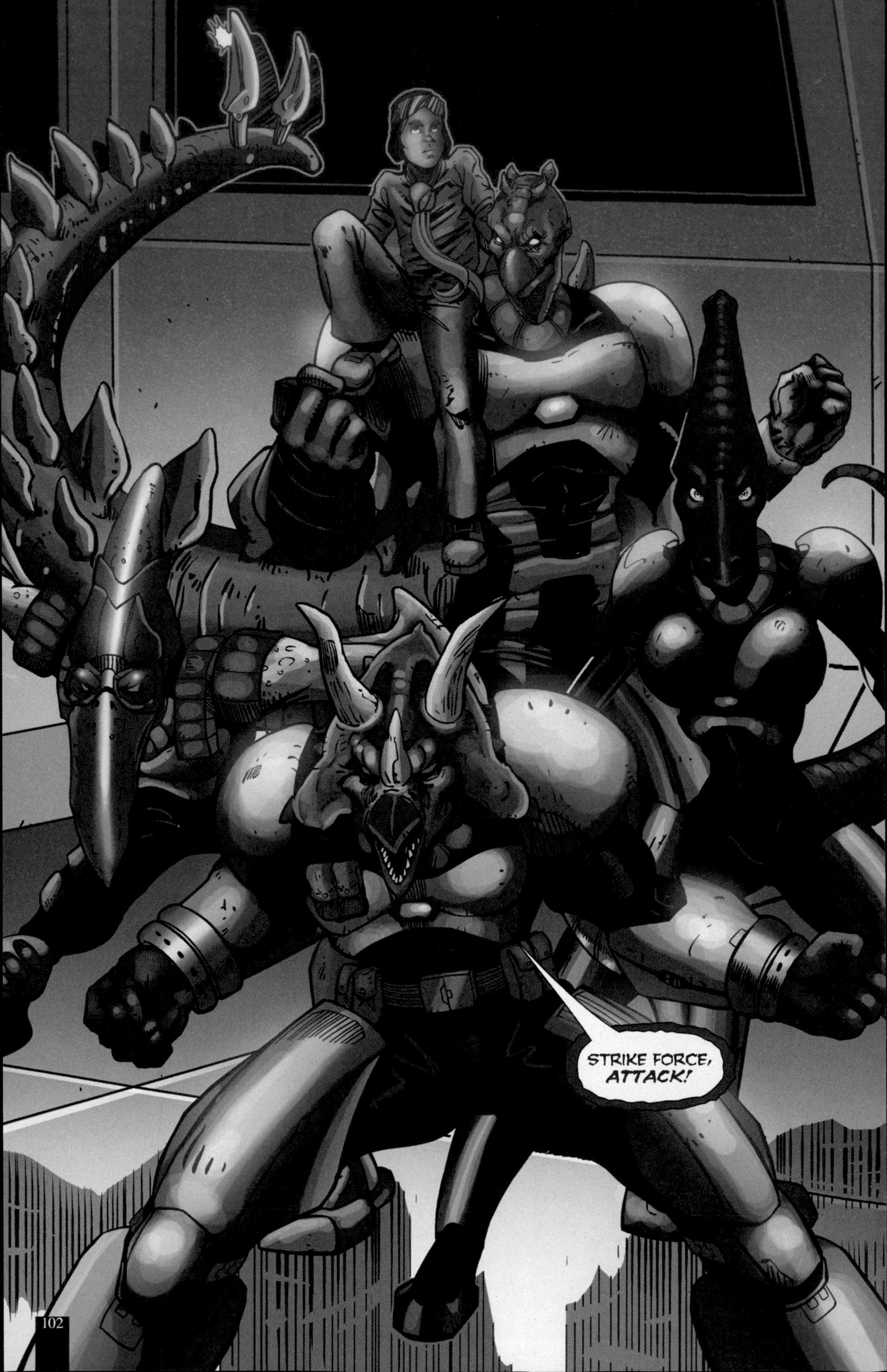
STRIKE FORCE, ATTACK!

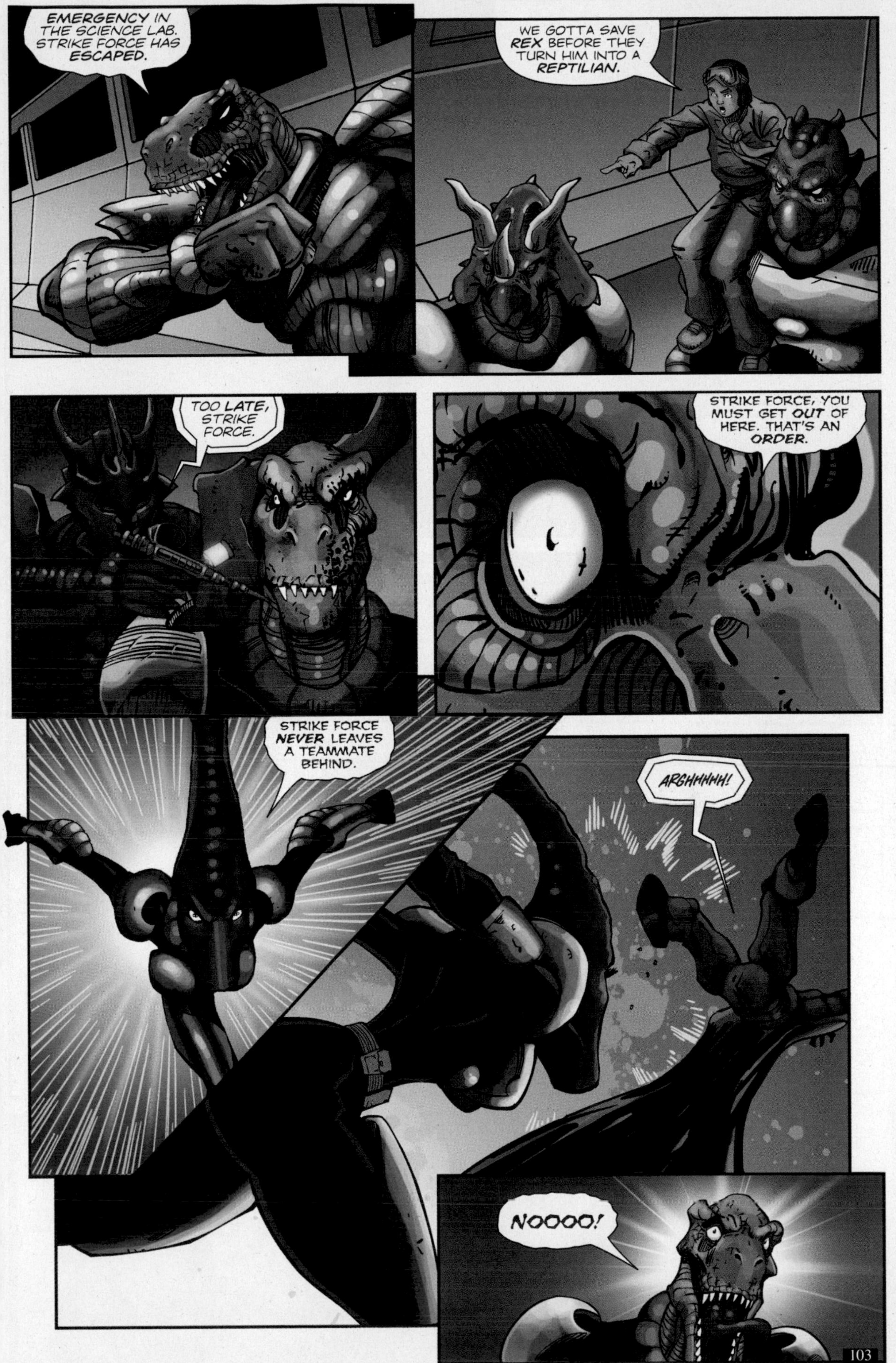
EMERGENCY IN THE SCIENCE LAB. STRIKE FORCE HAS ESCAPED.
WE GOTTA SAVE REX BEFORE THEY TURN HIM INTO A REPTILIAN.
TOO LATE, STRIKE FORCE.
STRIKE FORCE, YOU MUST GET OUT OF HERE. THAT'S AN ORDER.
STRIKE FORCE NEVER LEAVES A TEAMMATE BEHIND.
ARGHHHHH!
NOOOO!

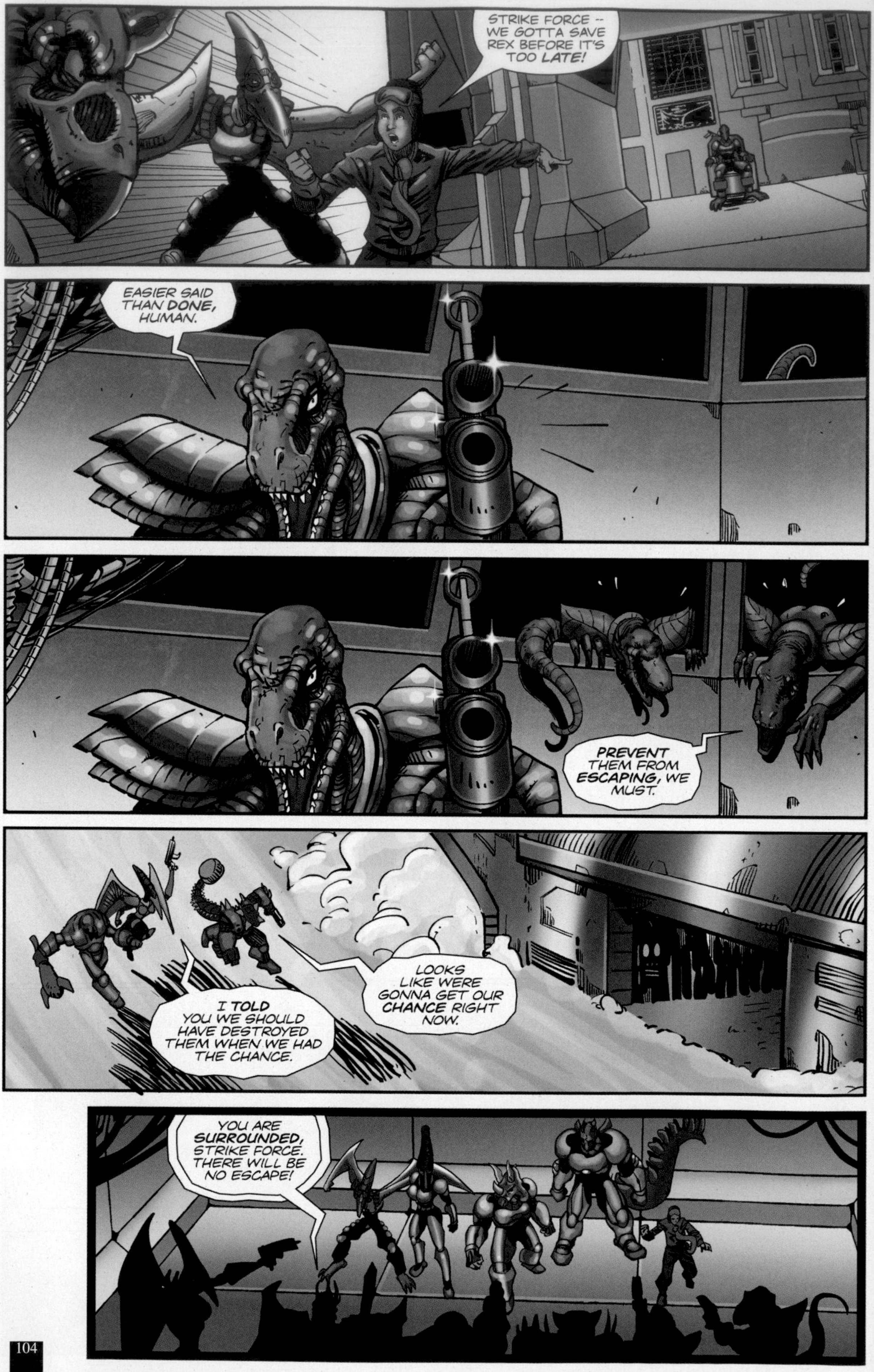
STRIKE FORCE -- WE GOTTA SAVE REX BEFORE IT'S TOO LATE!
EASIER SAID THAN DONE, HUMAN.
PREVENT THEM FROM ESCAPING, WE MUST.
I TOLD YOU WE SHOULD HAVE DESTROYED THEM WHEN WE HAD THE CHANCE.
LOOKS LIKE WERE GONNA GET OUR CHANCE RIGHT NOW.
YOU ARE SURROUNDED, STRIKE FORCE. THERE WILL BE NO ESCAPE!

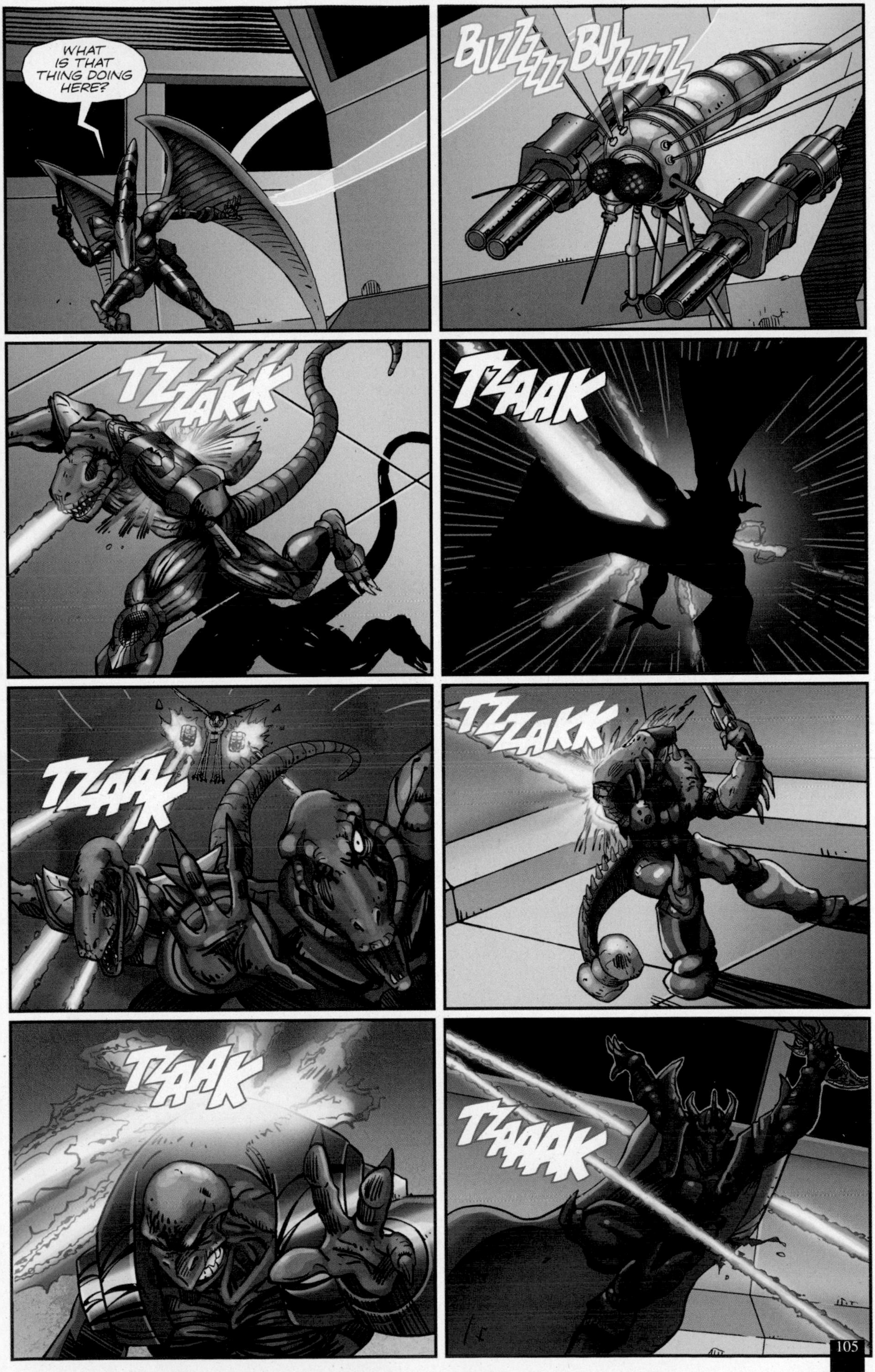
WHAT IS THAT THING DOING HERE?
BUZZZZZZ BUZZZZZZ
TZZAKK
TZAAK
TZAAK
TZZAKK
TZAAK
TZAAAK

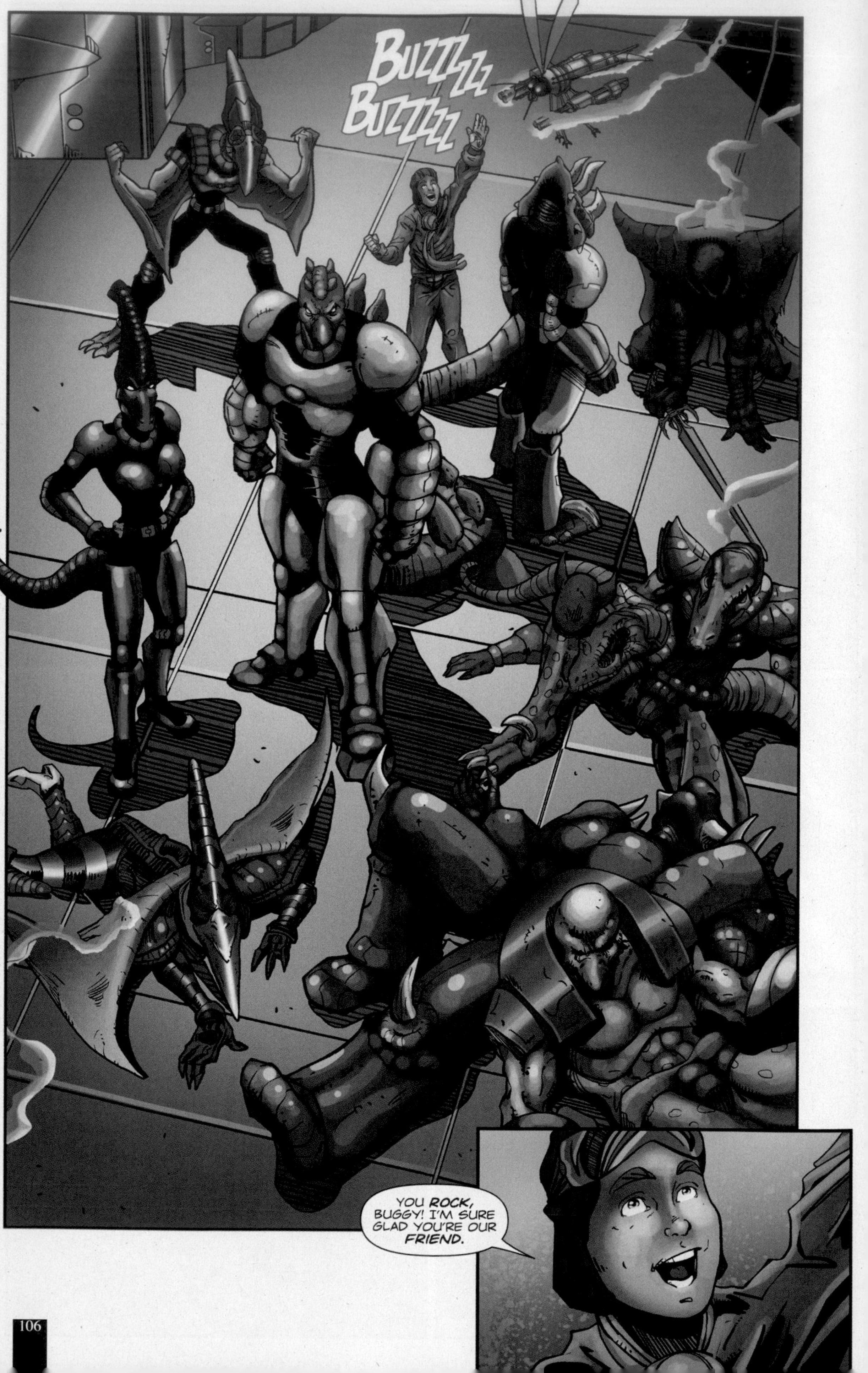
BUZZZZZ
BUZZZZZ
YOU ROCK, BUGGY! I'M SURE GLAD YOU'RE OUR FRIEND.

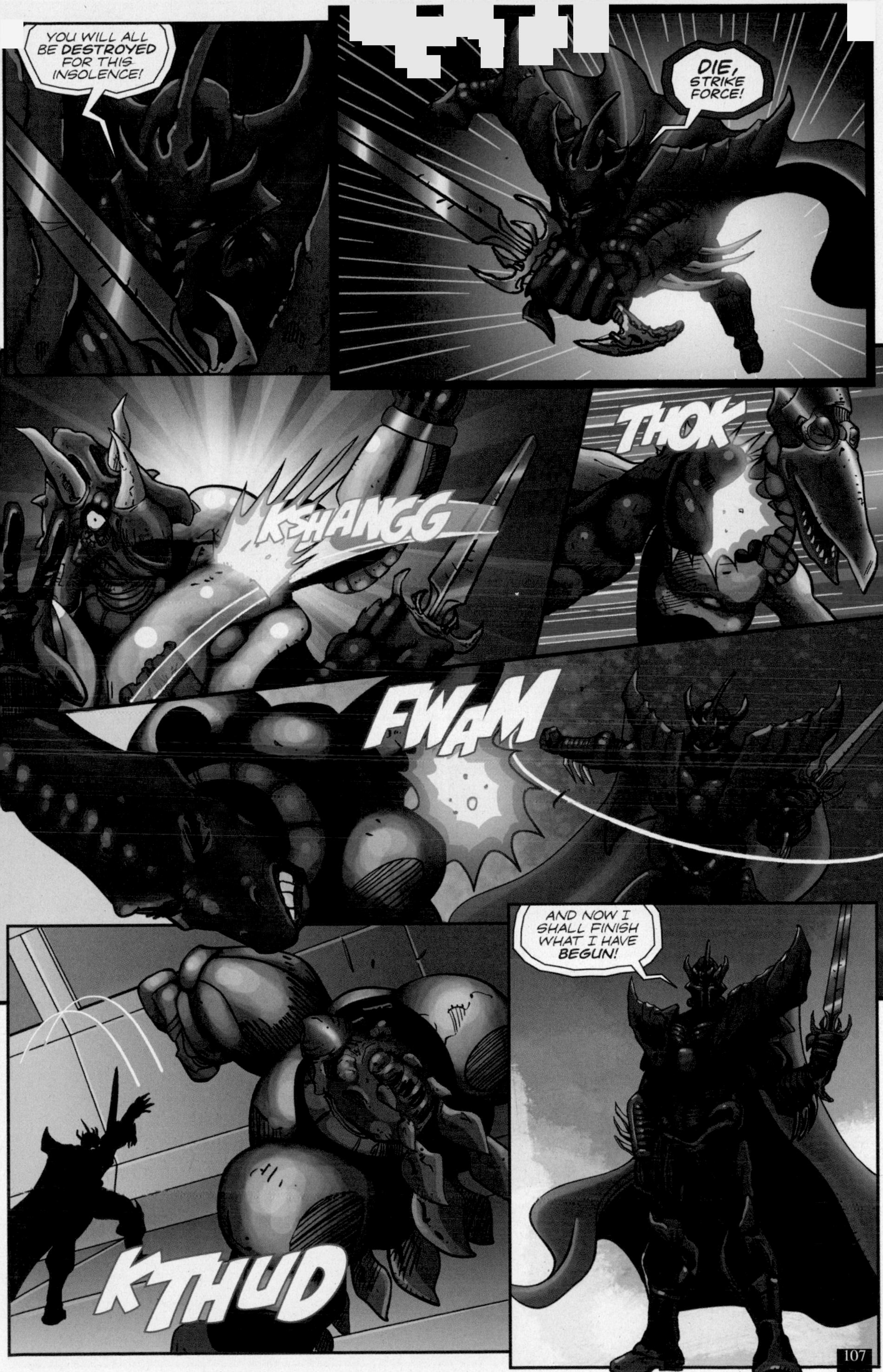
YOU WILL ALL BE DESTROYED FOR THIS INSOLENCE!
DIE, STRIKE FORCE!
KSHANGG
THOK
FWAM
KTHUD
AND NOW I SHALL FINISH WHAT I HAVE BEGUN!

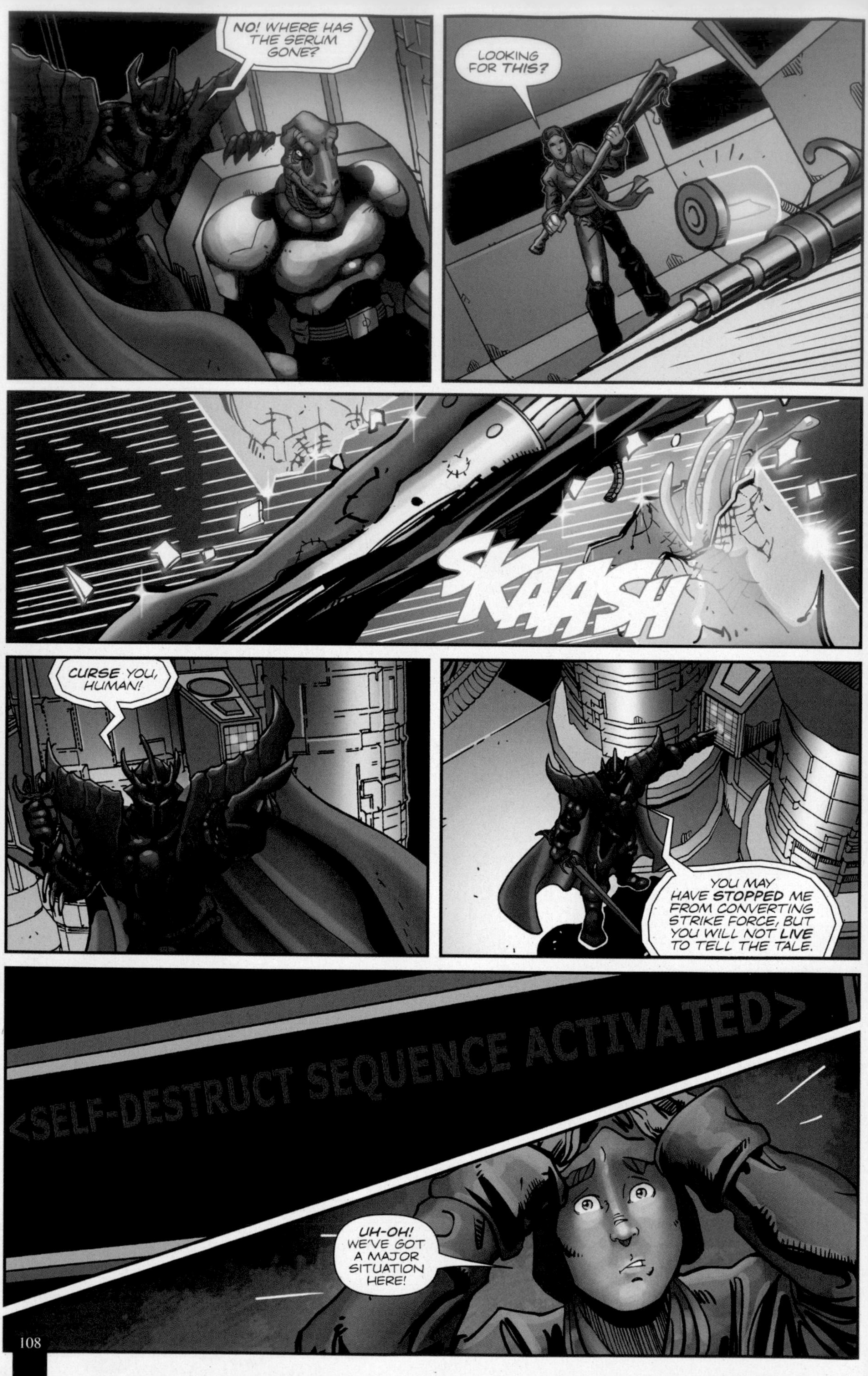
NO! WHERE HAS THE SERUM GONE?
LOOKING FOR THIS?
SKAASH
CURSE YOU, HUMAN!
YOU MAY HAVE STOPPED ME FROM CONVERTING STRIKE FORCE, BUT YOU WILL NOT LIVE TO TELL THE TALE.
<SELF-DESTRUCT SEQUENCE ACTIVATED>
UH-OH! WE'VE GOT A MAJOR SITUATION HERE!

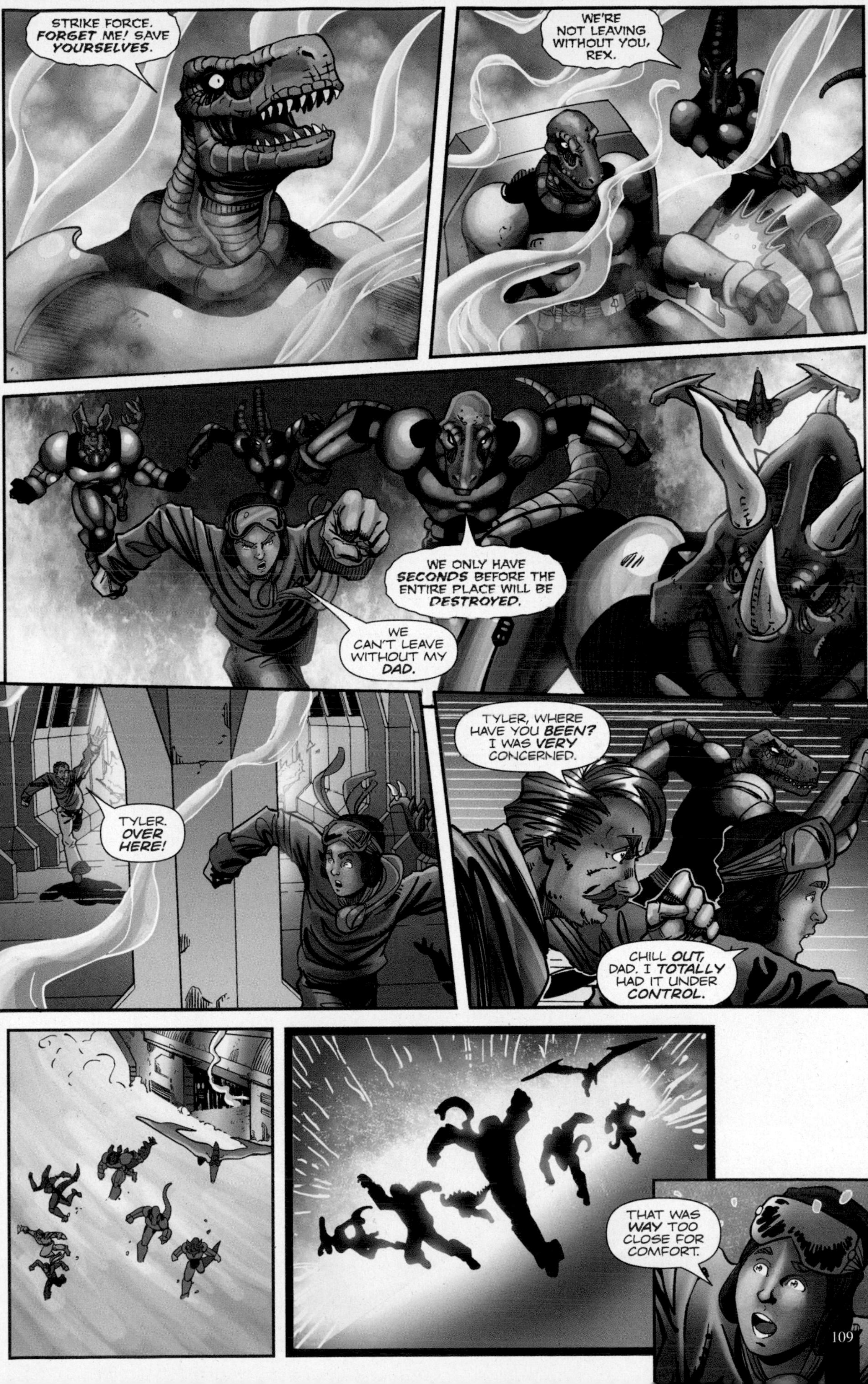
STRIKE FORCE. FORGET ME! SAVE YOURSELVES.
WE'RE NOT LEAVING WITHOUT YOU, REX.
WE ONLY HAVE SECONDS BEFORE THE ENTIRE PLACE WILL BE DESTROYED.
WE CAN'T LEAVE WITHOUT MY DAD.
TYLER. OVER HERE!
TYLER, WHERE HAVE YOU BEEN? I WAS VERY CONCERNED.
CHILL OUT, DAD. I TOTALLY HAD IT UNDER CONTROL.
THAT WAS WAY TOO CLOSE FOR COMFORT.

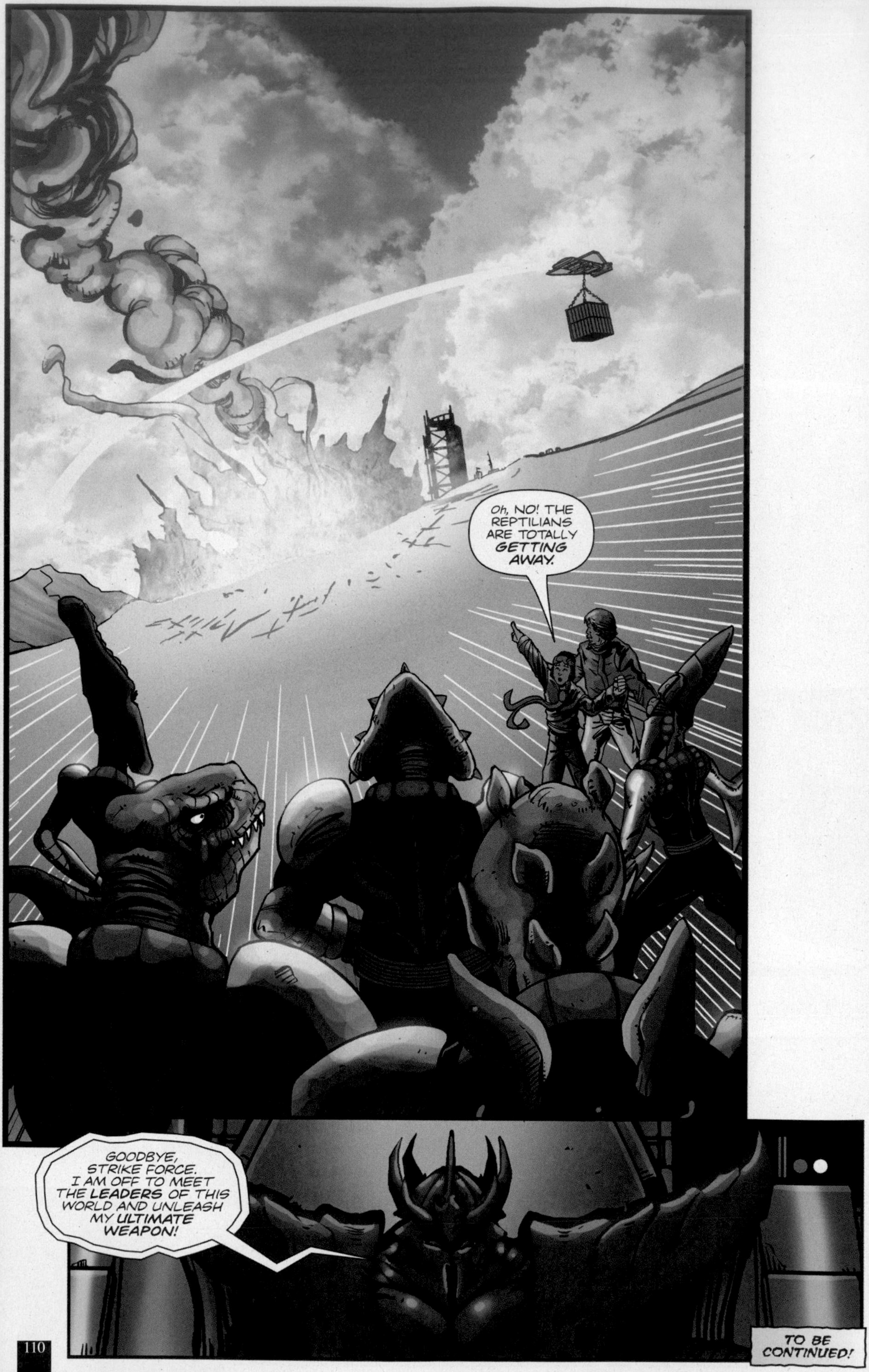
Oh, NO! THE REPTILIANS ARE TOTALLY GETTING AWAY.
GOODBYE, STRIKE FORCE. I AM OFF TO MEET THE LEADERS OF THIS WORLD AND UNLEASH MY ULTIMATE WEAPON!
TO BE CONTINUED!

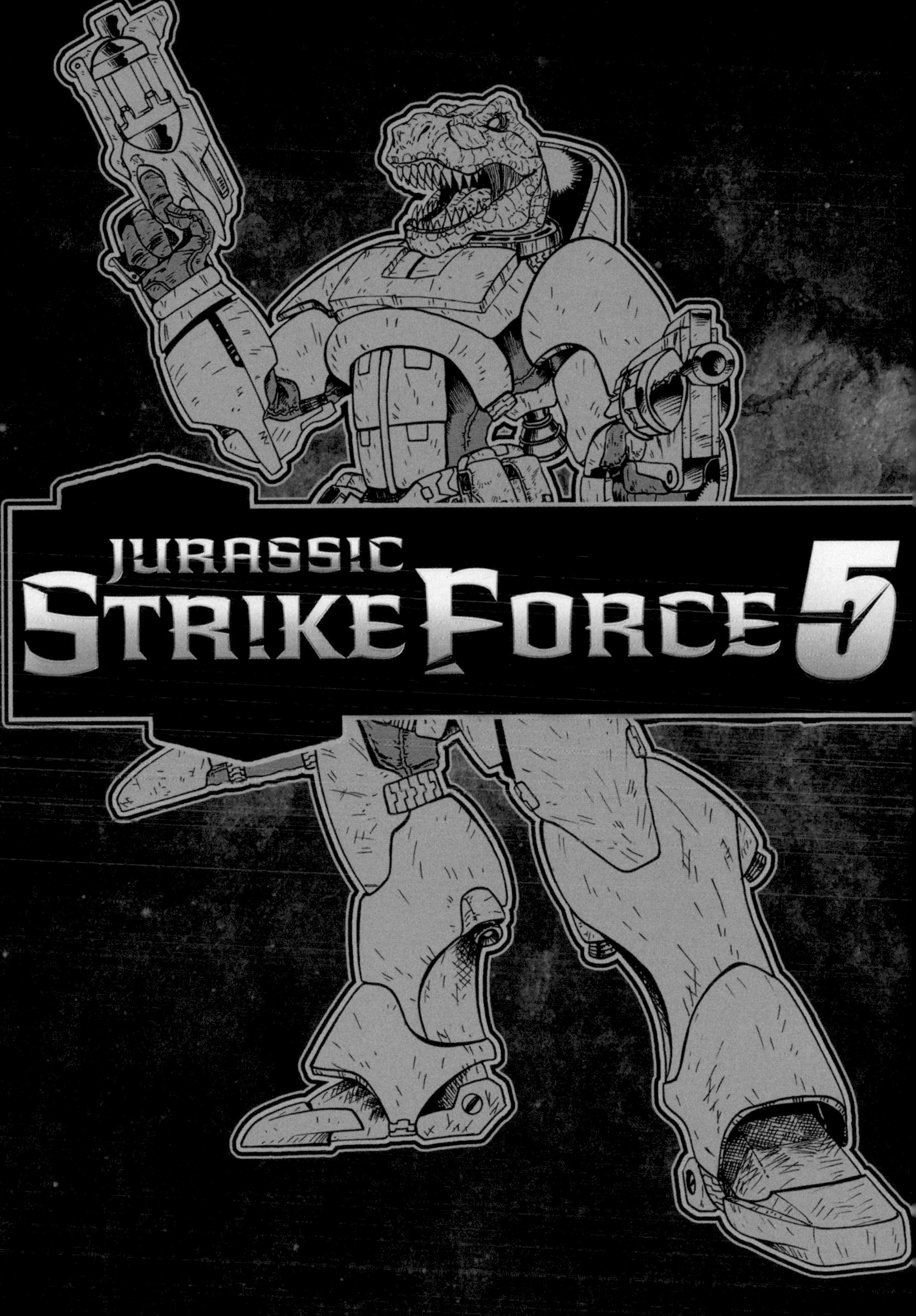
JURASSIC
STRIKE FORCE 5

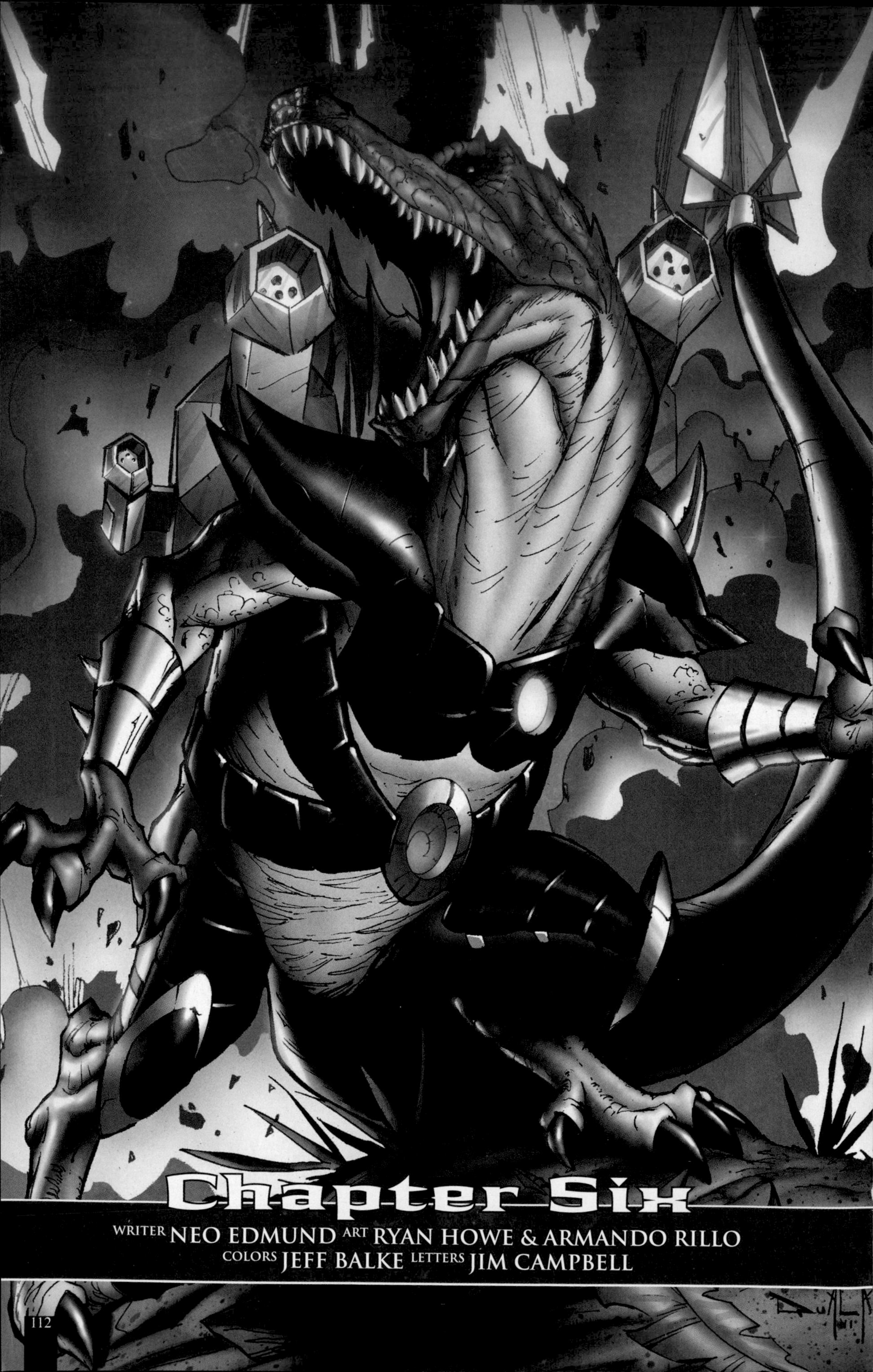

Chapter Six

WRITER NEO EDMUND ART RYAN HOWE & ARMANDO RILLO
COLORS JEFF BALKE LETTERS JIM CAMPBELL

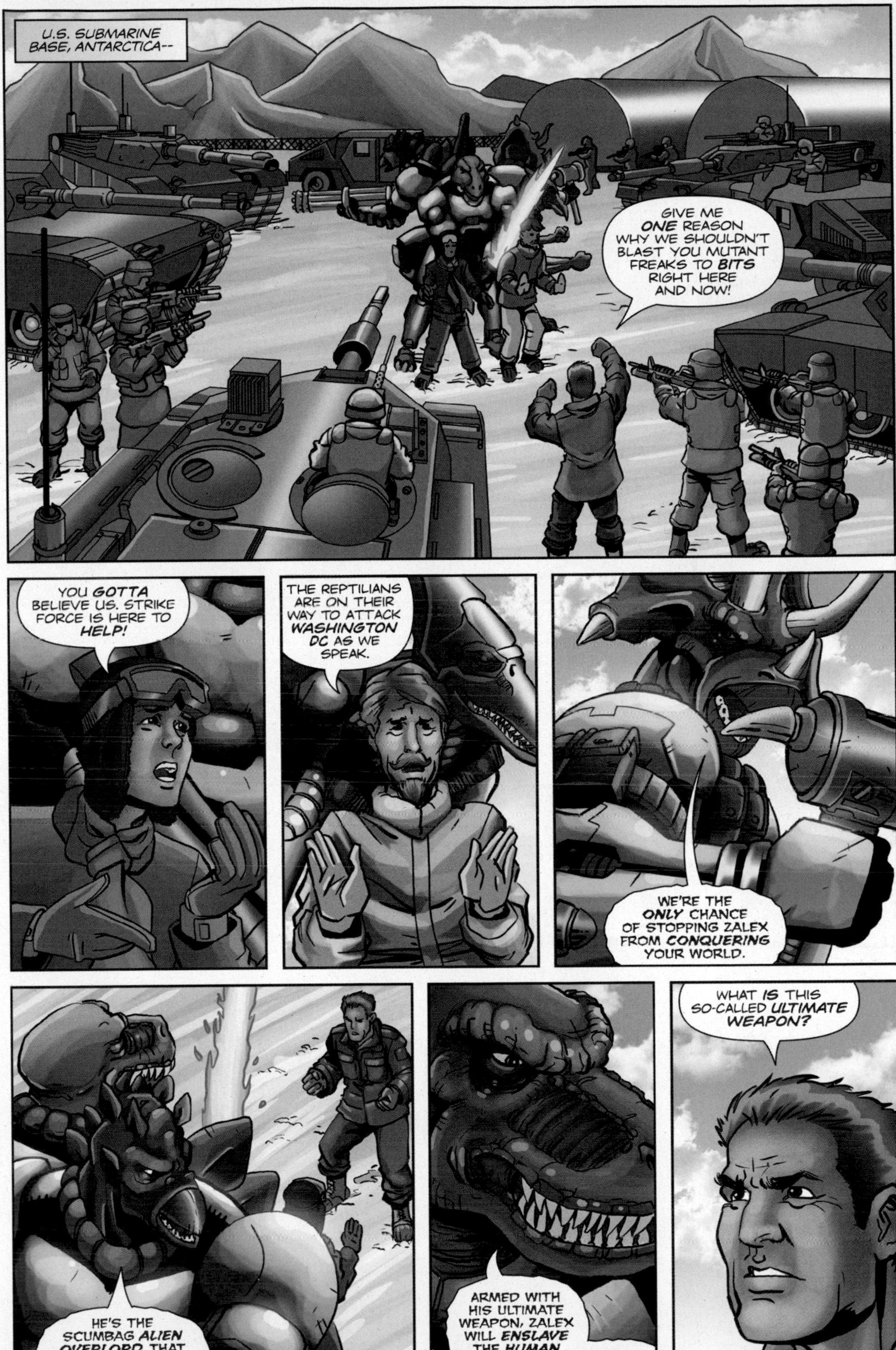
U.S. SUBMARINE BASE, ANTARCTICA--
GIVE ME ONE REASON WHY WE SHOULDN'T BLAST YOU MUTANT FREAKS TO BITS RIGHT HERE AND NOW!
YOU GOTTA BELIEVE US. STRIKE FORCE IS HERE TO HELP!
THE REPTILIANS ARE ON THEIR WAY TO ATTACK WASHINGTON DC AS WE SPEAK.
WE'RE THE ONLY CHANCE OF STOPPING ZALEX FROM CONQUERING YOUR WORLD.
HE'S THE SCUMBAG ALIEN OVERLORD THAT ATTACKED YOUR BASE AND HIJACKED ALL YOUR NUKES.
ARMED WITH HIS ULTIMATE WEAPON, ZALEX WILL ENSLAVE THE HUMAN RACE.
THEN THE ENTIRE GALAXY.
WHAT IS THIS SO-CALLED ULTIMATE WEAPON?

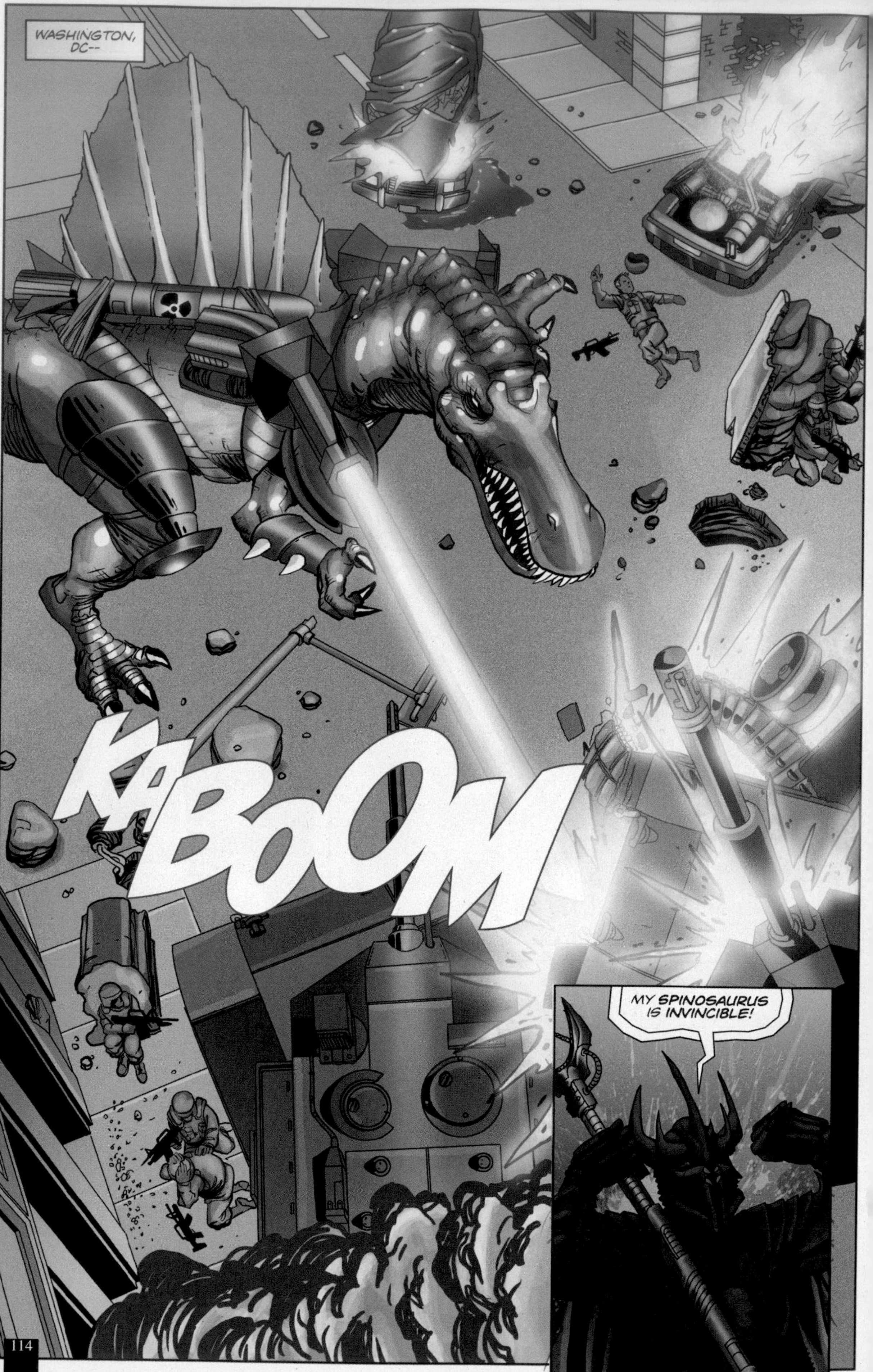
WASHINGTON, DC--
KABOOM
MY SPINOSAURUS IS INVINCIBLE!

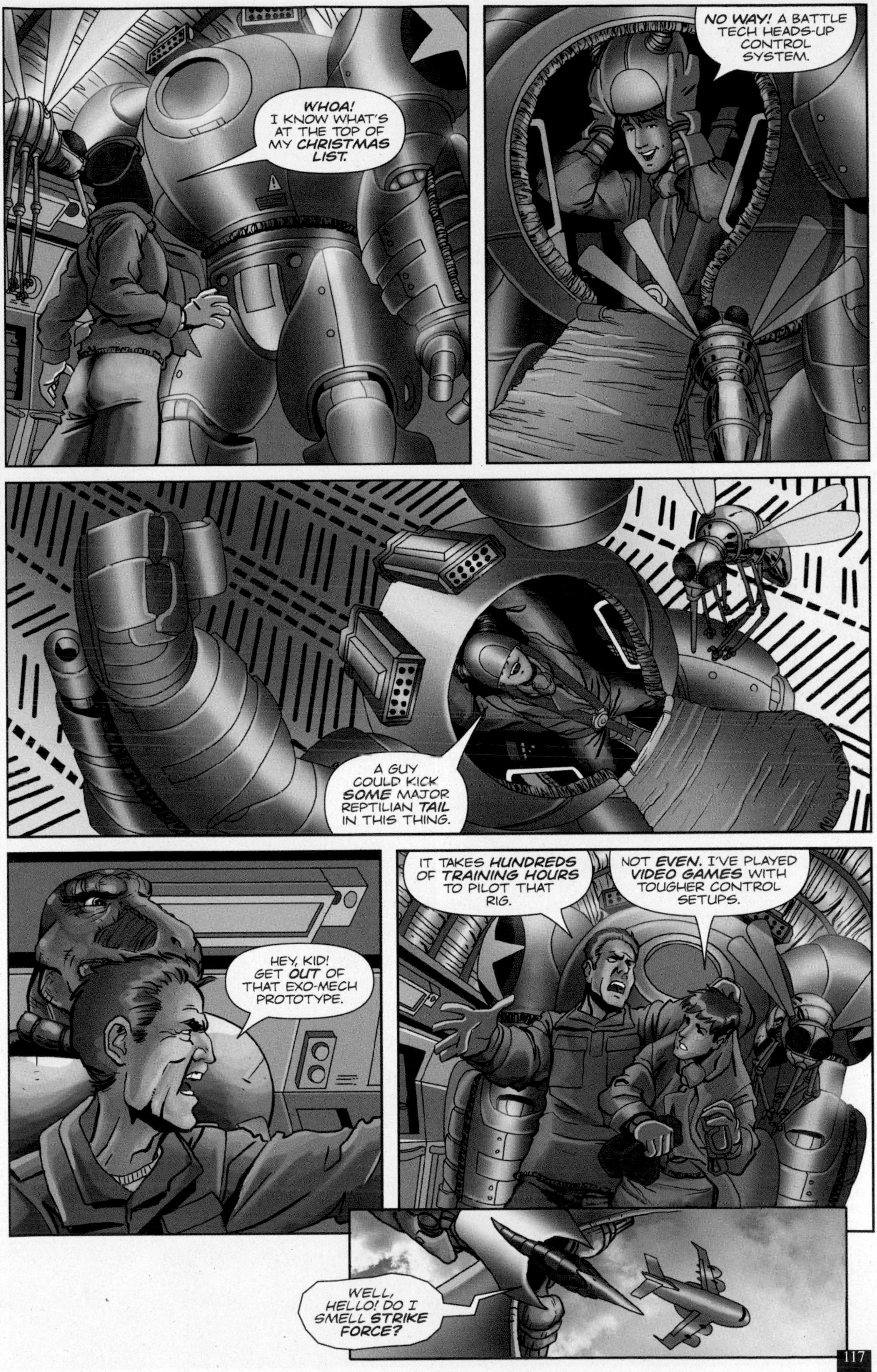
WHOA! I KNOW WHAT'S AT THE TOP OF MY CHRISTMAS LIST.
NO WAY! A BATTLE TECH HEADS-UP CONTROL SYSTEM.
A GUY COULD KICK SOME MAJOR REPTILIAN TAIL IN THIS THING.
HEY, KID! GET OUT OF THAT EXO-MECH PROTOTYPE.
IT TAKES HUNDREDS OF TRAINING HOURS TO PILOT THAT RIG.
NOT EVEN. I'VE PLAYED VIDEO GAMES WITH TOUGHER CONTROL SETUPS.
WELL, HELLO! DO I SMELL STRIKE FORCE?

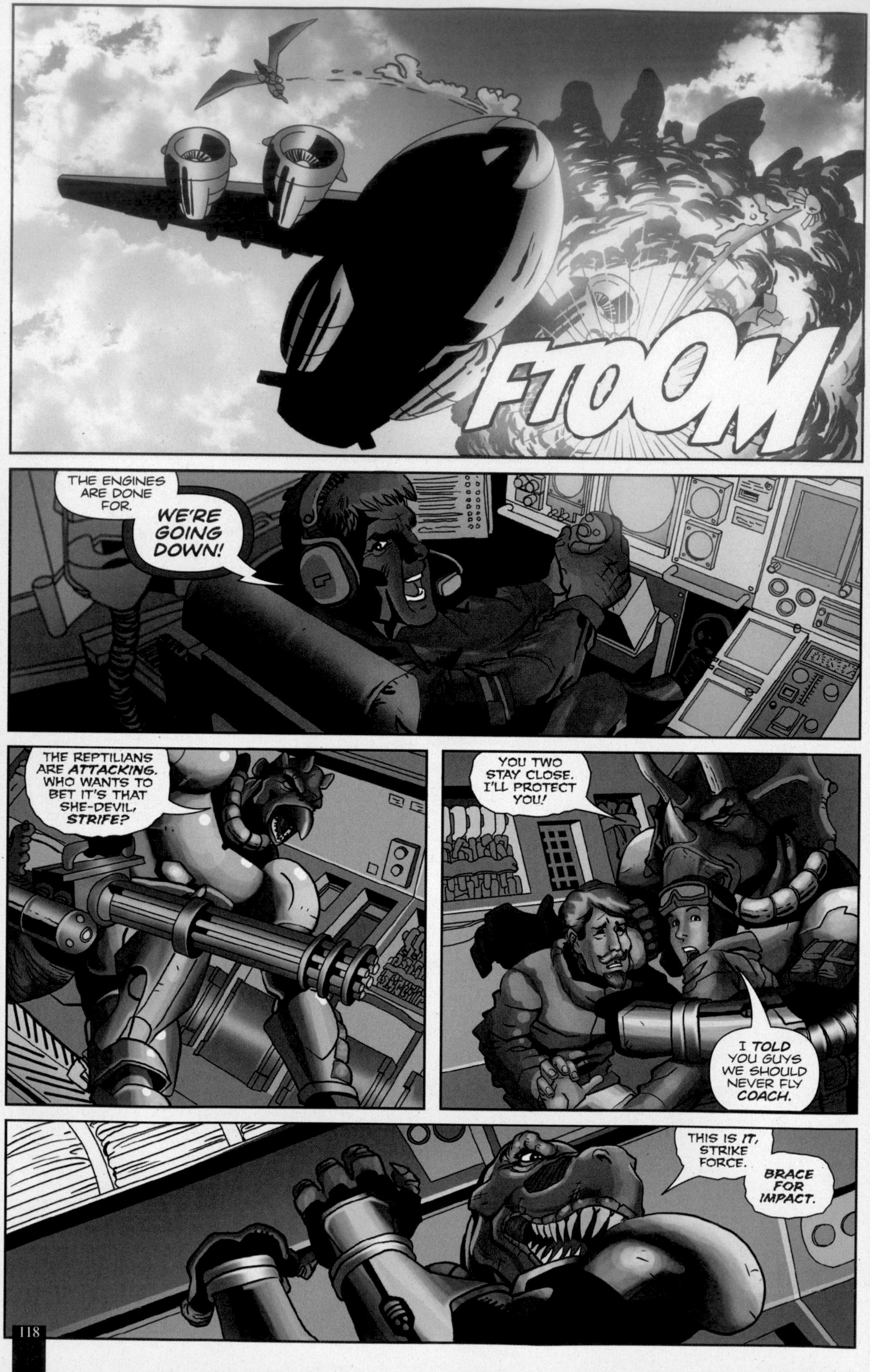
FTOOM
THE ENGINES ARE DONE FOR.
WE'RE GOING DOWN!
THE REPTILIANS ARE ATTACKING. WHO WANTS TO BET IT'S THAT SHE-DEVIL, STRIFE?
YOU TWO STAY CLOSE. I'LL PROTECT YOU!
I TOLD YOU GUYS WE SHOULD NEVER FLY COACH.
THIS IS IT, STRIKE FORCE.
BRACE FOR IMPACT.

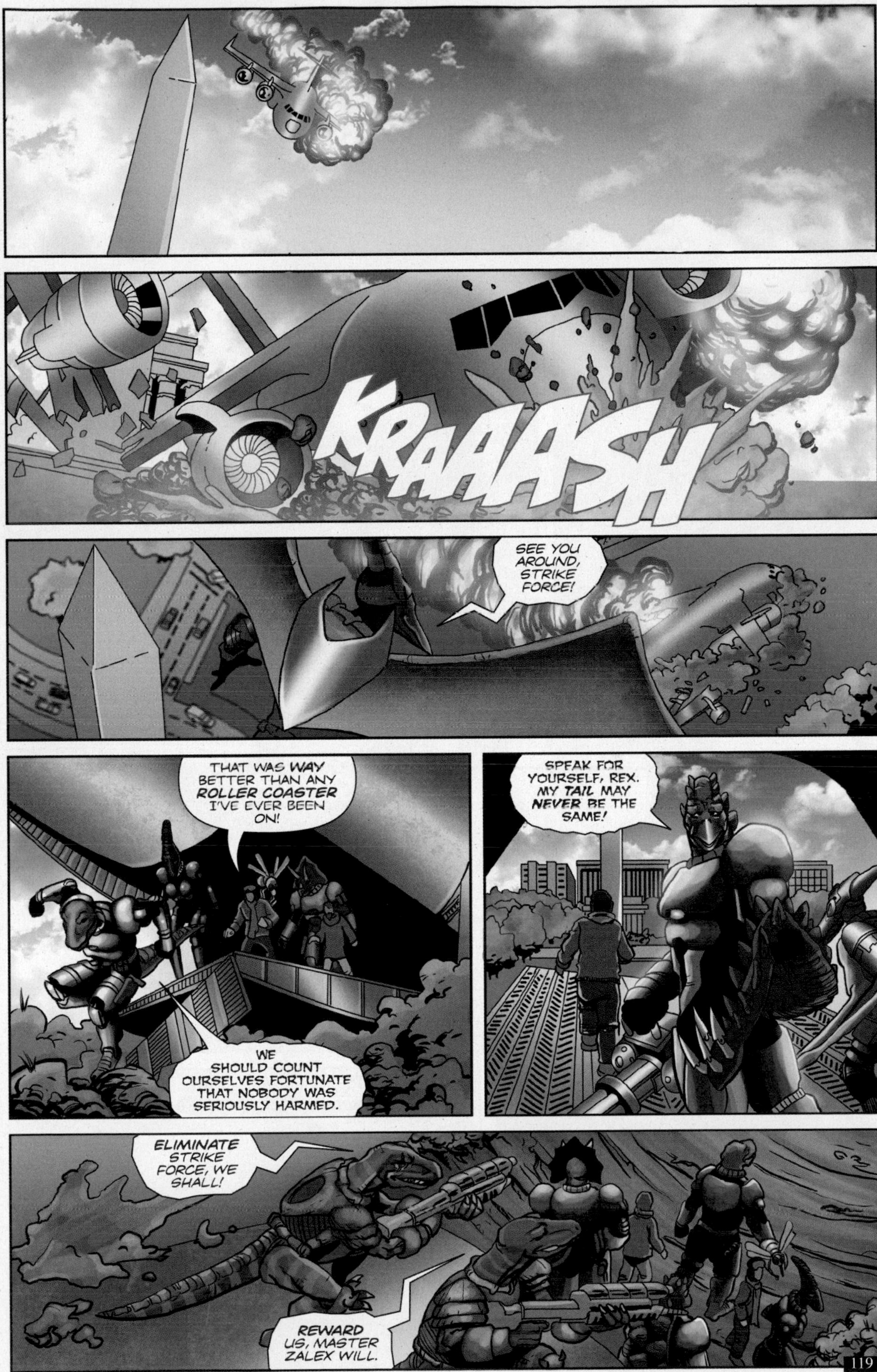
KRAAASH
SEE YOU AROUND, STRIKE FORCE!
THAT WAS WAY BETTER THAN ANY ROLLER COASTER I'VE EVER BEEN ON!
WE SHOULD COUNT OURSELVES FORTUNATE THAT NOBODY WAS SERIOUSLY HARMED.
SPEAK FOR YOURSELF, REX. MY TAIL MAY NEVER BE THE SAME!
ELIMINATE STRIKE FORCE, WE SHALL!
REWARD US, MASTER ZALEX WILL.

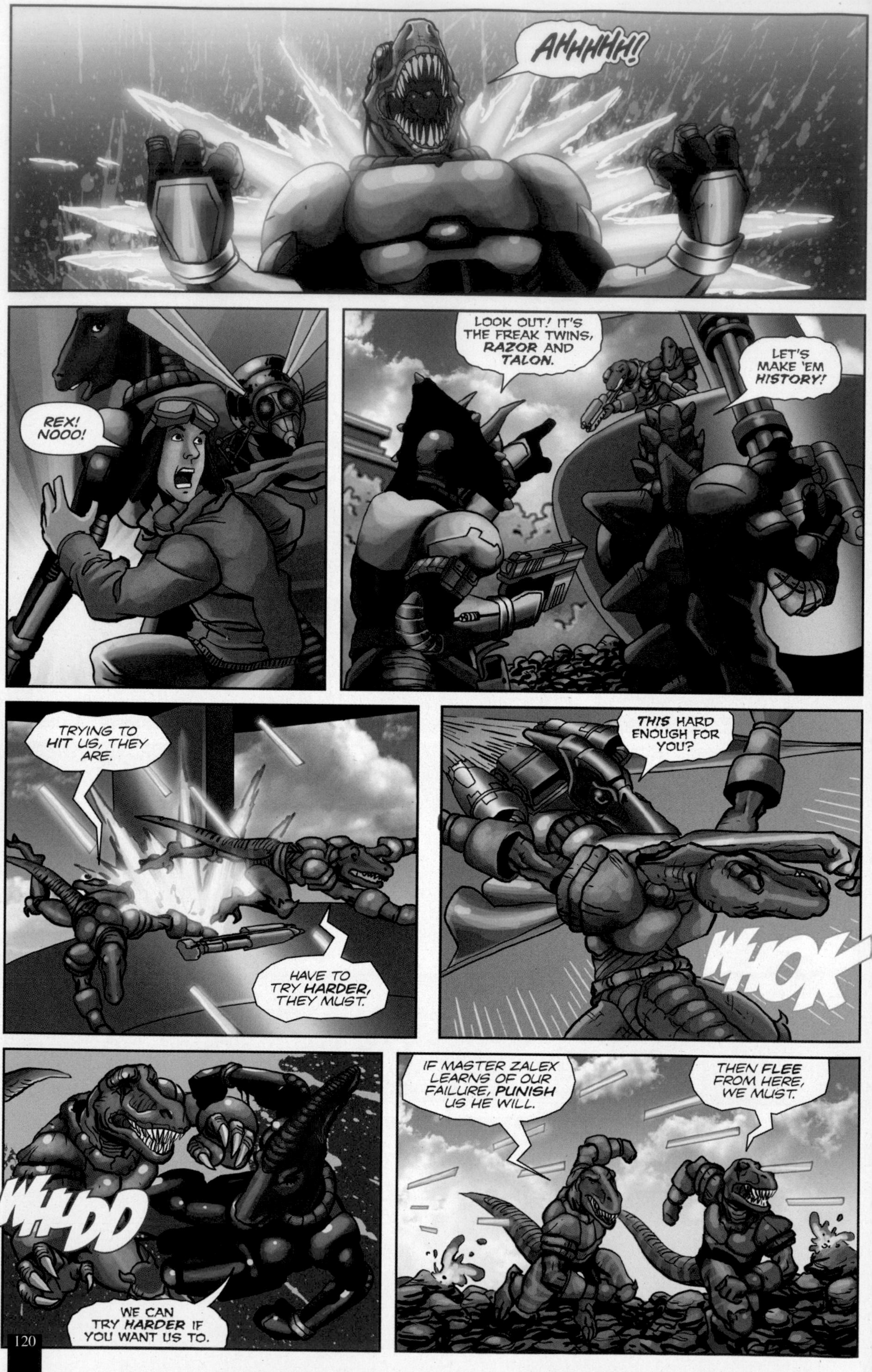

AHHHHH!!
REX! NOOO!
LOOK OUT! IT'S THE FREAK TWINS, RAZOR AND TALON.
LET'S MAKE 'EM HISTORY!
TRYING TO HIT US, THEY ARE.
HAVE TO TRY HARDER, THEY MUST.
THIS HARD ENOUGH FOR YOU?
WHOK
WHDD
WE CAN TRY HARDER IF YOU WANT US TO.
IF MASTER ZALEX LEARNS OF OUR FAILURE, PUNISH US HE WILL.
THEN FLEE FROM HERE, WE MUST.

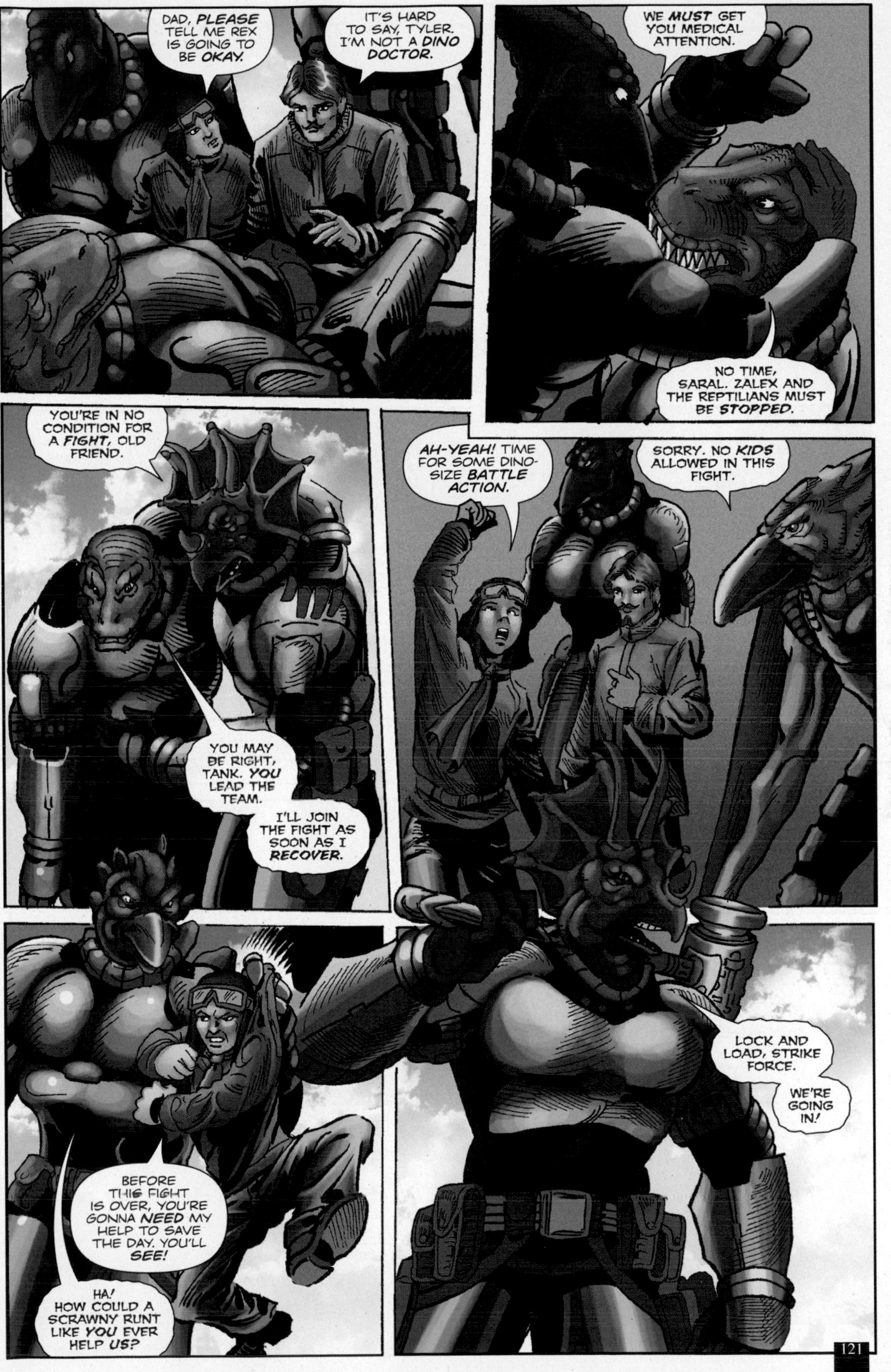
DAD, PLEASE TELL ME REX IS GOING TO BE OKAY.
IT'S HARD TO SAY, TYLER. I'M NOT A DINO DOCTOR.
WE MUST GET YOU MEDICAL ATTENTION.
NO TIME, SARAL. ZALEX AND THE REPTILIANS MUST BE STOPPED.
YOU'RE IN NO CONDITION FOR A FIGHT, OLD FRIEND.
YOU MAY BE RIGHT, TANK. YOU LEAD THE TEAM.
I'LL JOIN THE FIGHT AS SOON AS I RECOVER.
AH-YEAH! TIME FOR SOME DINO-SIZE BATTLE ACTION.
SORRY. NO KIDS ALLOWED IN THIS FIGHT.
BEFORE THIS FIGHT IS OVER, YOU'RE GONNA NEED MY HELP TO SAVE THE DAY. YOU'LL SEE!
HA! HOW COULD A SCRAWNY RUNT LIKE YOU EVER HELP US?
LOCK AND LOAD, STRIKE FORCE.
WE'RE GOING IN!

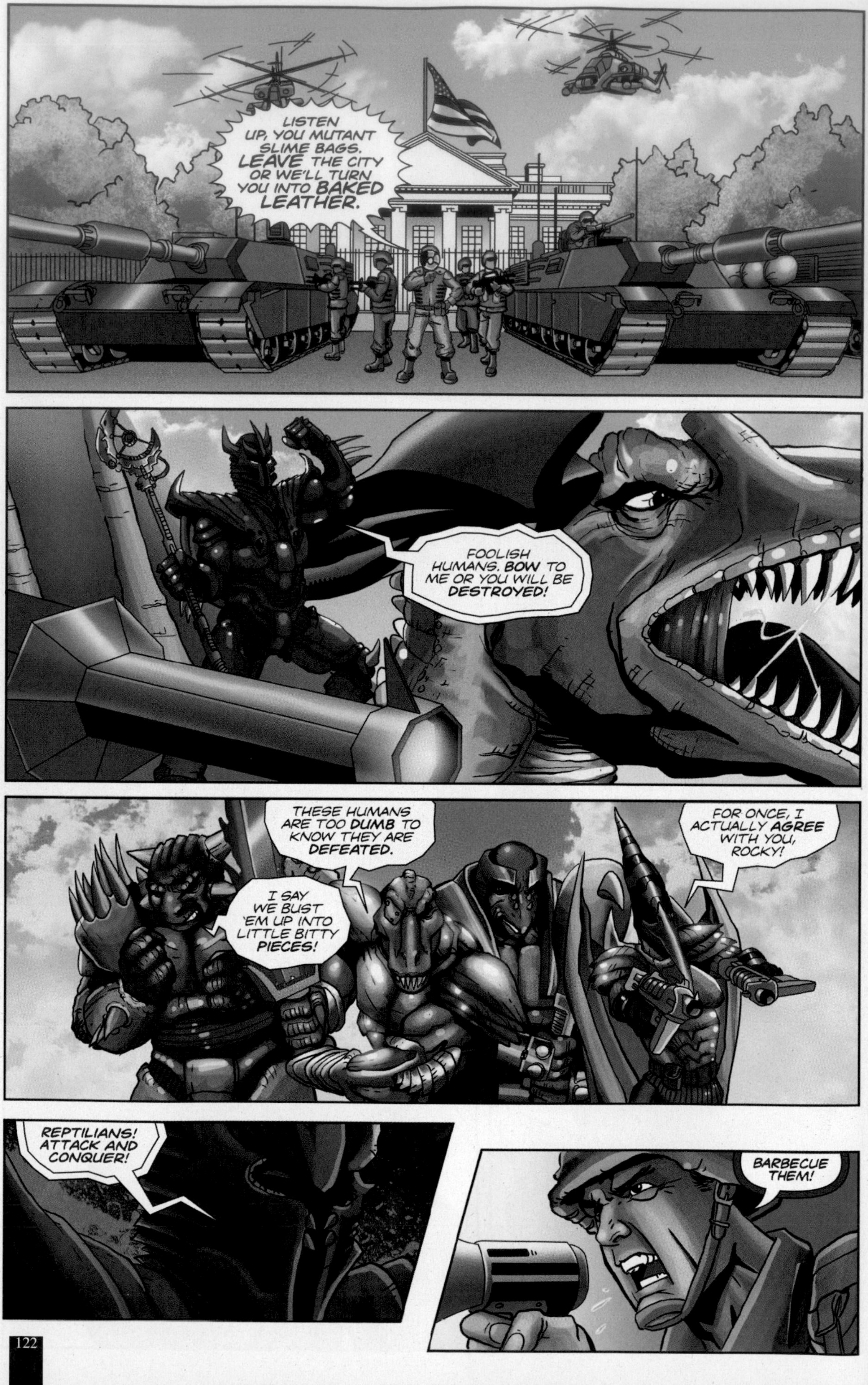
LISTEN UP, YOU MUTANT SLIME BAGS. LEAVE THE CITY OR WE'LL TURN YOU INTO BAKED LEATHER.
FOOLISH HUMANS. BOW TO ME OR YOU WILL BE DESTROYED!
THESE HUMANS ARE TOO DUMB TO KNOW THEY ARE DEFEATED.
I SAY WE BUST 'EM UP INTO LITTLE BITTY PIECES!
FOR ONCE, I ACTUALLY AGREE WITH YOU, ROCKY!
REPTILIANS! ATTACK AND CONQUER!
BARBECUE THEM!

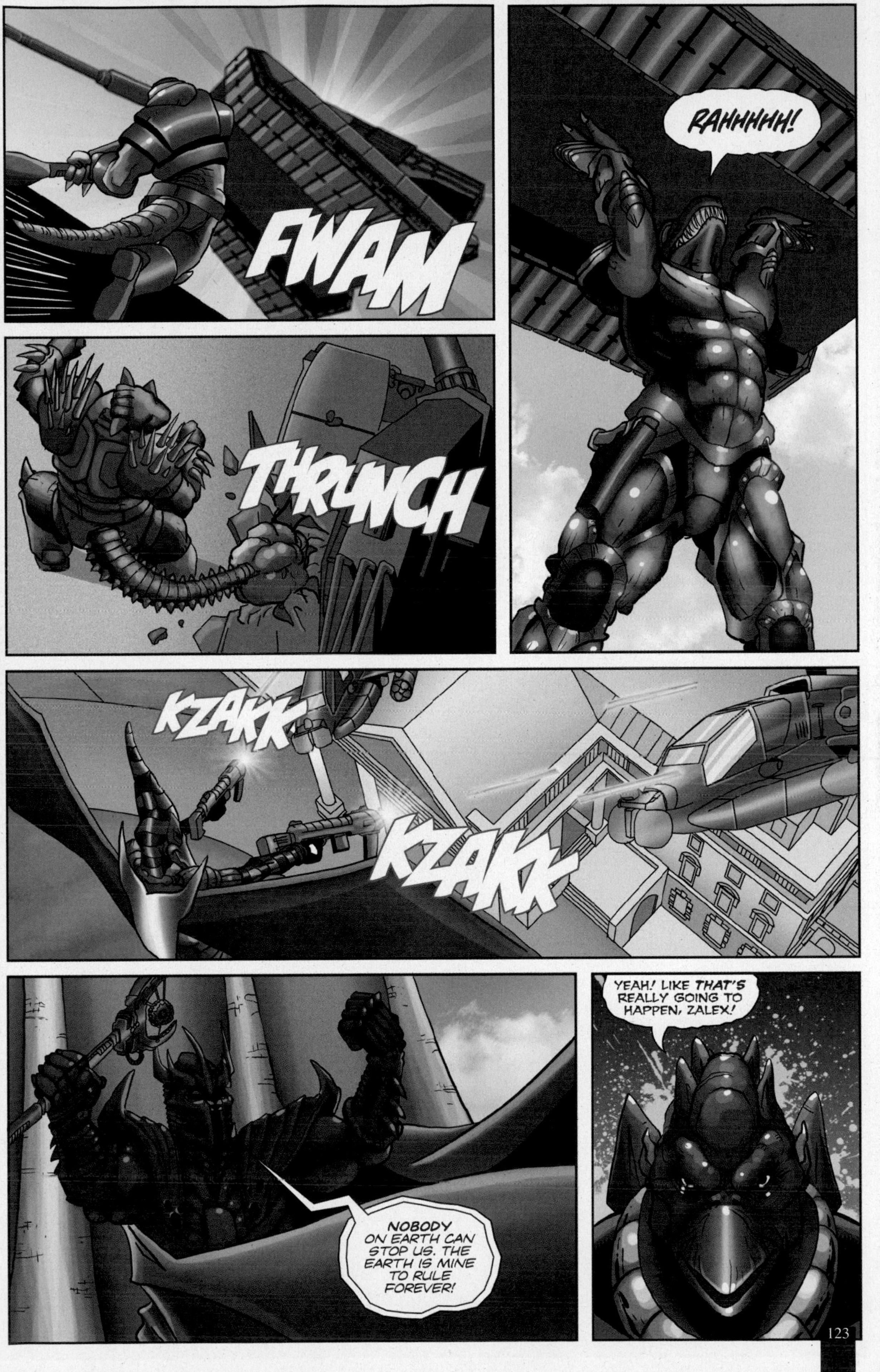
FWAM
RAHHHHH!
THRUNCH
KZAKK
KZAKK
NOBODY ON EARTH CAN STOP US. THE EARTH IS MINE TO RULE FOREVER!
YEAH! LIKE THAT'S REALLY GOING TO HAPPEN, ZALEX!

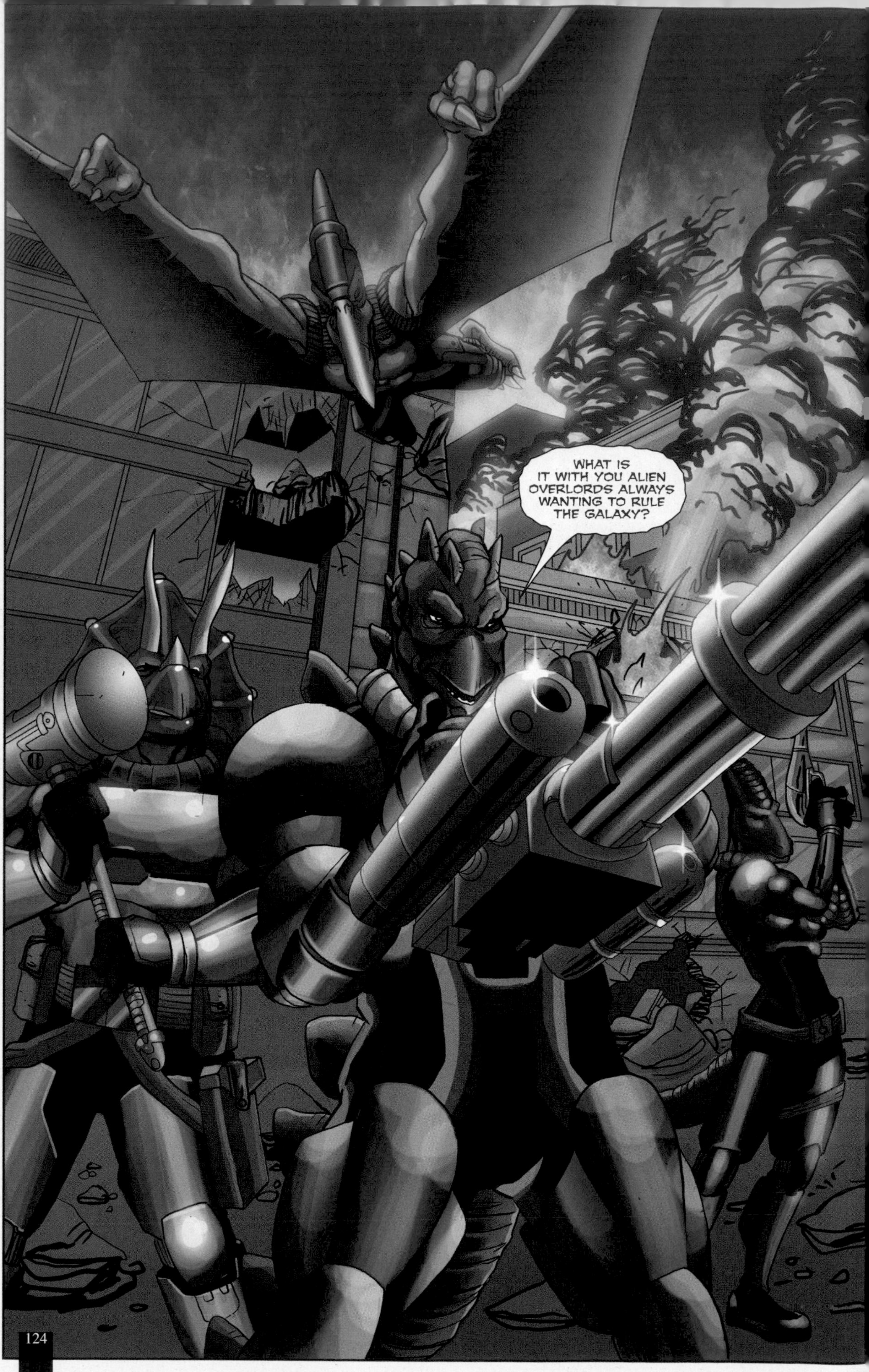
WHAT IS IT WITH YOU ALIEN OVERLORDS ALWAYS WANTING TO RULE THE GALAXY?

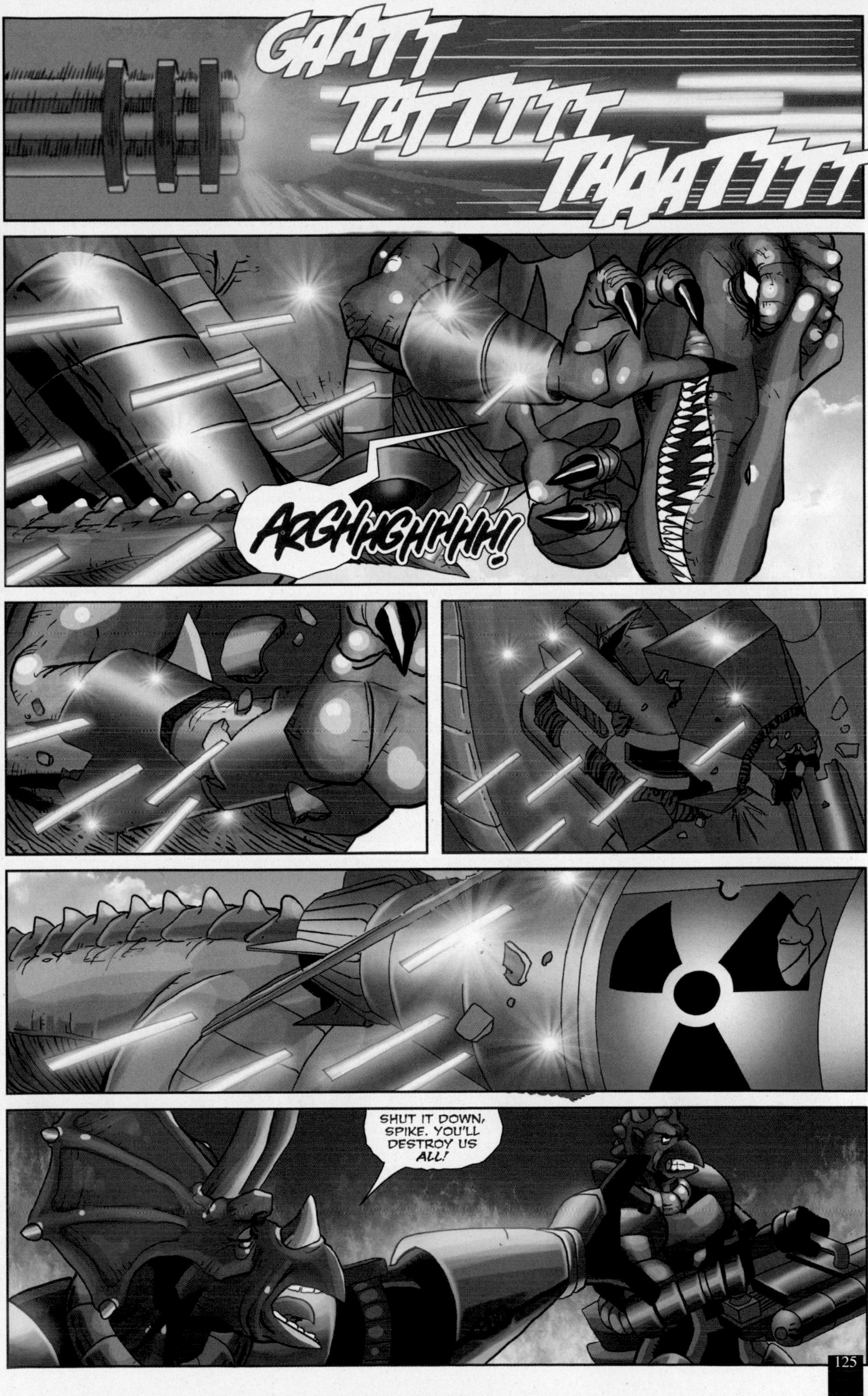
GAATT
TATTTTT
TAAATTTTT
ARGHHGHHHH!
SHUT IT DOWN, SPIKE. YOU'LL DESTROY US ALL!

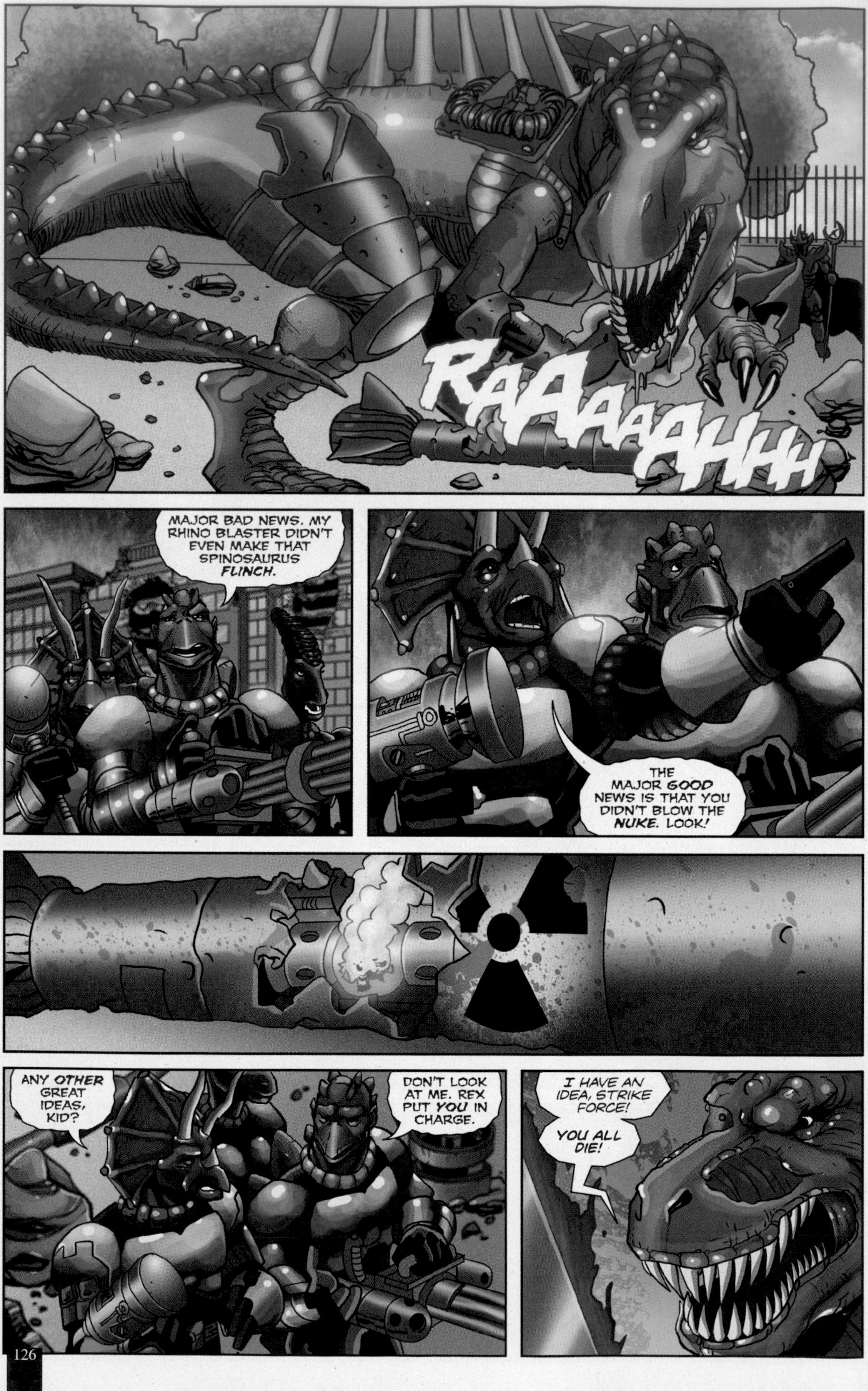
RAAAAAHHH
MAJOR BAD NEWS. MY RHINO BLASTER DIDN'T EVEN MAKE THAT SPINOSAURUS FLINCH.
THE MAJOR GOOD NEWS IS THAT YOU DIDN'T BLOW THE NUKE. LOOK!
ANY OTHER GREAT IDEAS, KID?
DON'T LOOK AT ME. REX PUT YOU IN CHARGE.
I HAVE AN IDEA, STRIKE FORCE!
YOU ALL DIE!

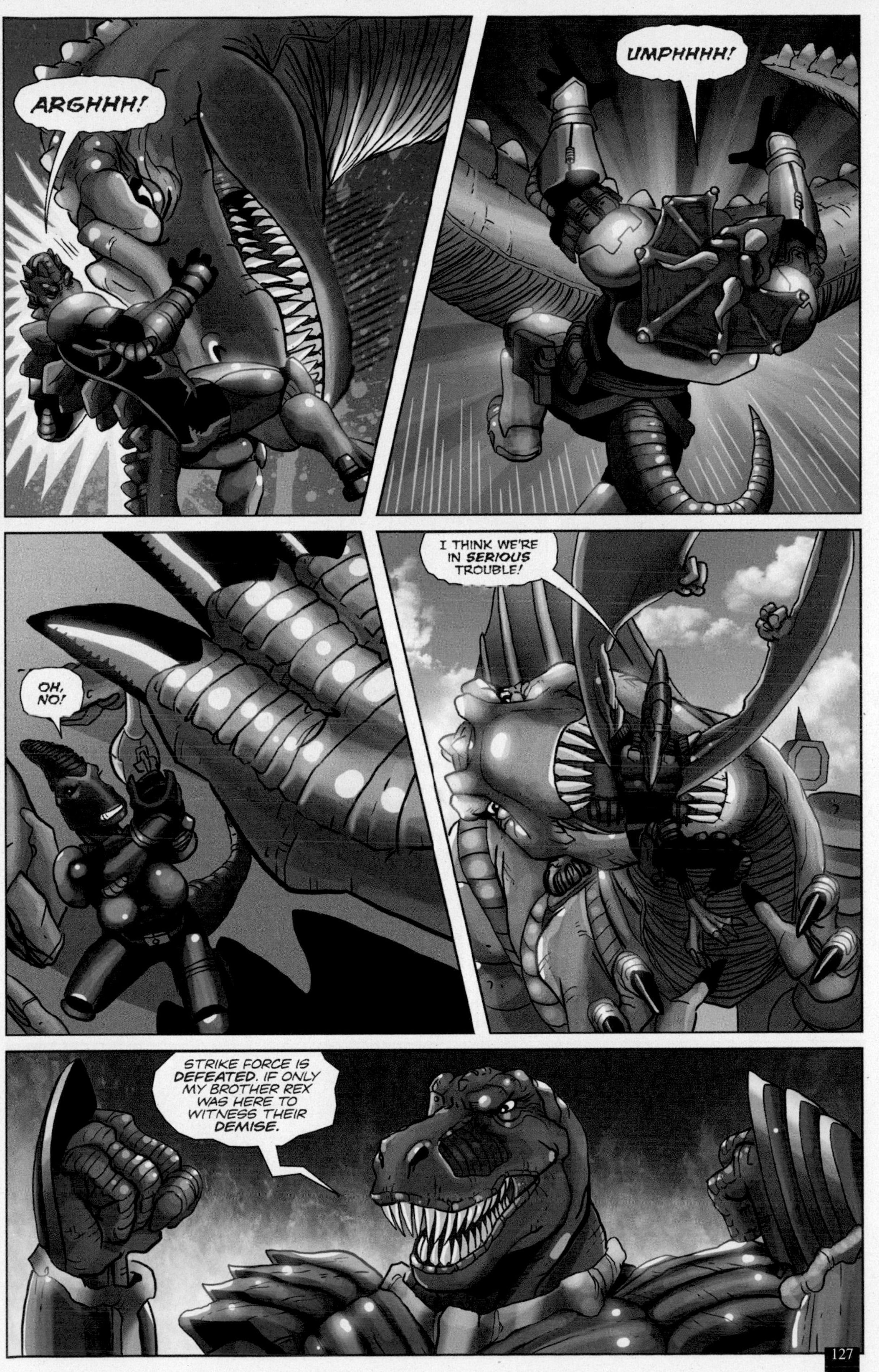
ARGHHH!
UMPHHHH!
OH, NO!
I THINK WE'RE IN SERIOUS TROUBLE!
STRIKE FORCE IS DEFEATED. IF ONLY MY BROTHER REX WAS HERE TO WITNESS THEIR DEMISE.

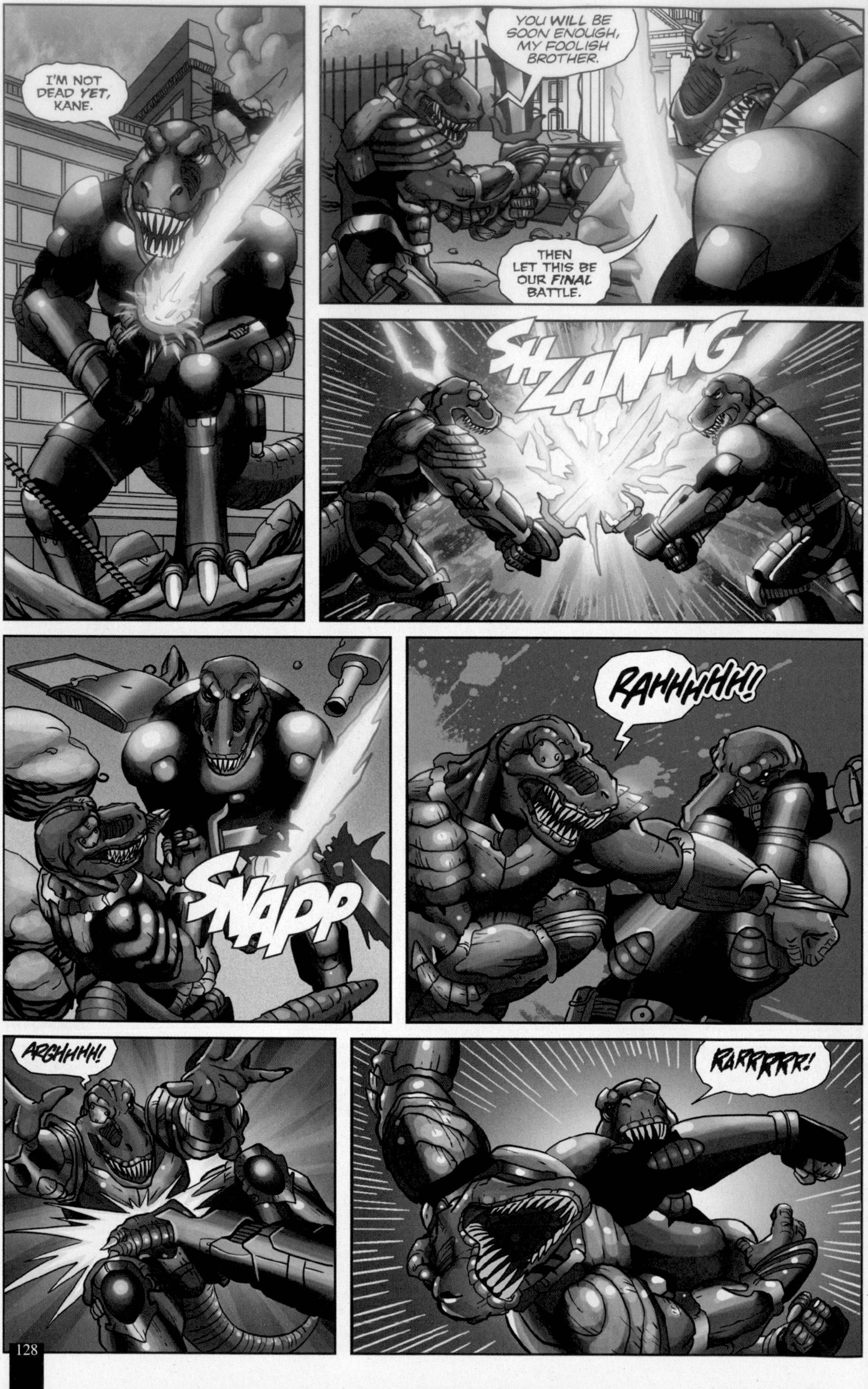
I'M NOT DEAD YET, KANE.
YOU WILL BE SOON ENOUGH, MY FOOLISH BROTHER.
THEN LET THIS BE OUR FINAL BATTLE.
SHZANNG
SNAPP
RAHHHHH!
ARGHHHH!
RARRRRR!

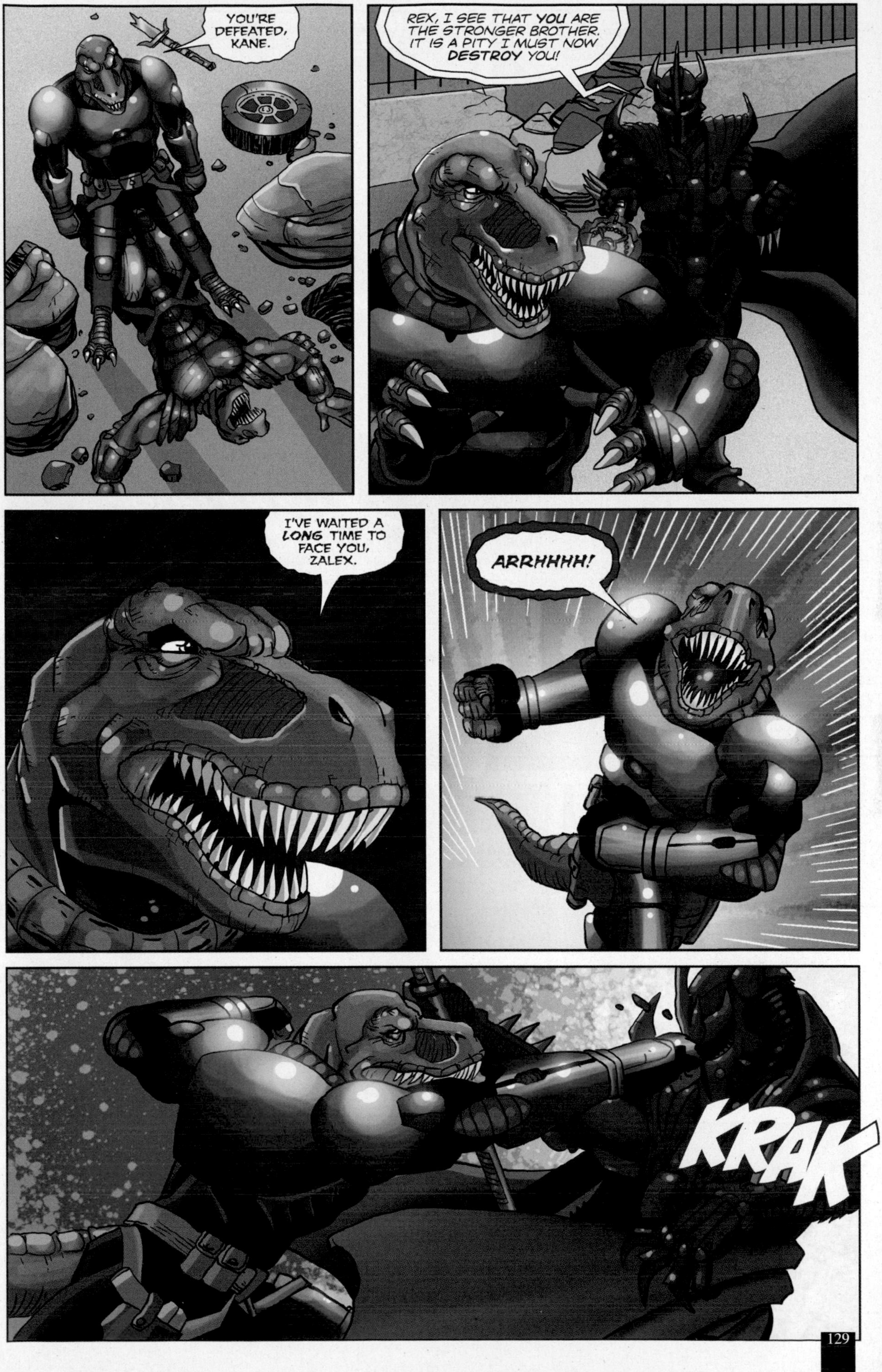
YOU'RE DEFEATED, KANE.
REX, I SEE THAT YOU ARE THE STRONGER BROTHER. IT IS A PITY I MUST NOW DESTROY YOU!
I'VE WAITED A LONG TIME TO FACE YOU, ZALEX.
ARRHHHH!
KRAK

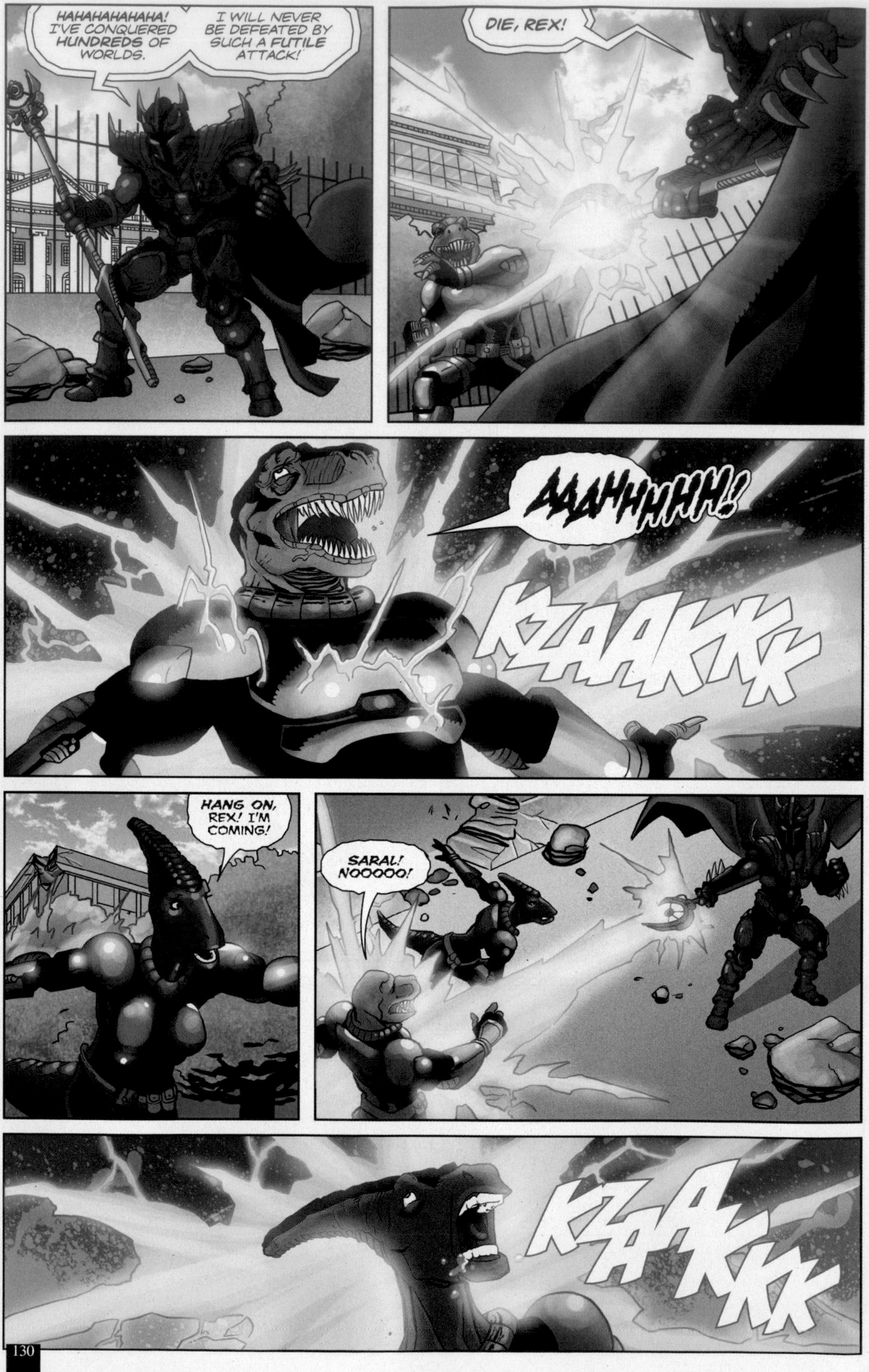
HAHAHAHAHAHA! I'VE CONQUERED HUNDREDS OF WORLDS.
I WILL NEVER BE DEFEATED BY SUCH A FUTILE ATTACK!
DIE, REX!
AAAHHHHH!
KZAAKKK
HANG ON, REX! I'M COMING!
SARAL! NOOOOO!
KZAAKKK

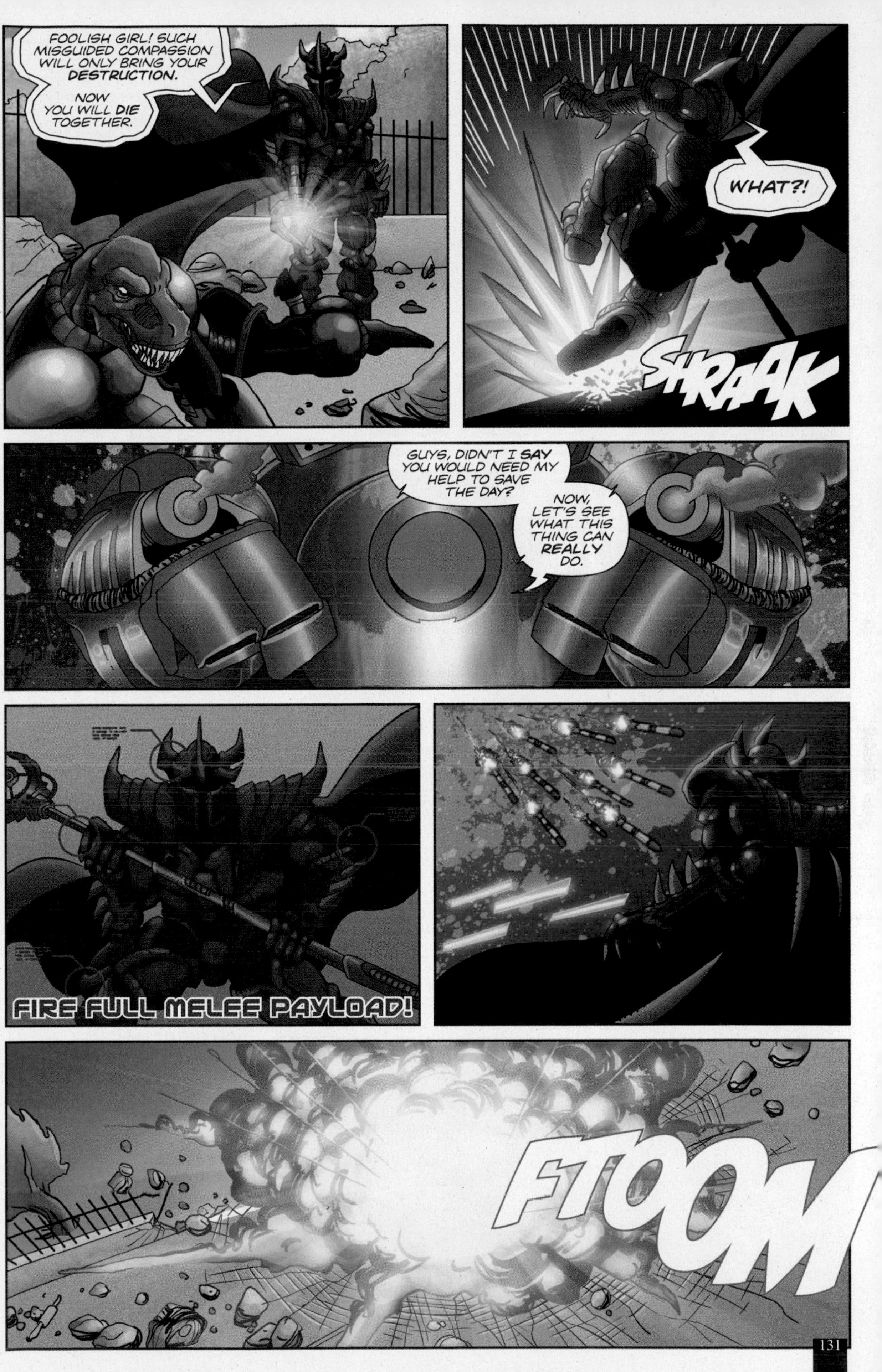
FOOLISH GIRL! SUCH MISGUIDED COMPASSION WILL ONLY BRING YOUR DESTRUCTION.
NOW YOU WILL DIE TOGETHER.
WHAT?!
SHRAAK
GUYS, DIDN'T I SAY YOU WOULD NEED MY HELP TO SAVE THE DAY?
NOW, LET'S SEE WHAT THIS THING CAN REALLY DO.
FIRE FULL MELEE PAYLOAD!
FTOOM

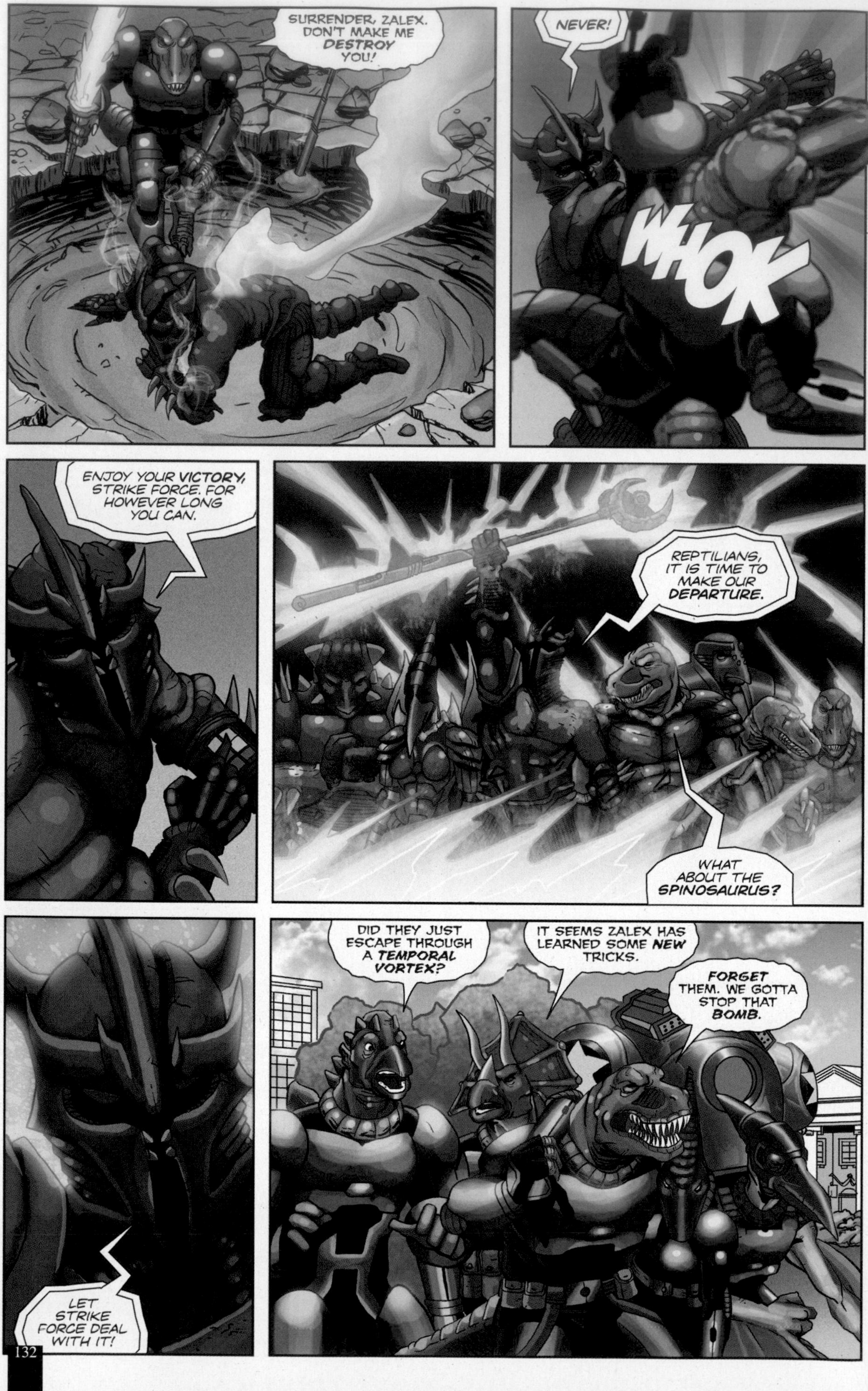
SURRENDER, ZALEX. DON'T MAKE ME DESTROY YOU!
NEVER!
WHOK
ENJOY YOUR VICTORY, STRIKE FORCE. FOR HOWEVER LONG YOU CAN.
REPTILIANS, IT IS TIME TO MAKE OUR DEPARTURE.
WHAT ABOUT THE SPINOSAURUS?
LET STRIKE FORCE DEAL WITH IT!
DID THEY JUST ESCAPE THROUGH A TEMPORAL VORTEX?
IT SEEMS ZALEX HAS LEARNED SOME NEW TRICKS.
FORGET THEM. WE GOTTA STOP THAT BOMB.

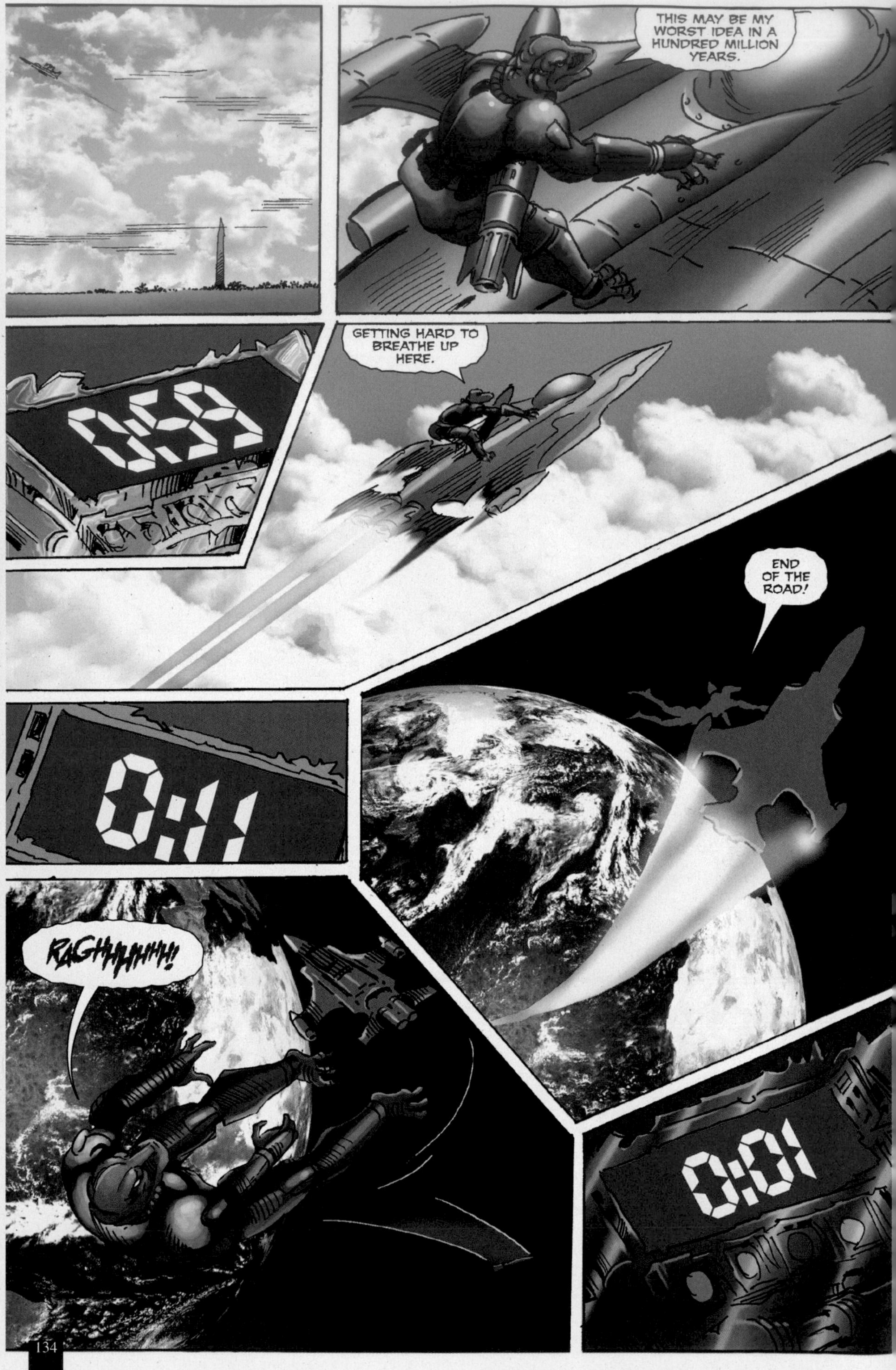
THIS MAY BE MY WORST IDEA IN A HUNDRED MILLION YEARS.
0:59
GETTING HARD TO BREATHE UP HERE.
0:11
END OF THE ROAD!
RAGHHHHHH!
0:01

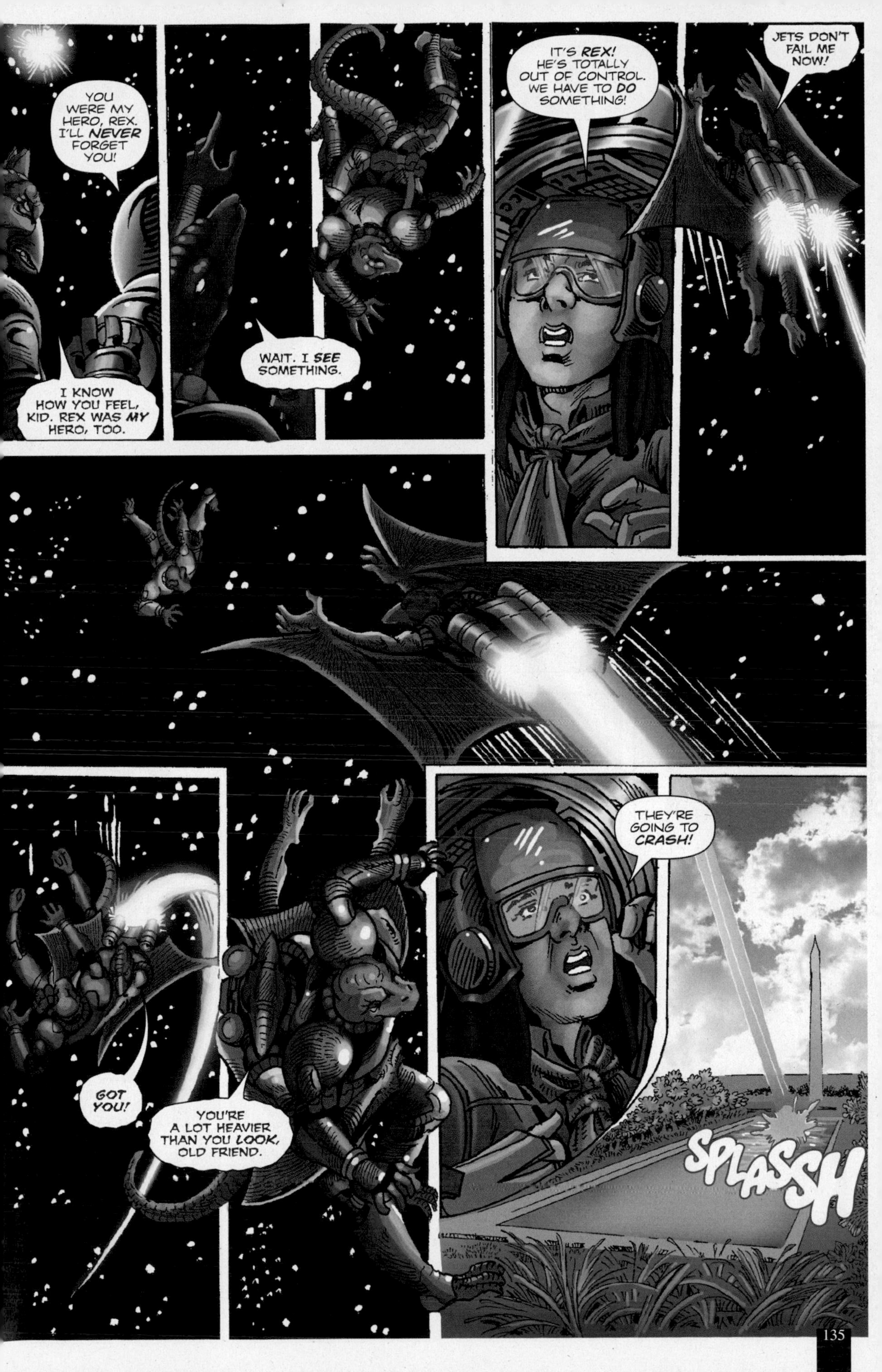

YOU WERE MY HERO, REX. I'LL NEVER FORGET YOU!
I KNOW HOW YOU FEEL, KID. REX WAS MY HERO, TOO.
WAIT. I SEE SOMETHING.
IT'S REX! HE'S TOTALLY OUT OF CONTROL. WE HAVE TO DO SOMETHING!
JETS DON'T FAIL ME NOW!
GOT YOU!
YOU'RE A LOT HEAVIER THAN YOU LOOK, OLD FRIEND.
THEY'RE GOING TO CRASH!
SPLASSH

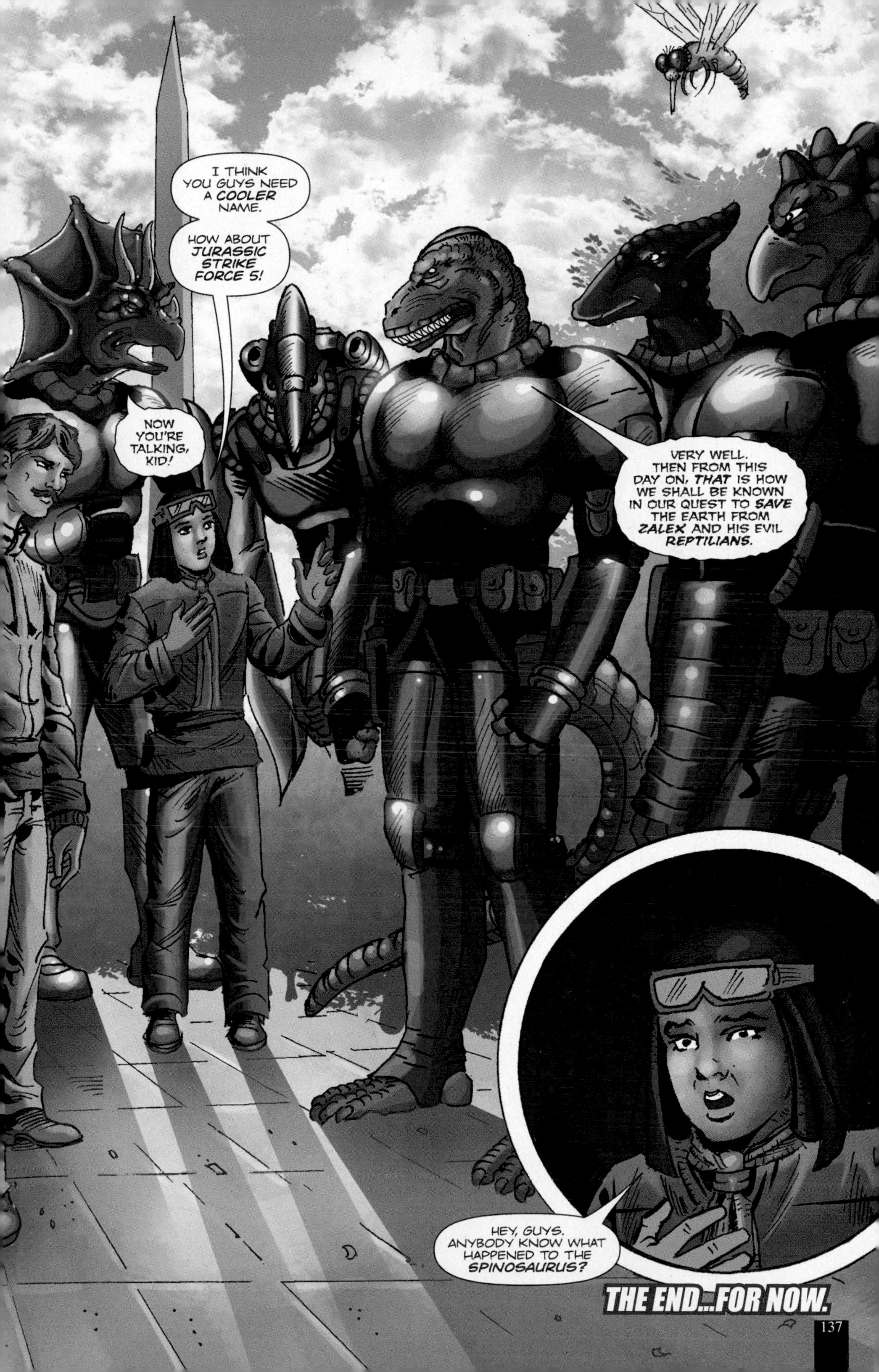
I THINK YOU GUYS NEED A COOLER NAME.
HOW ABOUT JURASSIC STRIKE FORCE 5!
NOW YOU'RE TALKING, KID!
VERY WELL. THEN FROM THIS DAY ON, THAT IS HOW WE SHALL BE KNOWN IN OUR QUEST TO SAVE THE EARTH FROM ZALEX AND HIS EVIL REPTILIANS.
HEY, GUYS. ANYBODY KNOW WHAT HAPPENED TO THE SPINOSAURUS?
THE END...FOR NOW.

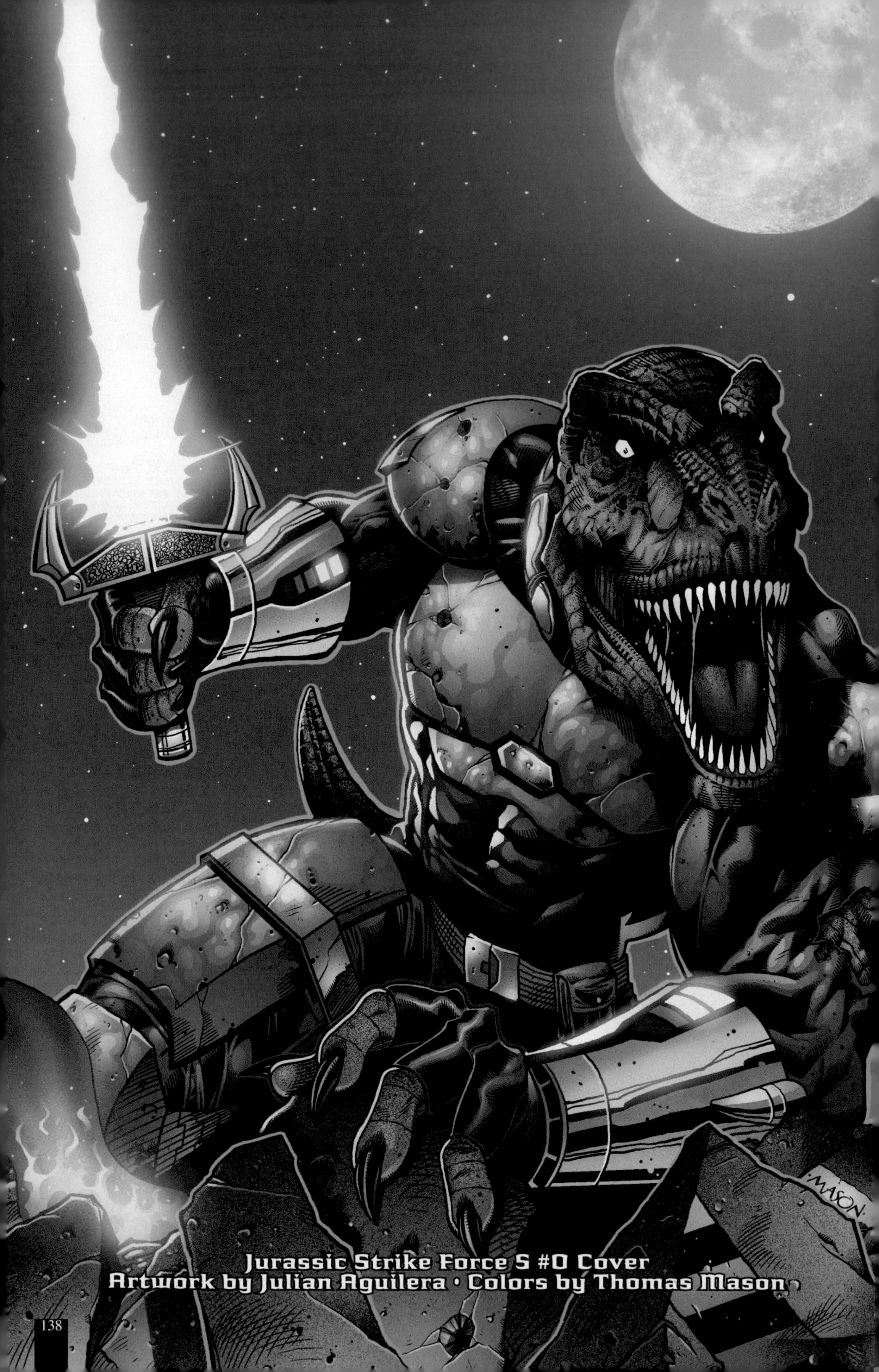
MASON

Jurassic Strike Force 5 #0 Cover
Artwork by Julian Aguilera · Colors by Thomas Mason

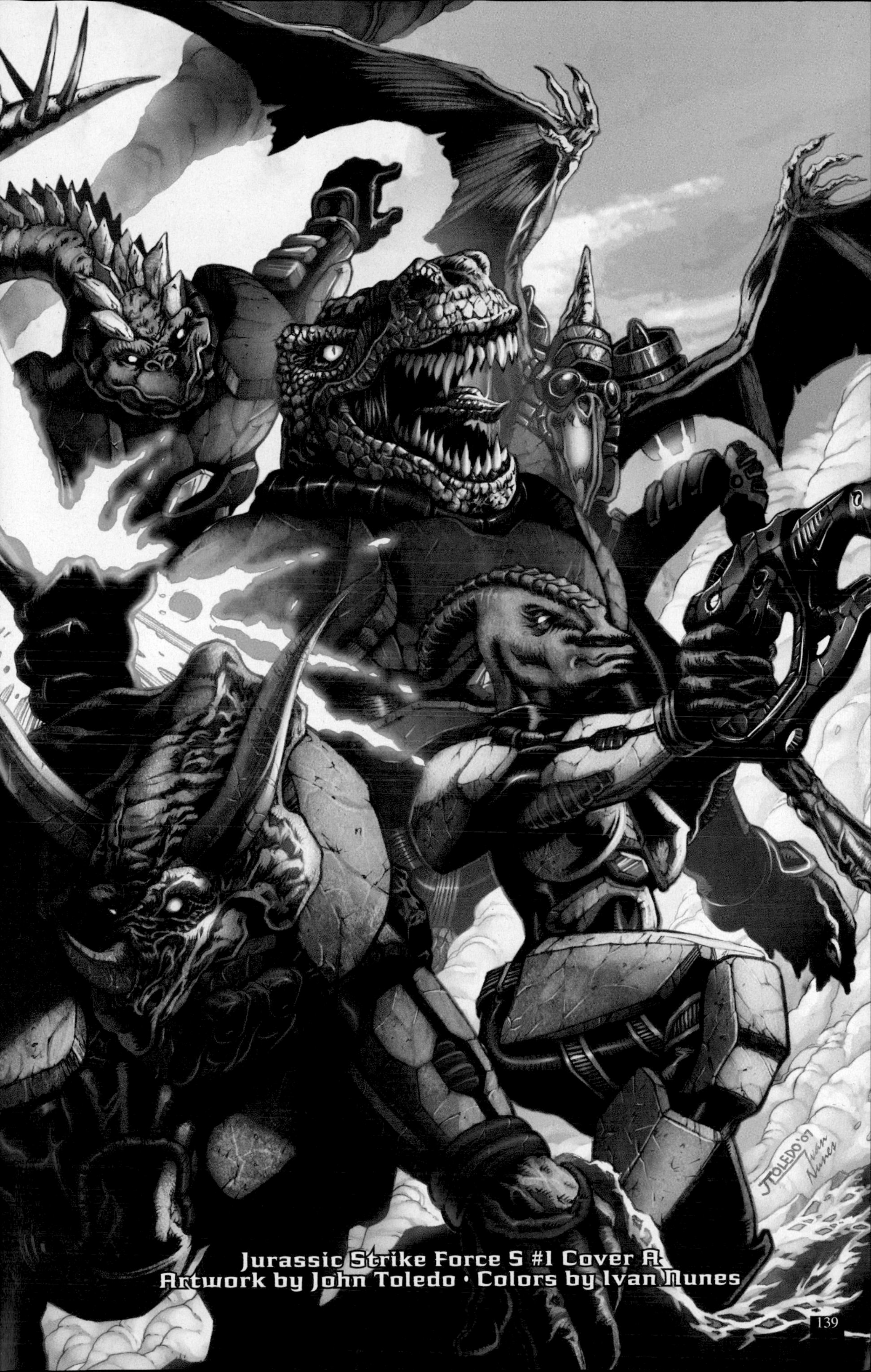
JTOLEDO '07
Ivan Nunes
Jurassic Strike Force 5 #1 Cover A
Artwork by John Toledo · Colors by Ivan Nunes

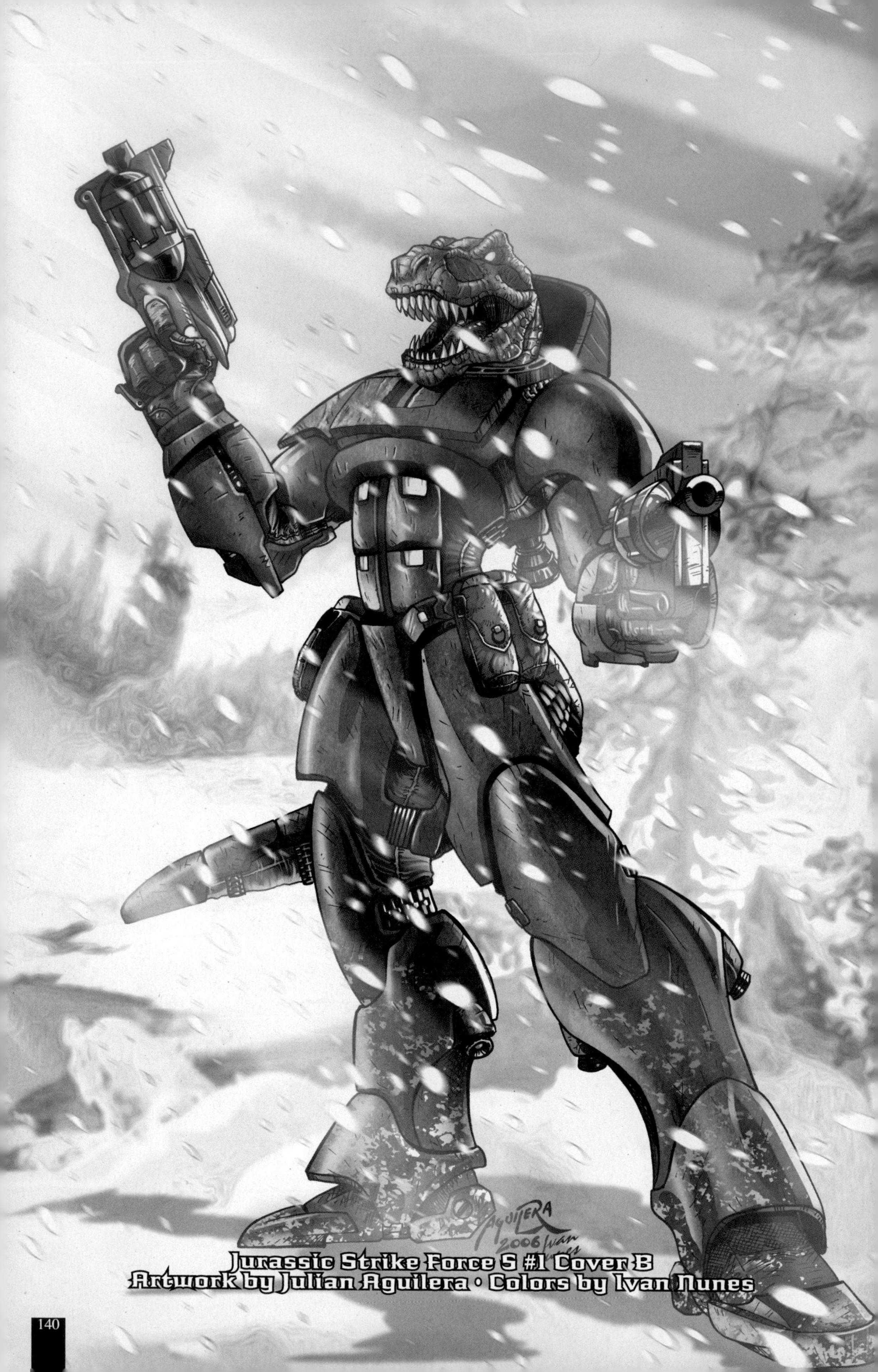
AGUILERA
2006

Jurassic Strike Force 5 #1 Cover B
Artwork by Julian Aguilera · Colors by Ivan Nunes

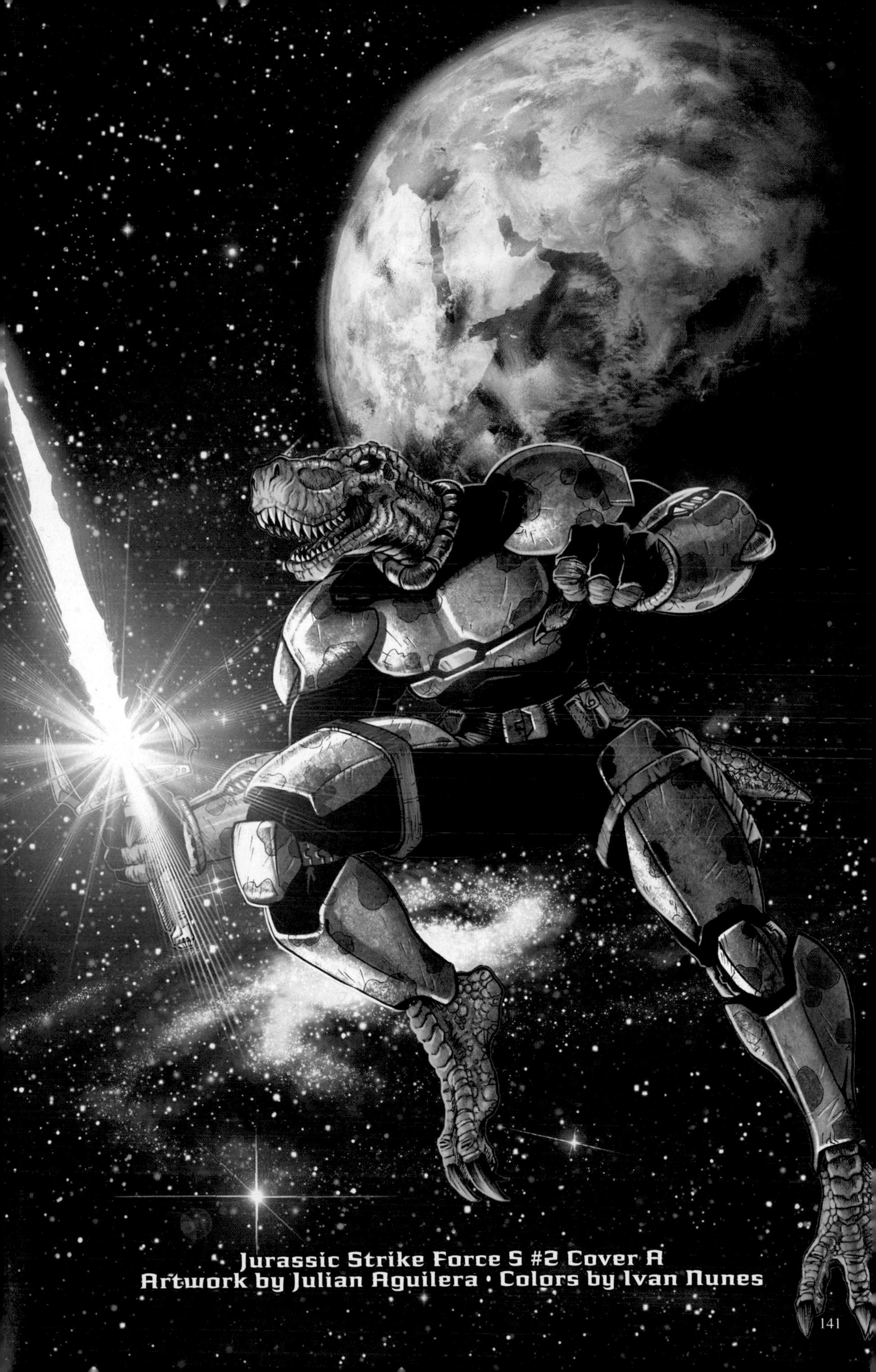

Jurassic Strike Force 5 #2 Cover A
Artwork by Julian Aguilera · Colors by Ivan Nunes

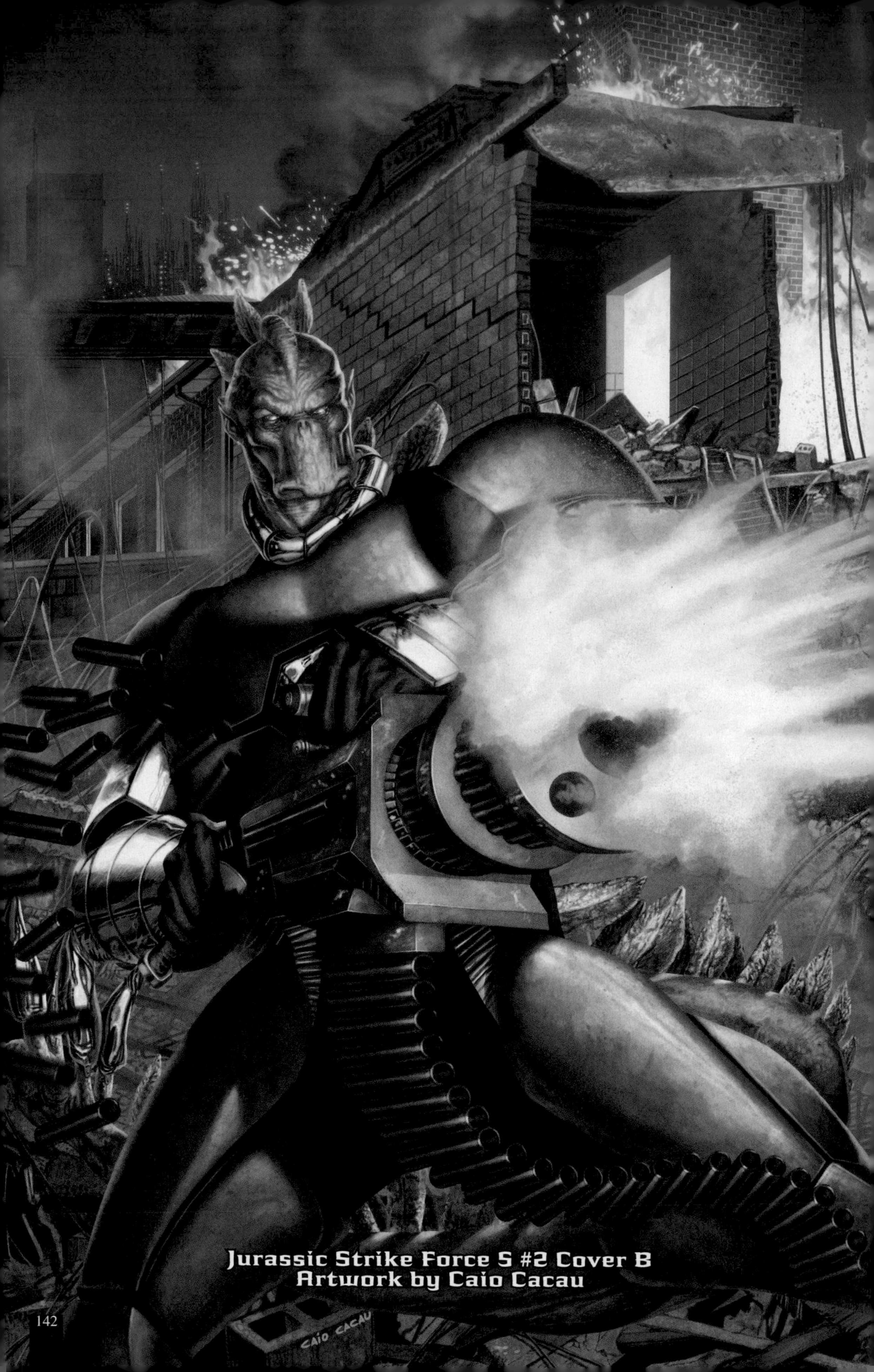
CAIO CACAU

Jurassic Strike Force 5 #2 Cover B
Artwork by Caio Cacau

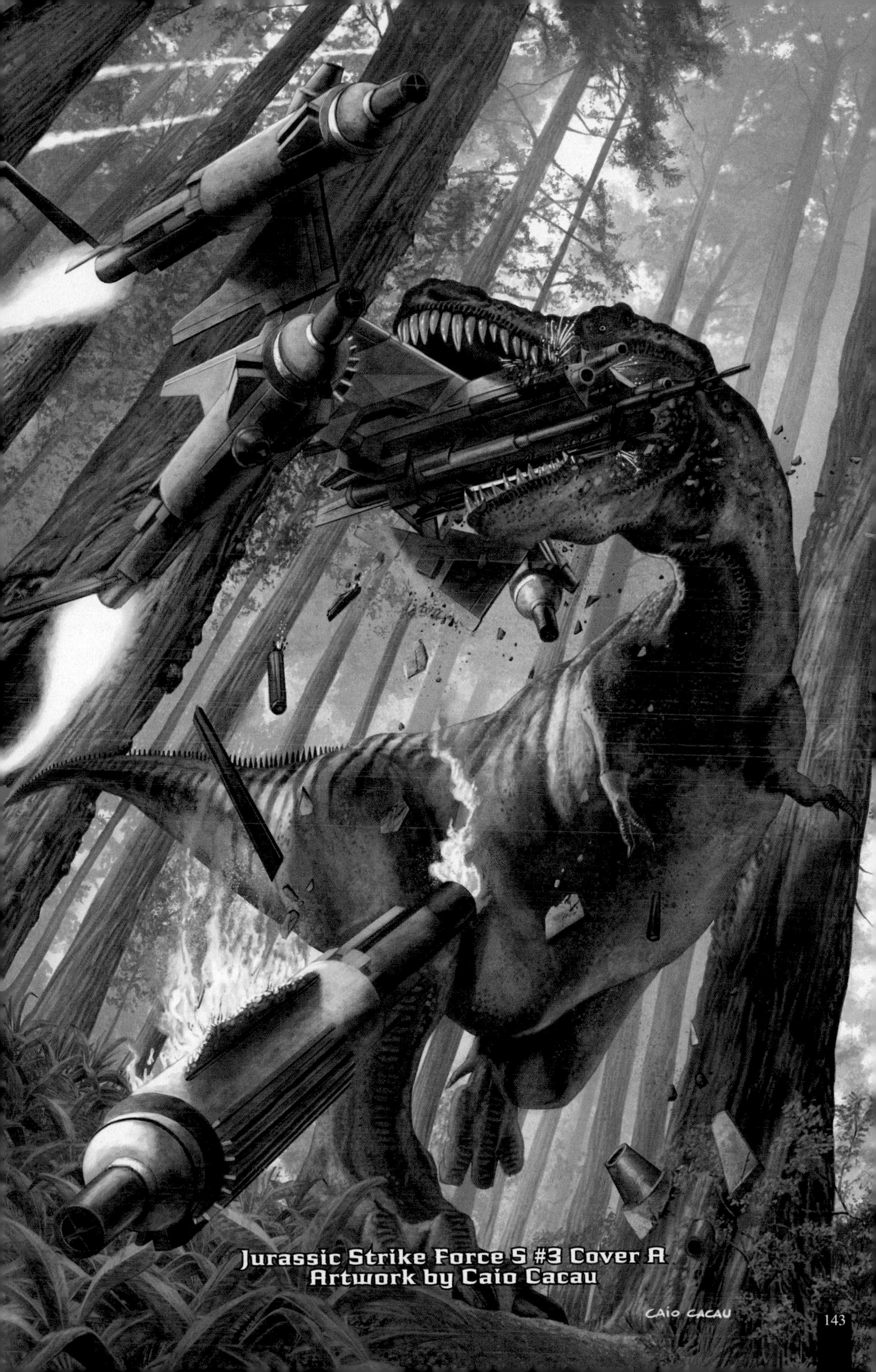
CAIO CACAU

Jurassic Strike Force 5 #3 Cover A
Artwork by Caio Cacau

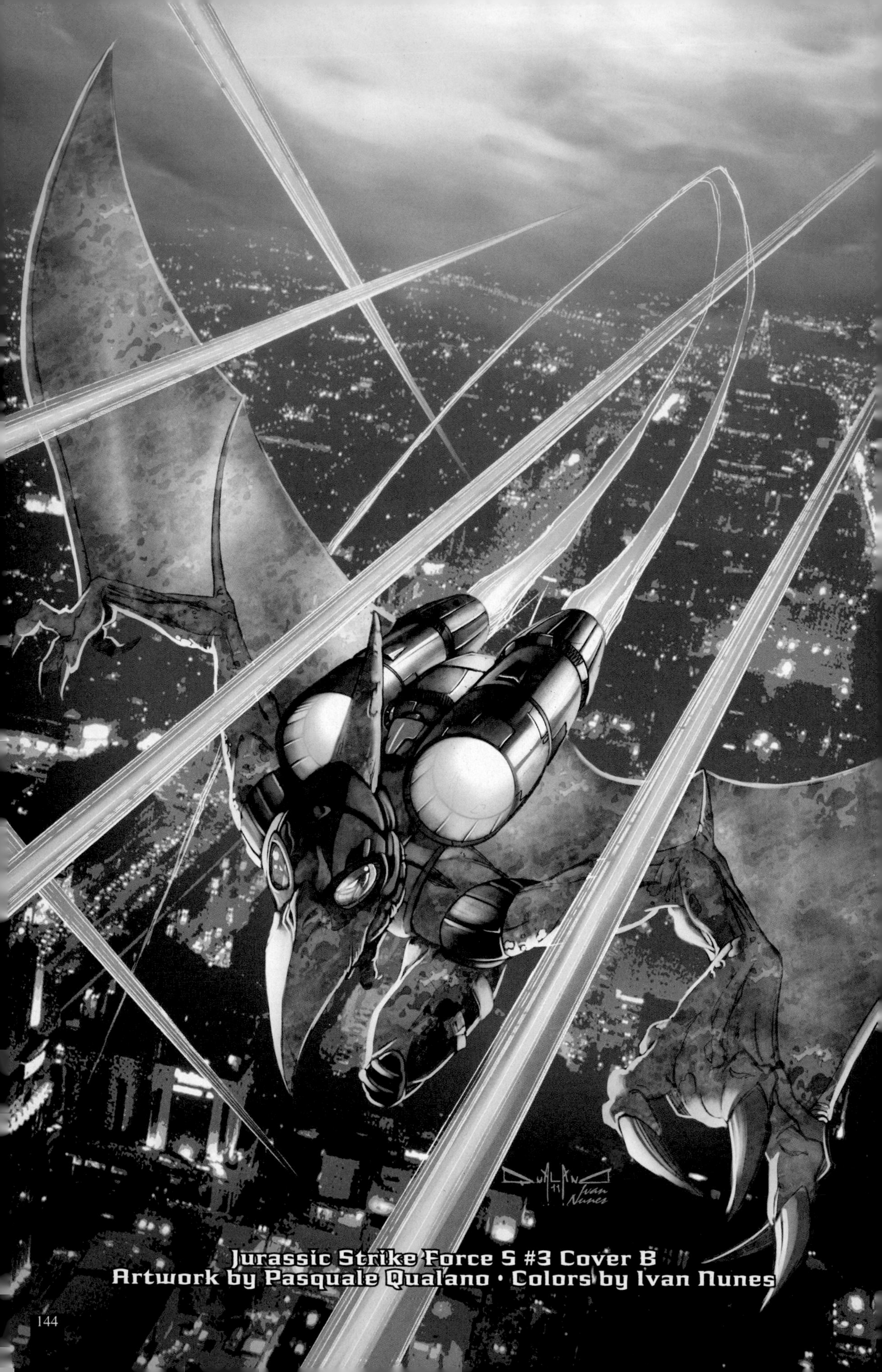

Jurassic Strike Force 5 #3 Cover B
Artwork by Pasquale Qualano • Colors by Ivan Nunes

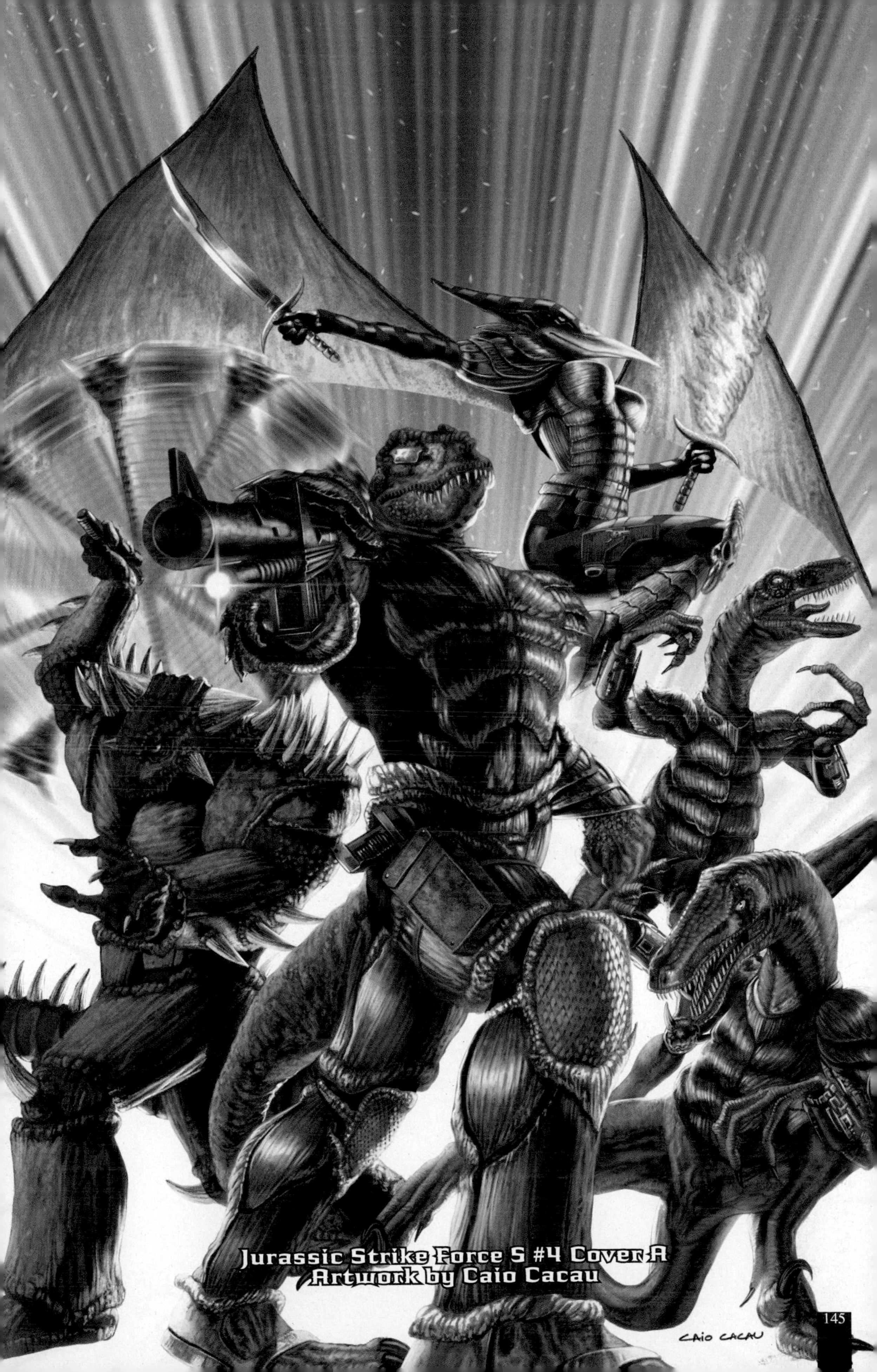
CAIO CACAU

Jurassic Strike Force 5 #4 Cover A
Artwork by Caio Cacau

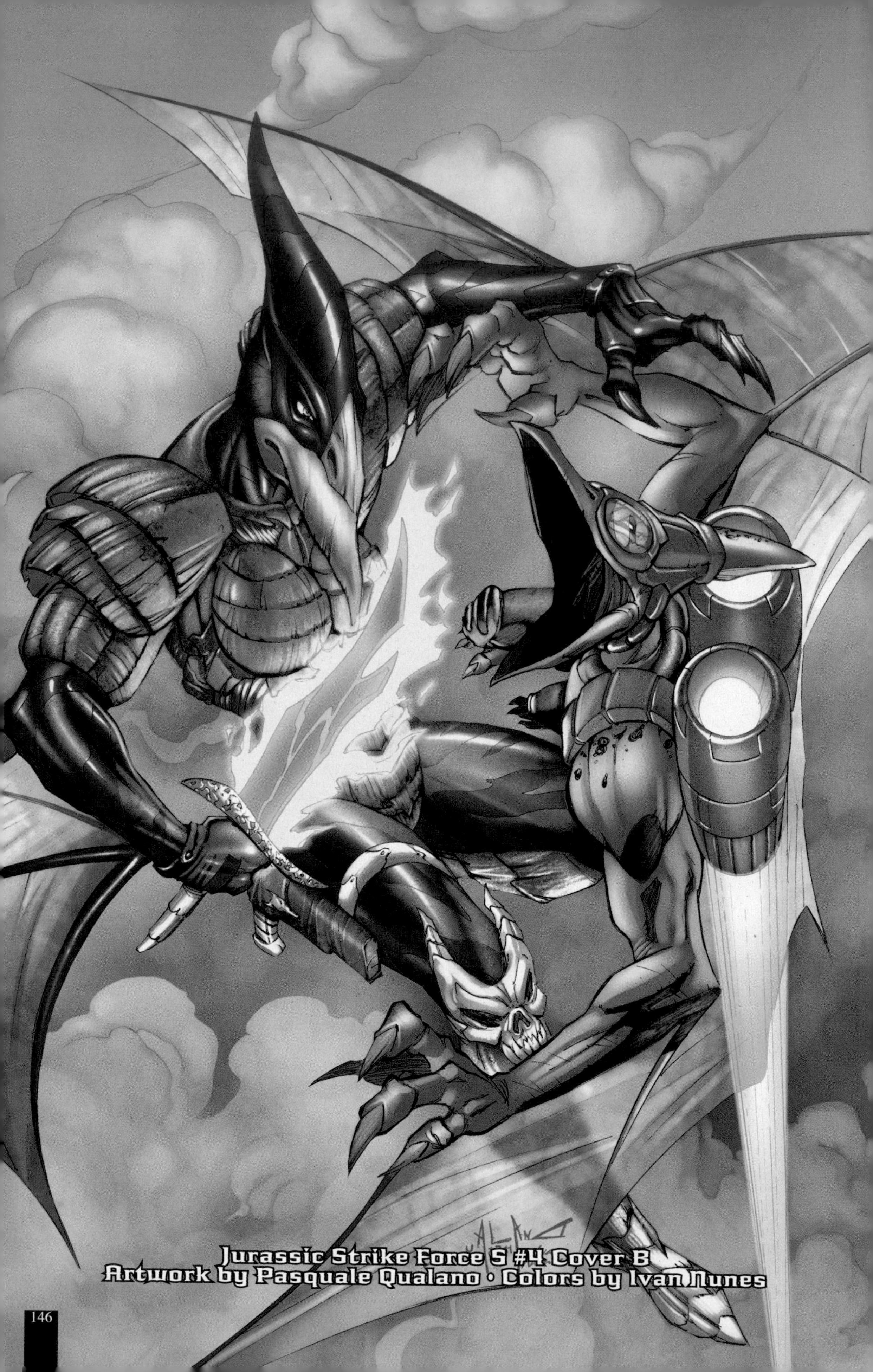

Jurassic Strike Force 5 #4 Cover B
Artwork by Pasquale Qualano • Colors by Ivan Nunes

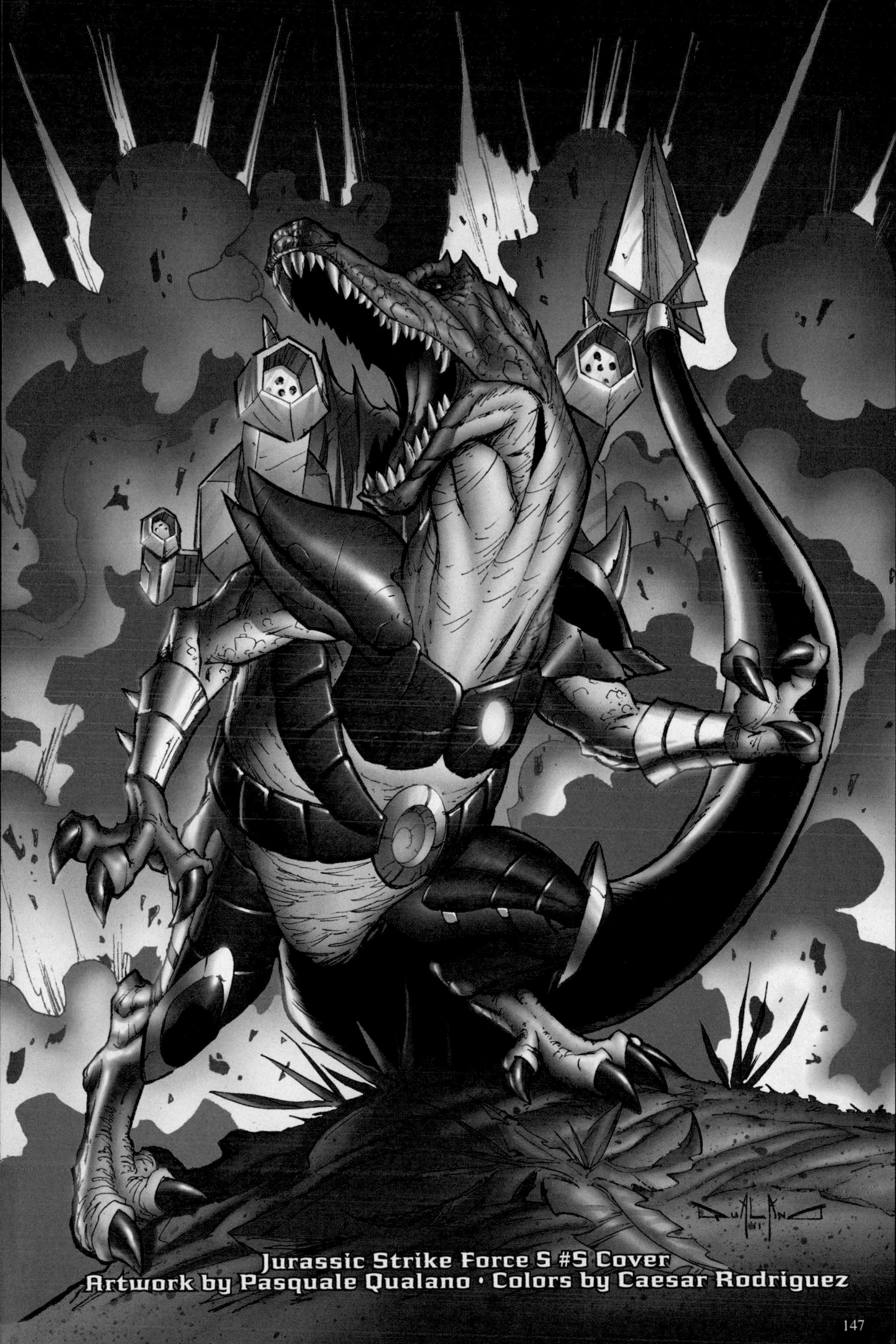

Jurassic Strike Force 5 #5 Cover
Artwork by Pasquale Qualano • Colors by Caesar Rodriguez

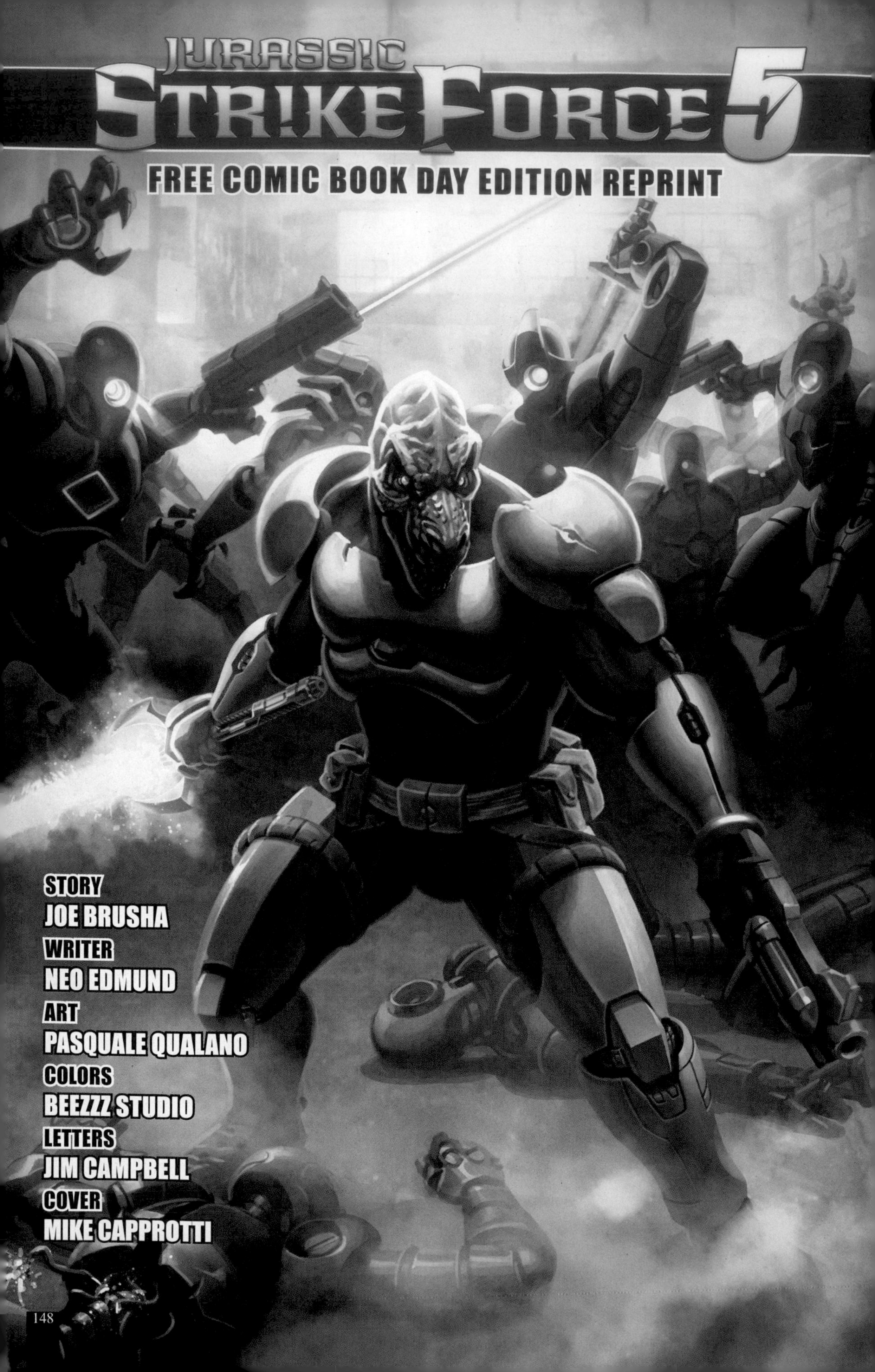
JURASSIC
STRIKE FORCE 5
FREE COMIC BOOK DAY EDITION REPRINT
STORY
JOE BRUSHA
WRITER
NEO EDMUND
ART
PASQUALE QUALANO
COLORS
BEEZZZ STUDIO
LETTERS
JIM CAMPBELL
COVER
MIKE CAPPROTTI

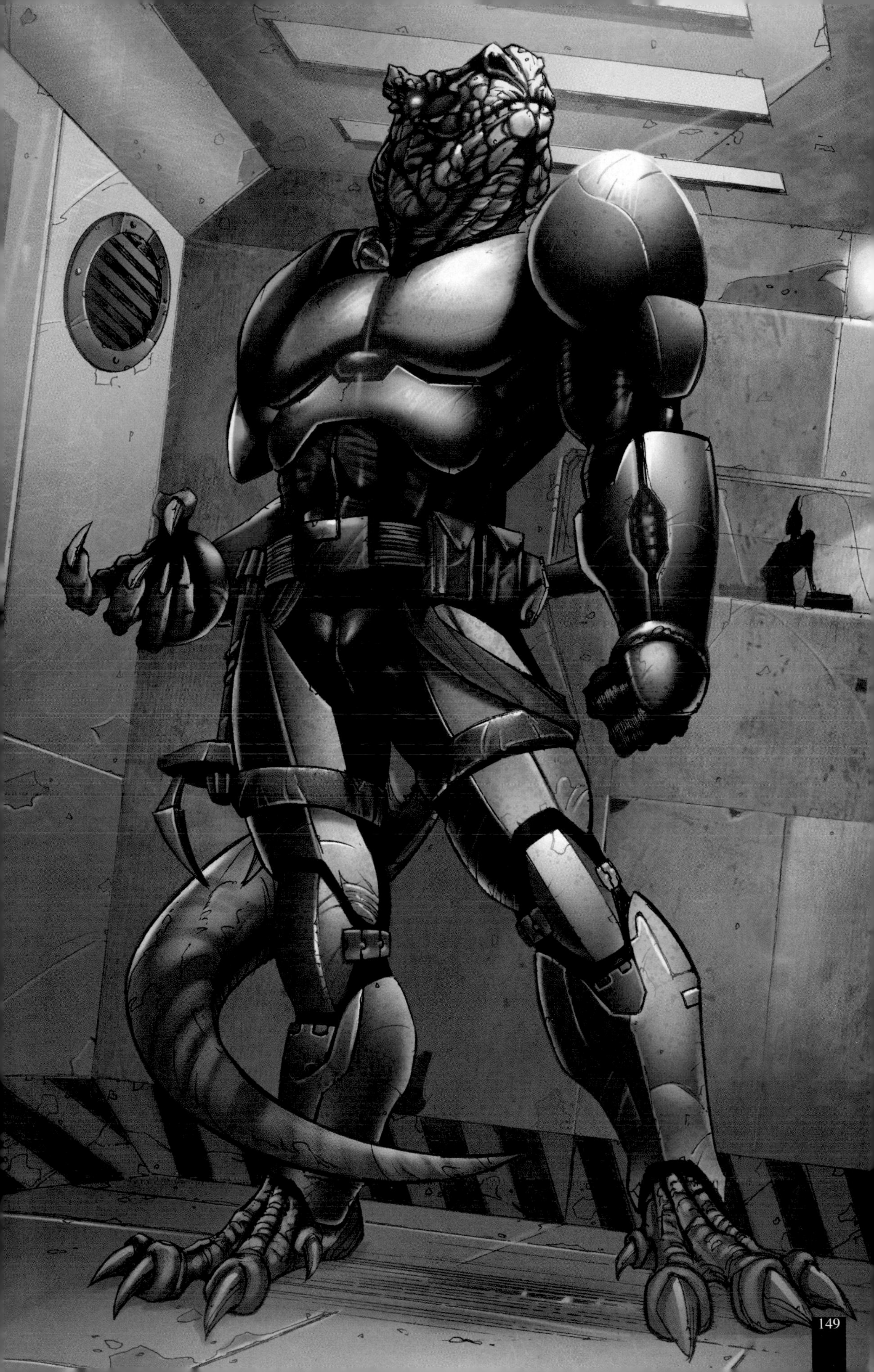

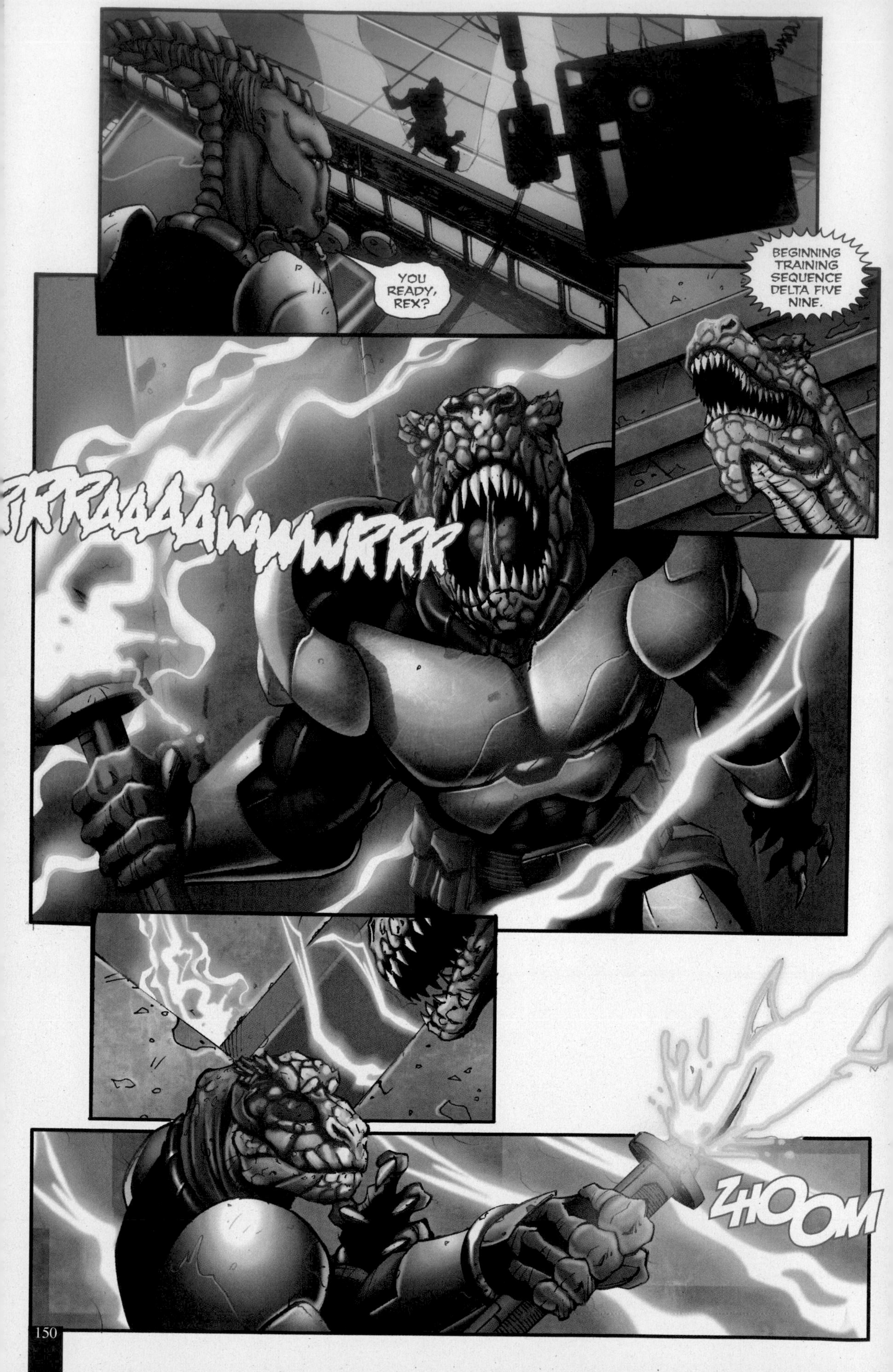
YOU READY, REX?
BEGINNING TRAINING SEQUENCE DELTA FIVE NINE.
RRRAAAAWWWRRR
ZHOOM

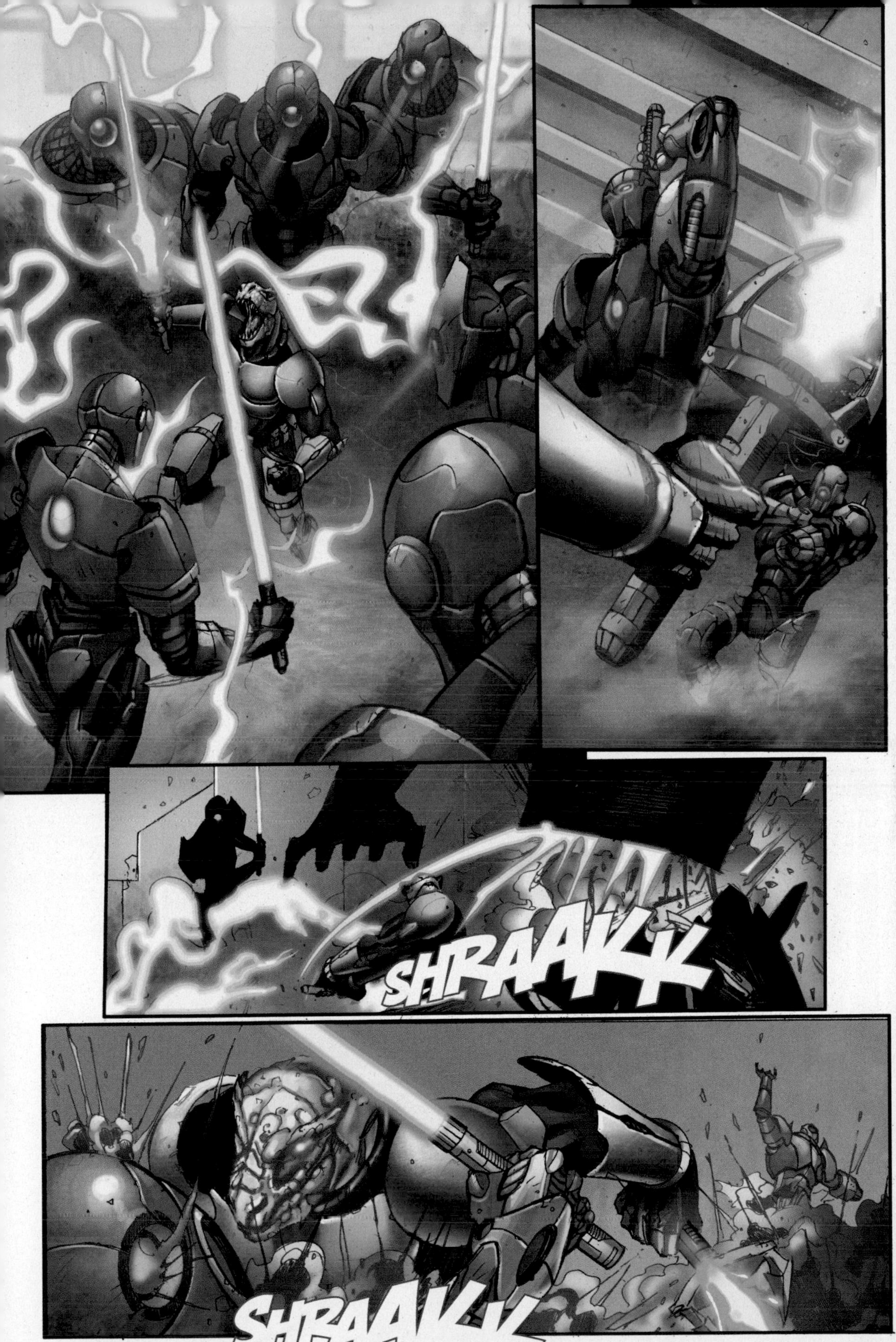
SHRAAKK
SHRAAKK

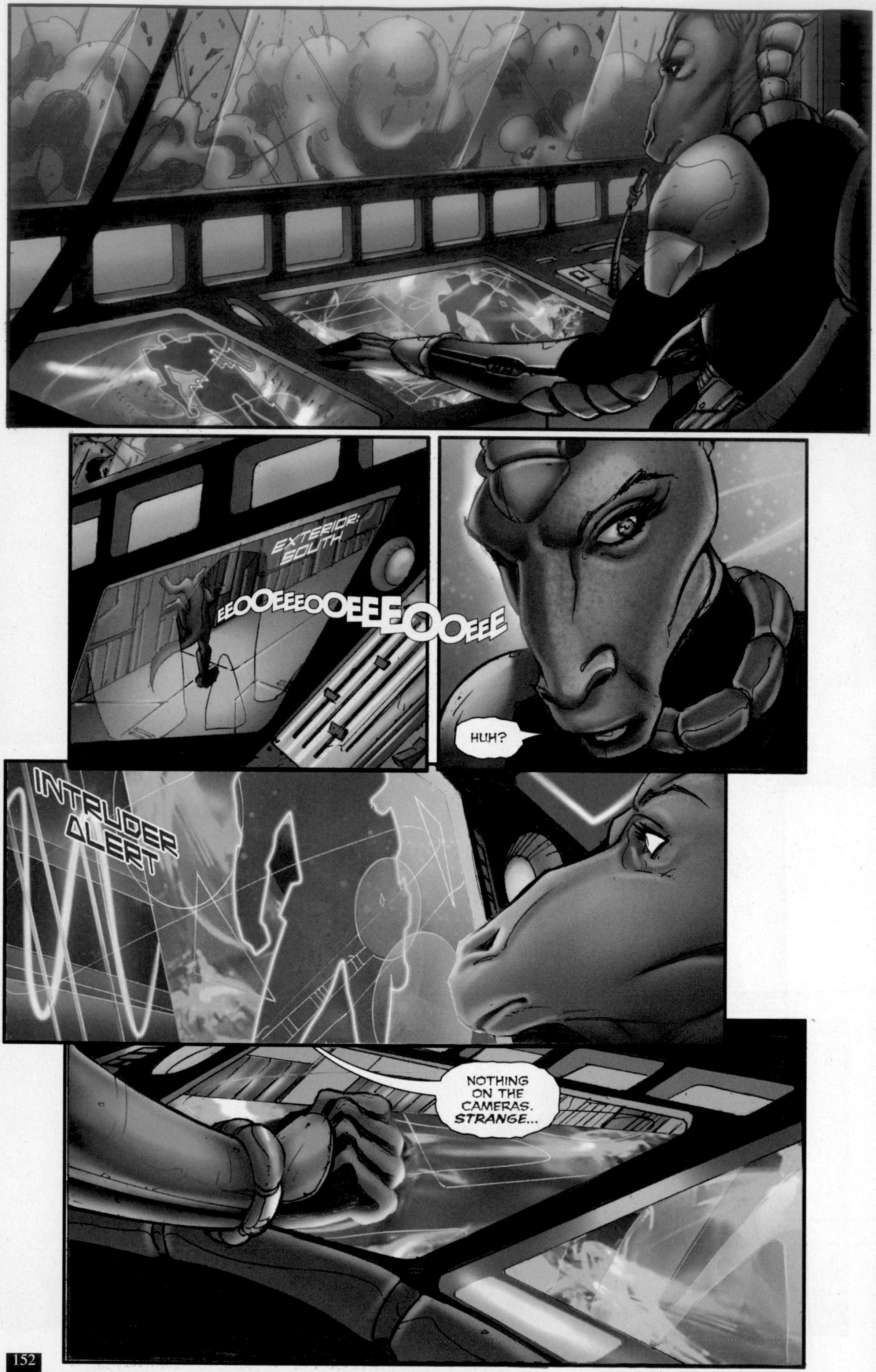
EXTERIOR: SOUTH
EEOOEEEOOEEEOOEEE
HUH?
INTRUDER ALERT
NOTHING ON THE CAMERAS. STRANGE...

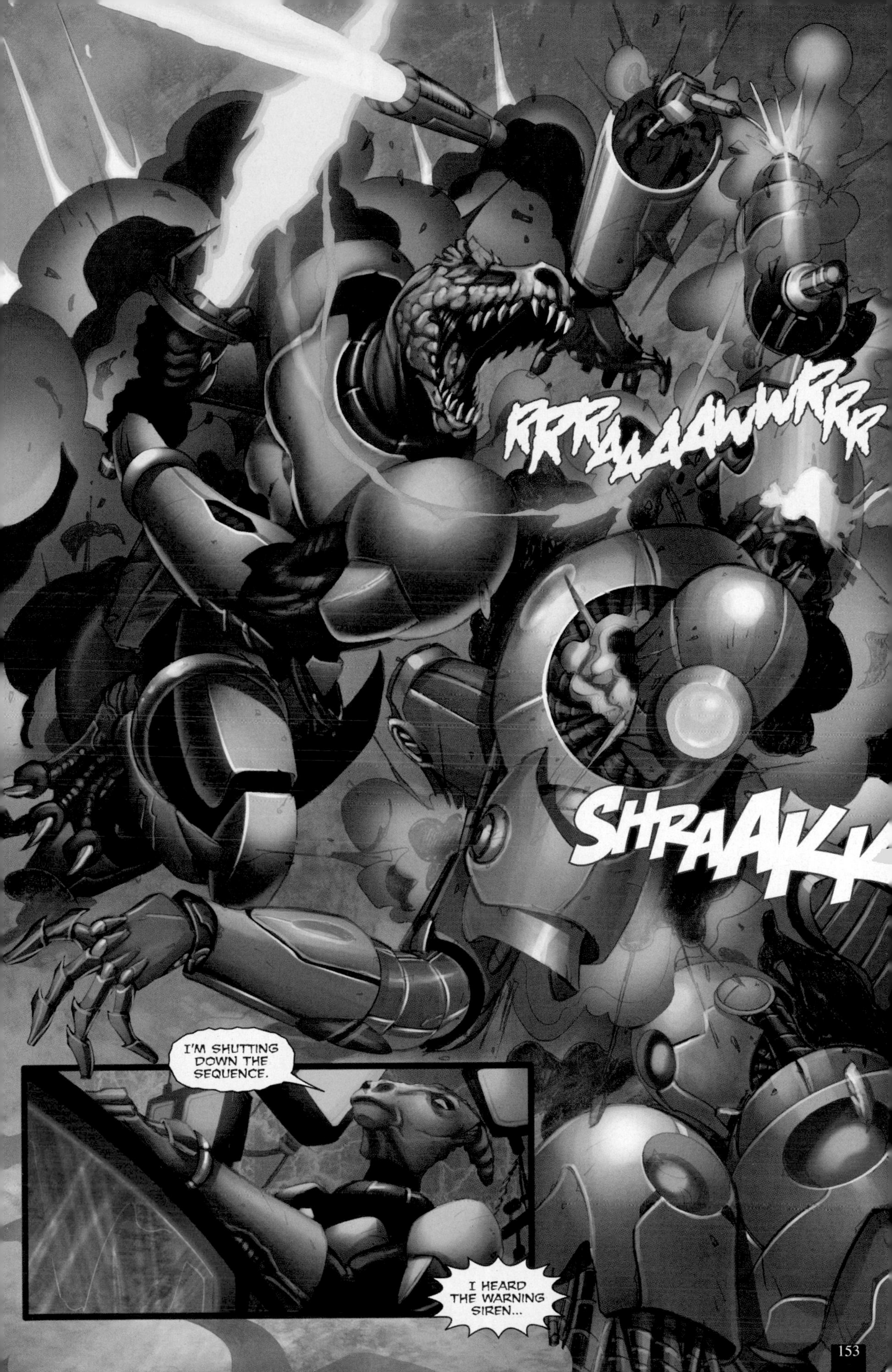
RRRAAAAWWRRR
SHRAAKK
I'M SHUTTING DOWN THE SEQUENCE.
I HEARD THE WARNING SIREN...

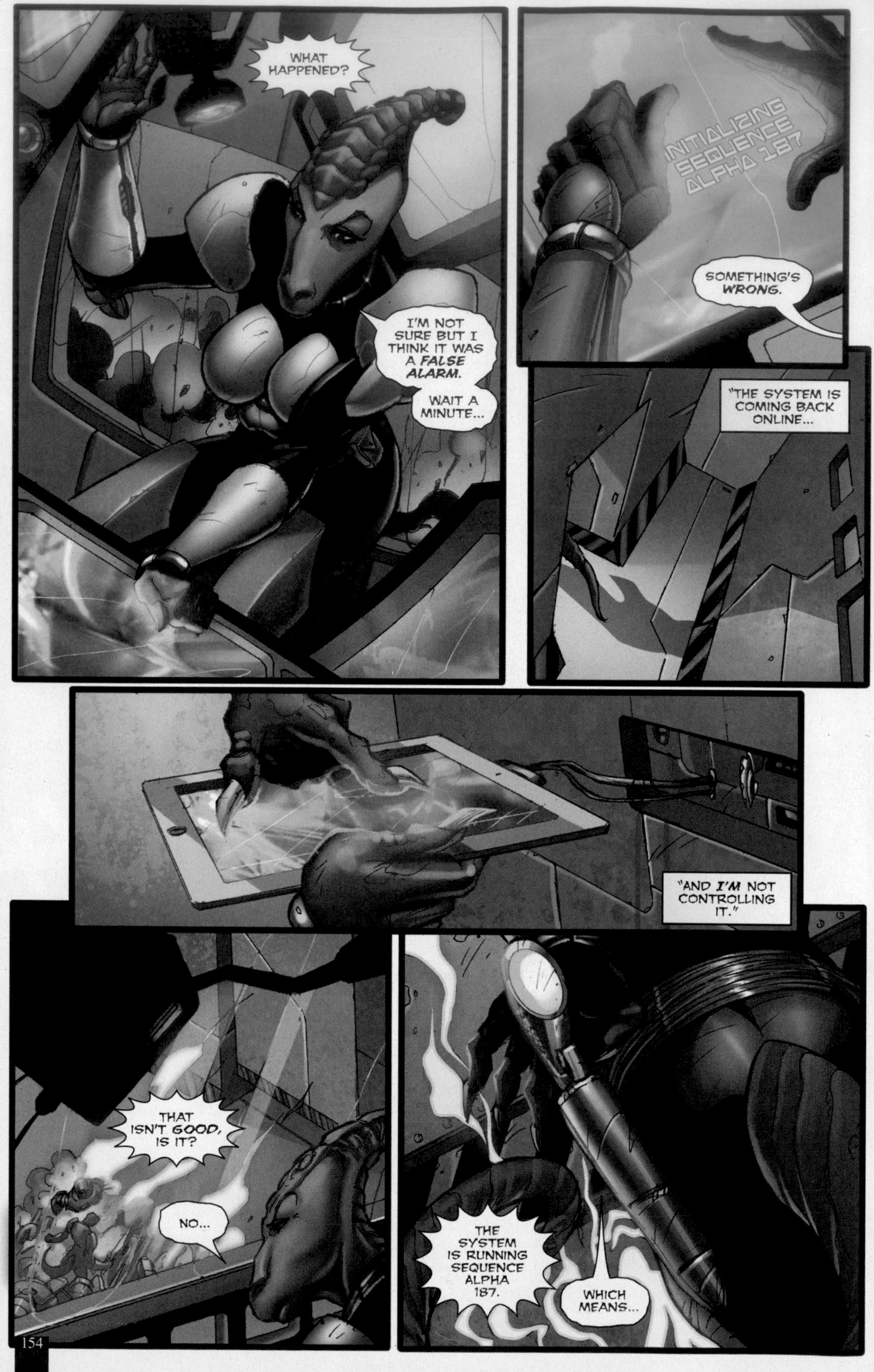
WHAT HAPPENED?
INITIALIZING SEQUENCE ALPHA 187
SOMETHING'S WRONG.
I'M NOT SURE BUT I THINK IT WAS A FALSE ALARM.
WAIT A MINUTE...
"THE SYSTEM IS COMING BACK ONLINE...
"AND I'M NOT CONTROLLING IT."
THAT ISN'T GOOD, IS IT?
NO...
THE SYSTEM IS RUNNING SEQUENCE ALPHA 187.
WHICH MEANS...

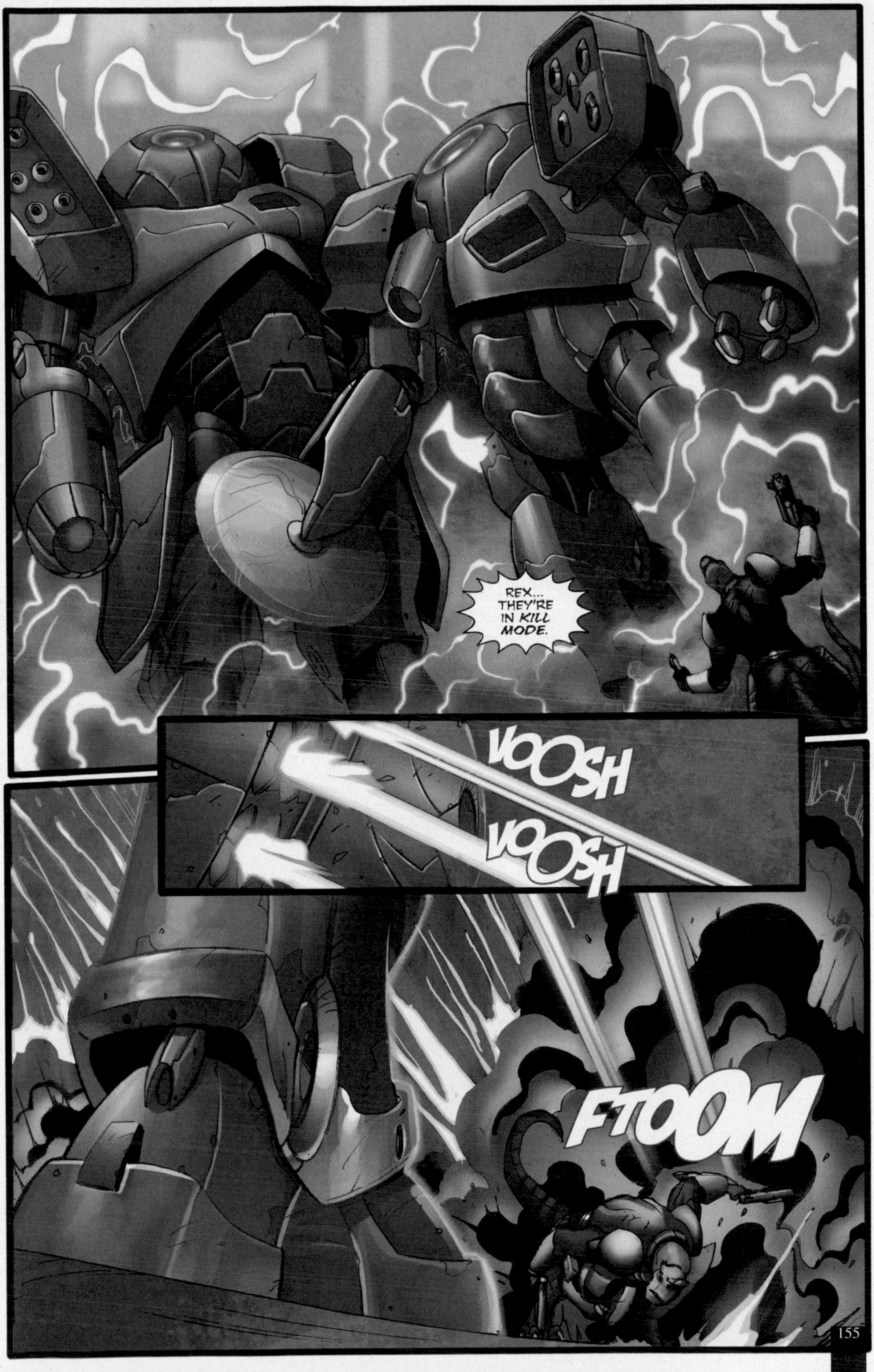
REX... THEY'RE IN KILL MODE.
VOOSH
VOOSH
FTOOM

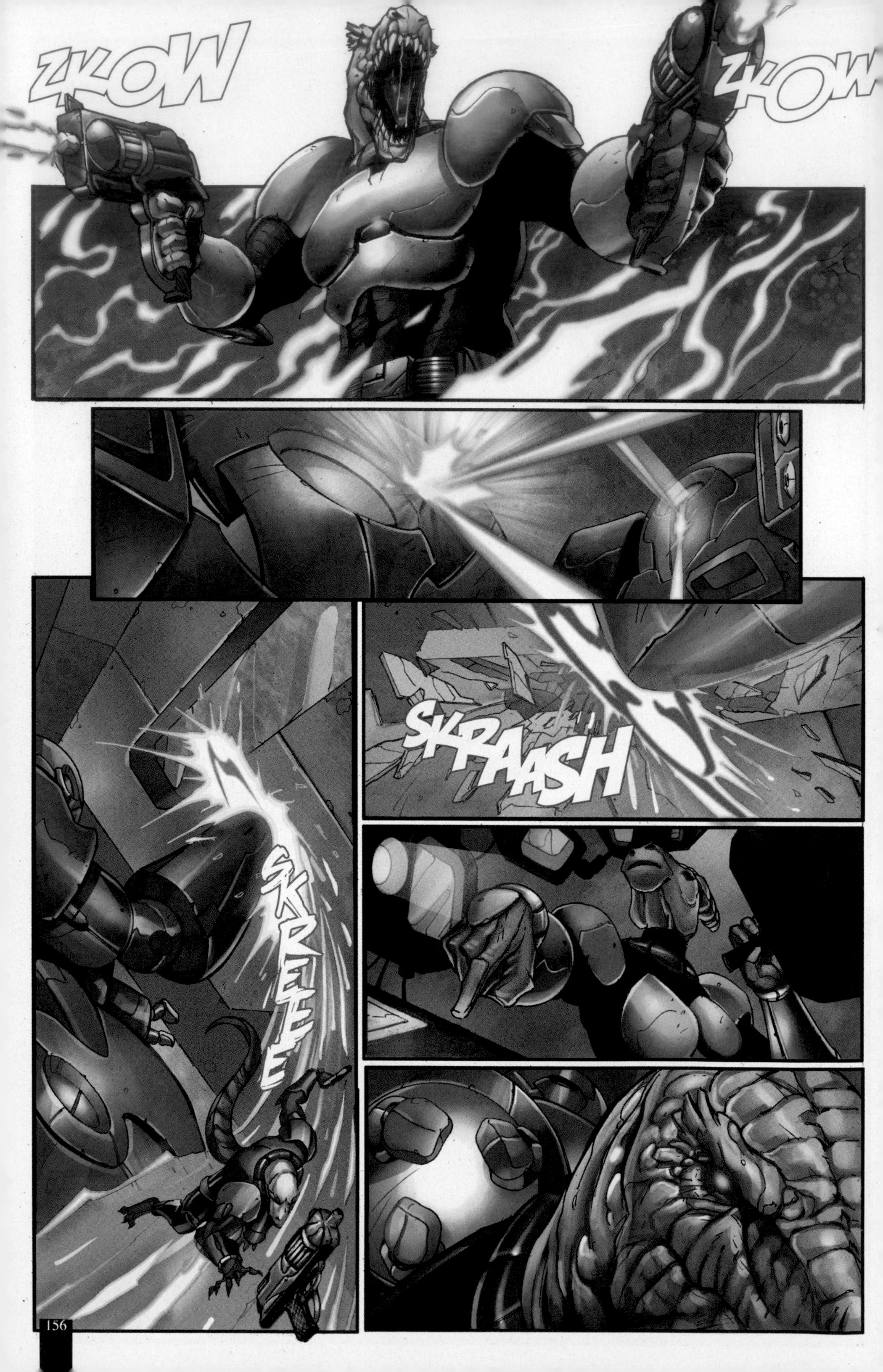
ZKOW
ZKOW
SKRAASH
SKREEEE

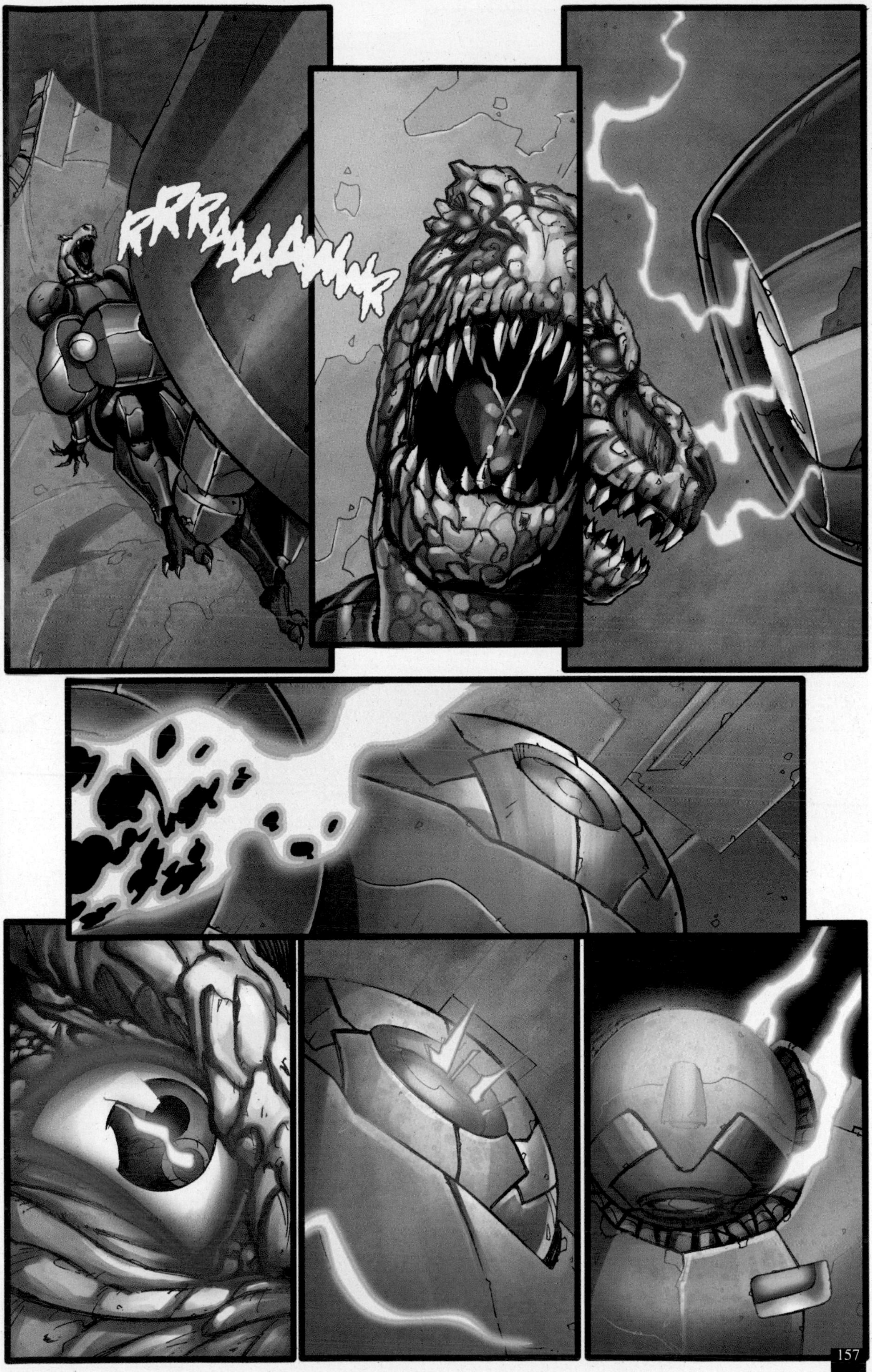
RRRAAAAWWR

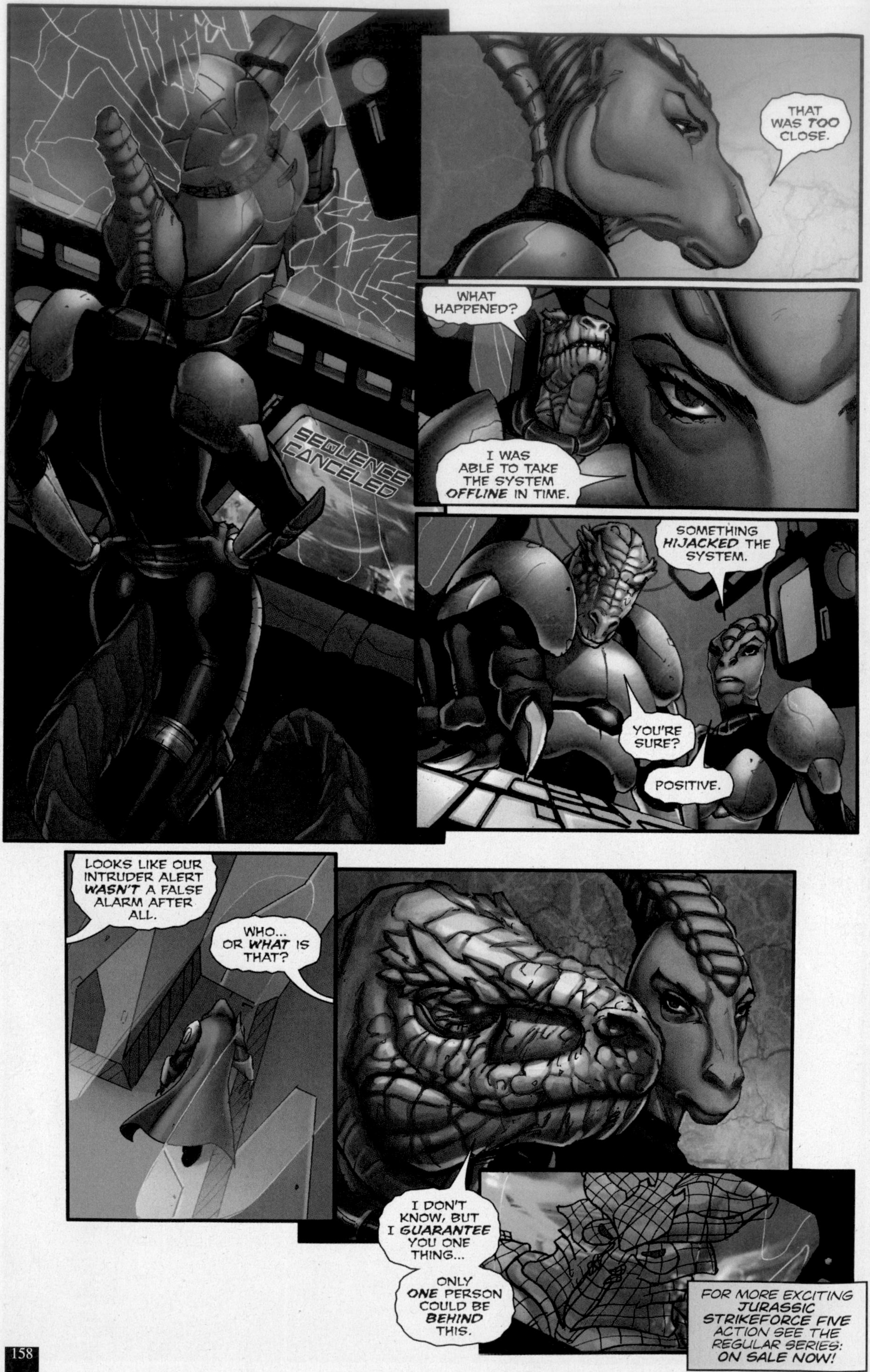
SEQUENCE CANCELED
THAT WAS TOO CLOSE.
WHAT HAPPENED?
I WAS ABLE TO TAKE THE SYSTEM OFFLINE IN TIME.
SOMETHING HIJACKED THE SYSTEM.
YOU'RE SURE?
POSITIVE.
LOOKS LIKE OUR INTRUDER ALERT WASN'T A FALSE ALARM AFTER ALL.
WHO... OR WHAT IS THAT?
I DON'T KNOW, BUT I GUARANTEE YOU ONE THING...
ONLY ONE PERSON COULD BE BEHIND THIS.
FOR MORE EXCITING JURASSIC STRIKEFORCE FIVE ACTION SEE THE REGULAR SERIES: ON SALE NOW!

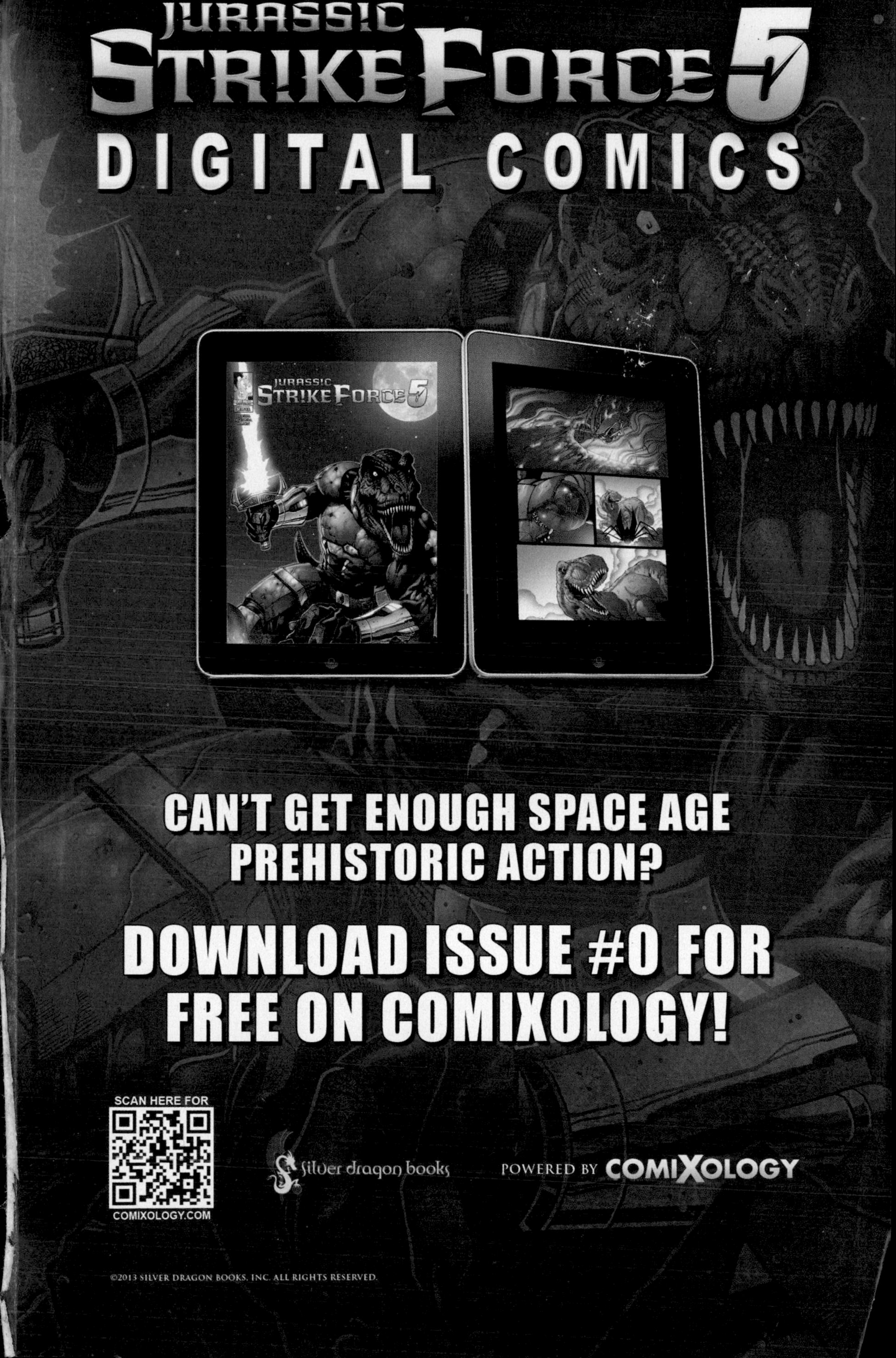
JURASSIC
STRIKE FORCE 5
DIGITAL COMICS
JURASSIC
STRIKE FORCE 5
CAN'T GET ENOUGH SPACE AGE PREHISTORIC ACTION?
DOWNLOAD ISSUE #0 FOR FREE ON COMIXOLOGY!
SCAN HERE FOR
COMIXOLOGY.COM
silver dragon books
POWERED BY COMIXOLOGY
©2013 SILVER DRAGON BOOKS, INC. ALL RIGHTS RESERVED.

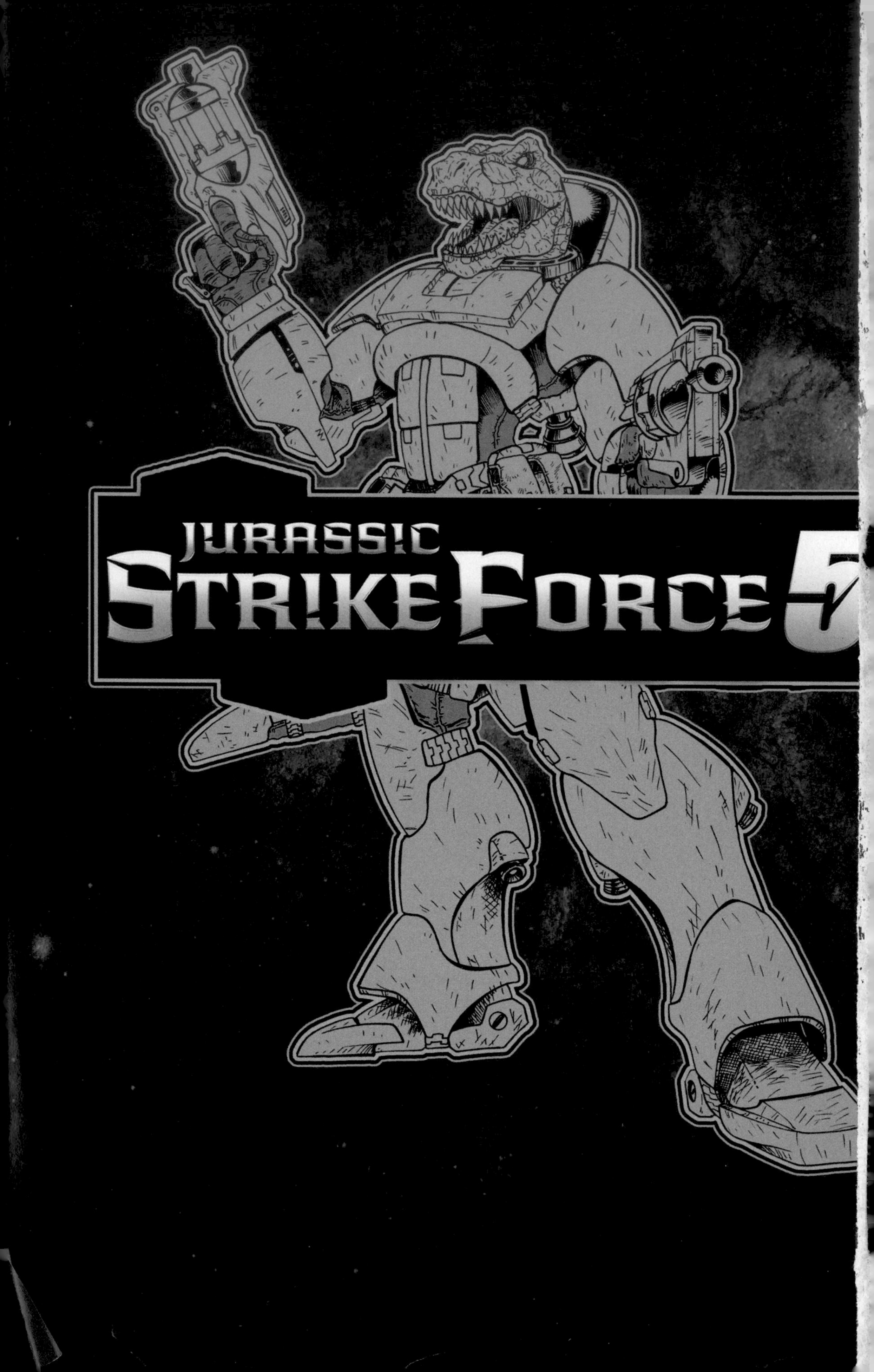
JURASSIC
STR!KE FORCE 5